P9-DSZ-119

CONDUCTORS
A NEW GENERATION

*Orpheus in the New World: The Symphony
Orchestra as an American Cultural Institution*

CONDUCTORS

A NEW GENERATION

PHILIP HART

CHARLES SCRIBNER'S SONS / NEW YORK

Library of Congress Cataloging in Publication Data

Hart, Philip.
  Conductors: a new generation.

    1. Conductors (Music)—Biography.   I. Title.
ML402.H37   785'.092'2 [B]   79–18083
ISBN 0–684–16389–6

1 3 5 7 9 11 13 15 17 19   F/C   20 18 16 14 12 10 8 6 4 2

ACKNOWLEDGMENT is gratefully made to the following for permission to publish excerpts from articles and reviews: *The Boston Globe*; *The Chicago Tribune*; *L'Express*, September 13, 1977; Field Enterprises, Inc. for excerpts from reviews by Bernard Jacobson, November 8, 1970, June 25, 1971, August 11, 1972 in *The Chicago Daily News*; General Gramophone Publications, Ltd.; Suvi Raj Grubb; Guardian Publications, Ltd.; *High Fidelity*; *International Herald Tribune*; *The Los Angeles Times* for excerpts from a review by Martin Berkheimer, © 1972 The Los Angeles Times; The Metropolitan Opera Association; William Morrow and Company; Newsweek, Inc. for excerpts from "At Long Last Lulu," © 1977 by Newsweek, Inc. All rights reserved; *The New Yorker* for excerpts from reviews by Andrew Porter and Winthrop Sargent; *New York Magazine* for excerpts from a review by Alan Rich, © 1977 by the NYM Corporation; *The New York Times*, © 1963, 1968, 1969, 1971, 1972, 1973, 1974, 1975, 1978, 1979 by The New York Times Company; *The Observer*; *Opera* for excerpt from a review by Peter Dannenberg; *Opera News*; Penguin Books Ltd.; *The Philadelphia Inquirer*, March 5, 1978; Polydor Inc.; *The San Francisco Chronicle*; *The San Francisco Examiner*; *Saturday Review*; *Time,* The Weekly Newsmagazine; copyright Time Inc. 1963; *The Washington Post*; and Charles Scribner's Sons.

TEXT PHOTO CREDITS

CLAUDIO ABBADO, DANIEL BARENBOIM, JAMES LEVINE, ZUBIN MEHTA, and RICCARDO MUTI—*Clive Barda*; ANDREW DAVIS—*Toronto Symphony Orchestra*; EDO DE WAART—*Mike Evans*; SEIJI OZAWA—*Deutsche Grammophon*.

ACKNOWLEDGMENTS

My most important acknowledgment must be to the eight conductors who are the subject of this book. Each supplied factual information, permitted attendance at working rehearsals, and articulately expressed opinions that are the very heart of this project. Moreover, all corrected and clarified information I had obtained elsewhere. Each conductor permitted me to tape substantial portions of our talks. Where no other source is specifically cited for extended direct quotations, it is these recorded interviews.

For factual information I relied on a variety of publications; where such information has been of critical importance, I have cited the source in my text. The *New York Times* on microfilm was exceptionally important in verifying dates and other facts. The New Mexico State Library in Santa Fe and the Zimmerman and Fine Arts libraries at the University of New Mexico in Albuquerque were extraordinarily cooperative in assisting me with their periodical files. Another source of periodical material were the press files of several orchestras, especially for reviews of performances.

Much of the information in an interview with Daniel Barenboim in *L'Express* published September 13, 1977, duplicates material I have found elsewhere, but that interview also suggested other areas for further investigation. Where I have quoted that interview, the translation is my own.

A number of people in several cities and, in many cases, affiliated with major music organizations rendered invaluable help of all kinds to me. I list them here according to city and organization:

In Boston: Richard Dyer of the *Boston Globe*. At the Boston Symphony Orchestra, Peter Gelb, Thomas Morris, Thomas D. Perry, and Michael Steinberg.

CONDUCTORS

In Chicago: At the Chicago Symphony Orchestra, John S. Edwards, Carl Fasshauer, Edward Druzinsky, Margaret Hillis, Peter Jonas, Gordon Peters, Milton Preves, and Kenneth Utz and his public relations staff. Thomas Willis at Northwestern University. Edward Gordon and Earle Ludgin of the Ravinia Festival Association.

In Los Angeles: At the Los Angeles Philharmonic, Ernest Fleischmann, Sidney and Teresa Harth, Orrin Howard and his public relations staff, and Jaye Rubanoff. Martin Bernheimer and Albert Goldberg at the *Los Angeles Times*. William Severns of the Music Center.

In New York: Sheldon Gold. David Hamilton. Wendy Hanson and David Reuben at the Metropolitan Opera. At the New York Philharmonic, Charles Croce, Frank Milburn, Carlos Moseley, Jack Murphy, and Albert K. Webster. Andrew Porter. Harold Shaw. Marvin Shoffer. Gideon Waldrop. Ronald Wilford.

In Philadelphia: Anthony Cecchia. At the Philadelphia Orchestra, Mary Crouse, Louis Hood, Joseph Santarlasci, and Boris Sokoloff.

In San Francisco: Philip S. Boone. Robert Commanday and Alfred Frankenstein of the *San Francisco Chronicle*. At the San Francisco Symphony Association, Virginia Cochrane, Peter Pastreich, Connie Rylee, and Joseph A. Scafidi.

In Toronto: Stephen Adler and Walter Homburger at the Toronto Symphony Orchestra.

In Florence: Massimo Bogianckino at the Teatro Comunale.

In London: Edward Greenfield. Nicola Wallis at the European Community Youth Orchestra. Diana Rix of Harold Holt, Limited. Stephen Crabtree of the London Philharmonic Orchestra. Michael Kaye of the London Symphony Orchestra.

The above listing is not actually complete, because there were several individuals who provided important help and asked to remain anonymous.

CONTENTS

For Margaret

INTRODUCTION

Any asino *can conduct—but to*
make music—eh? Is difficile!
Toscanini

RELAXING on a warm afternoon many years ago in his dressing room
at the Ravinia Festival—the North Shore suburban summer home of
the Chicago Symphony Orchestra—Pierre Monteux was discussing conducting with his old friend Walter Piston. "You go like this," he said,
giving his characteristically firm downbeat, "and they begin. It's very
simple." Then his bright little black eyes became more serious. "I remember once I conducted the Berlin Philharmonic in the Beethoven
First Symphony. No matter how I tried to beat it, we couldn't begin
the first movement together. You know, it is very hard. Even in the
concert it was not good. A while later, the Berlin Philharmonic came
to Paris with Furtwängler. The Beethoven First was on the program,
so I went—just to see. You know how his downbeat was—a sort of
shudder sometimes. That's what he did, and they all came in perfectly."

As an art reaching beyond technique, conducting can no more be
explained in precise terms than can Horowitz's piano tone or the light
in Rembrandt's painting. Real conducting, that is, as opposed to beat-
ing time. All one needs for the latter is some technique and a certain
physical facility. Real conducting involves a lot more. Call it charisma,
if you will—not necessarily the charisma that merely excites the audience
but the commanding personal magnetism that so controls one hundred
musicians that their performance communicates musical excitement to
the audience, despite the fact that every player may regard himself as a
better musician and have a quite different concept of how the music

(ix)

should go. Conductors are the only musicians whose instrument is a human one.

Some players swear that such communication comes from the eyes, from the expression on the conductor's face, or from the expressive grace of his body and gestures. Others say that all they have to do is watch the very end of the baton: if the conductor is a good one, everything is concentrated there. How, then, does one explain Herbert von Karajan, who conducts with his eyes closed, or the late Leopold Stokowski and his imitators, who have disdained the use of the baton? How much of a conductor's "message" is imparted in rehearsal, and how much left to the concert? George Szell wanted everything letter-perfect by the last rehearsal, leaving nothing to chance in the performance. Sir Thomas Beecham won his way into the hearts of many an orchestra with the shortest possible and seemingly improvisatory rehearsals, and captivated his audiences with the spontaneity of his performances. There is no fixed formula for great conducting any more than for any true artistic achievement or, for that matter, for leadership in any field of endeavor. That is one of the fascinating things about conducting—the source of its variety and its mystery.

Books on music history and conducting technique tell us that in the total perspective of Western music, conducting is a relatively recent phenomenon. Musicosociologists find provocative implications in contrasting the "democracy" of chamber music with the "autocracy" of the conductor, some seeing the latter as an ominous symptom of modern society. Musicopsychologists discuss the conductor as a father figure and explain the militance of unionized orchestral musicians as filial resentment of parental domination. The emergence of orchestral music and opera as public performance arts, available to all classes of society rather than just the aristocracy in its palaces or in its private boxes at the *teatro lyrico,* is an important historical development. It unquestionably affected the emergence of the conductor as a major figure in music performance, no longer a composer directing his own and others' music. Conversely, the evolution of the old-style *Kapellmeister* into the modern charismatic maestro has been a major force in the proliferation of symphony orchestras and opera companies and in arousing wider public interest in serious music. It has also had a profound effect on the kind of music that is being written—and not written—by the composers of our time. The shift from composer conducting to composer-conductor and finally to conductor alone has more than historic interest, for the latter retains, as an interpreter of music, significant vestiges of the creative force that his predecessors had.

In fact, one of the crucial issues of conducting today is this matter of interpretive license, and every conductor has his own views on this question, his own models in earlier generations of conductors. A convenient, if simplistic, way of expressing this nowadays is to set up a polarity between Arturo Toscanini at one extreme and Wilhelm Furtwängler at the other. One could create other polarities of this sort—Felix Weingartner versus Willem Mengelberg, Richard Strauss versus Gustav Mahler, Felix Mendelssohn versus Richard Wagner. In simplified terms, Toscanini, Weingartner, Strauss, and Mendelssohn represented an effort to play the composers' scores in a reasonably literal manner, as opposed to the inclination of Furtwängler, Mengelberg, Mahler, and Wagner to interpret music more freely, explained partly as subjective expression but more frequently as instinctual insight into the "music between the notes." It is said that Mengelberg would justify the idiosyncracies of his Beethoven interpretations by claiming that he had learned Beethoven from Franz Wüllner, who had studied with Anton Schindler, who had been a protégé of Beethoven. Thanks to the phonograph, we know how unreliable such appeals to tradition can be.

The phonograph and tape recorder have played an important part for the last five decades both in documenting many composers' own performances and in providing models in general interpretation from one generation to the next. Although one might, in theory at least, have once traced a tradition of Wagnerian interpretation from the Master himself through Levi to Mottl and Muck, there is no real certainty that the later generations truly reflected the original. In fact, in the case of Wagnerian interpretation, there was a quite different line through Hans Richter to Pierre Monteux, with an equal claim to authenticity. In our own time, even though Stravinsky was not a brilliant conductor, he was a very precise one, at least until his old age; his performance intentions in many of his records are beyond question. But how many conductors today show, in performances of such works as *Le Sacre du Printemps,* that they are aware of the composer's well-documented concept? Some conductors are more concerned with speculative musicology in restoring authentic baroque performance practices than they are with respecting the explicit intentions of composers working in this century.

If conductors with access to such recordings and to scores far more precisely notated than those of a century ago so habitually indulge their interpretive creativity, it becomes somewhat difficult to place too much credence in protestations of "fidelity to the composer" as an interpretive ideal. Anyone upholding Toscanini as the champion of fidelity should talk to musicians who played under him or read a fascinating book written by one of them, Samuel Antek's *This Was Toscanini,* still the best account of how this great conductor actually made music. From it one can learn several facts about Toscanini as a conductor that contribute to understanding his unique genius. It was a fact that Toscanini believed in maintaining a more uniform tempo than most of his colleagues did, because Toscanini believed that the composer wanted it that way—a belief based as much on his own temperament as on historical evidence. Moreover, Toscanini could alter a composer's scoring on the same grounds— his own conviction of what the composer wanted—but he did so less frequently than many others. What dominated all this was the fierce intensity of his temperament, which demanded clarity of orchestral texture, precision of ensemble and rhythm, an Italianate singing line, and total involvement of himself no less than of his players. In the end, it was the force of his personality—or charisma, for want of a better term —that fused these elements together and achieved their projection by his orchestras.

Furtwängler's search for the "melos" of a composition—the creative spirit behind the written notes—had the same objective as Toscanini's determination to convey what he believed the composer set down. Their differences were differences of temperament and cultural background, not of artistic integrity. In the right context Toscanini would admit to reading between the notes of a Beethoven score, just as Furtwängler's profound general knowledge of music and of the specific score before him was indispensable in his search for its inner, essential meaning. Since both were complete and great conductors, their respective techniques and ultimate results were part of a seamless whole—their totality as human individuals.

In addition to documenting a composer's own performances, the phonograph plays another role for modern conducting: for more than fifty years, recordings, imperfectly from the beginning but constantly improving in fidelity and increasing in influence, have documented the evolution of conducting in our time. Recordings are replacing the person-to-person, teacher-pupil, or master-protégé chain whereby the technical and interpretive traditions of conducting are passed on. As a young conductor in Dresden, Fritz Reiner not only heard Richard Strauss conduct his own and other composers' music but also traveled frequently to Berlin and Leipzig to hear Artur Nikisch conduct. Ernest Bloch, who heard Mahler, Mengelberg, and Walter at one time or another over a span of more than forty years, considered Mengelberg to be more in the tradition of Mahler than was Bruno Walter, usually regarded as Mahler's most faithful disciple. But memories are fallible, especially when filtered through highly creative minds. We have no documentation of Mahler as a conductor, scarcely any of Nikisch, and woefully little of Strauss in his own or others' music. But Mengelberg's conducting is reasonably well preserved on records, especially that at the end of his long career. In fact, the whole generation of Toscanini, Furtwängler, Mengelberg, Koussevitzky, Weingartner, and Stokowski is the first to be so well documented, and our knowledge of subsequent conductors has progressively increased in quantity and quality of reproduction. Although few of the eight subjects of this book actually heard in person many of the conductors of that first reasonably well-documented generation, they all have access to a far better experience of the conducting tradition of the past fifty years than did their counterparts fifty years ago.

Another conducting phenomenon of the past fifty years deserves mention here: the gradual disappearance of the martinet among conductors. It is now the exception rather than the rule to find autocracy in instructing players in rehearsal or in the hiring and firing of them, certainly to the degree that prevailed in the years before World War II. We have the musicians' unions and, more important, individual orchestra committees to thank for this far more humane relation between conductors and the musicians they command. The comment attributed to George Szell that "a conductor cannot be a good guy and make a great orchestra" no longer represents the prevailing view. Nor is there necessarily any general validity to record producer Goddard Lieberson's observation "Show me an orchestra that likes its conductor, and I will show you a bad orchestra."

Does this mean that we are coming to the end of an era of extraordinary orchestral perfection? Is it possible today to have orchestras playing with the fire of the New York Philharmonic under Toscanini, the brilliant precision of the Chicago Symphony under Reiner, the opulence of the Philadelphia Orchestra under Stokowski and Ormandy or the Boston Symphony under Koussevitzky, or the jewellike chamber-music quality of the Cleveland Orchestra under Szell? If the greatness of those orchestras was achieved at a human price, younger conductors are seeking their own and possibly quite different kind of greatness on a first-name basis with their players.

Just what is meant by "a new generation" in the title of this book? What is a generation? In a family, it is easy to define children, grandchildren, great-grandchildren, parents, aunts and uncles, grandparents, and so on. In history, it is possible to talk meaningfully about a post-Napoleonic or a pre–World War generation. Certain great creative figures can define a generation: the *Eroica* and *Le Sacre du Printemps* were watersheds in musical composition. The lines are harder to draw in the interpretive arts: the Casals or Toscanini who so completely breaks with the past does, to be sure, have a strong influence on those who follow, but he does not affect the course of music history as decisively as Beethoven, Wagner, or Stravinsky did.

The eight subjects of this book are highly personal choices, in some respects arbitrary ones. The decision to concentrate on younger artists was both personal and arbitrary: I was simply more interested in devoting my time and energy to them than to older figures, whose work I already knew and whose ideas and comments on music were already familiar. I wanted to explore conductors from whom I, as someone professionally involved in symphonic music for over a generation (that word again!), might learn something new. Once that decision was made, along with the quantitative considerations of book length and time span of work, I did proceed with a certain logic in establishing the criteria that guided my choices.

My subjects had to enjoy a reasonably well established international reputation. I had to believe that they stood a good chance of ranking in their profession a couple of decades hence as such artists as Solti, Bernstein, and Karajan do today. Some objective criteria helped me determine stature, among them recordings and engagements with major orchestras and opera companies here and abroad.

The most important criterion was opinion in the music profession itself—peer evaluation. I talked with administrators, critics, other conductors and soloists, and orchestral players; many a grain of salt had to leaven the individual opinions I heard, but their aggregate was indispensable to my final choice. One of my subjects would never have been included here except that so many professionals whom I respected urged me to consider him. The serious music profession is often accused of being a tight little world stretching from Fifty-seventh Street to the Piazza della Scala, so exclusive that it can ruin the career of a talented youngster whom it arbitrarily ignores or rejects. I do not share that view. It is conceivable that there is hidden away somehow or somewhere a greatly gifted conductor wanting a career who has not been given a chance by that aggregation of composers, performers, critics, teachers, administrators, and informed laymen that we call the "music world." But I doubt it very much.

If anything, under pressure to provide conductors for an increasing number of orchestras playing more and more concerts, the system is pushing mediocre talents and immature conductors too far and too rapidly. I certainly do not mean to predict that every talented conductor will succeed: there are some tragic figures, even some contemporaries of those chosen here, whose careers have been ruined, or at best stunted, by bad judgment on their part or by premature exploitation. To discuss them candidly by name here might injure what chance they have for recovery.

From my own little niche in professional music activity, I had some acquaintance and knowledge of many of the subjects of this book long before I ever thought of it. I have a vivid recollection of the final stages of two Dimitri Mitropoulos competitions in which Claudio Abbado and Edo de Waart were among the winners, and I recall comments of colleagues on the promise each showed then. Many years ago, I briefly met Daniel Barenboim and Zubin Mehta in contexts that had nothing to do with conducting. Seiji Ozawa I recall as a very shy young assistant to Leonard Bernstein when the latter visited Juilliard to work with some students there. None of these encounters was as meaningful as the four years when I knew and worked with James Levine at Juilliard—I as an administrator of performances, he as an extremely impressive young performer. I mention these as instances of a worker in the limited music world encountering and recognizing extraordinary talent long before it bursts upon the world at large.

From the outset, there has been a built-in bias in this book: I wanted to write about conductors who interested me and whose work I liked and respected, even if I ran the danger of sounding like a Pollyanna. I did much of my preliminary screening with records, both commercially released and pirated, for I wanted to get as broad a view of a prospect's work as I could. Knowing the limitations and distortions inherent in records, I met and heard all of my eight choices, and quite a few others, before settling on my final list. From a purely logistical point of view, my subjects had to be "available": that is, they had to be where I could hear them at work and talk with them. Most important, they had to be agreeable to my writing about them; this presented less of a problem than might be expected, for few conductors, especially young ones, are publicity-shy. However, I wanted no unwilling subjects, nor would I go behind their backs. Happily, no conductor that I really wanted to write about was not available. They were most gracious in helping me attend rehearsals and concerts with major orchestras and opera companies. All agreed to talk with me, on and off the record, but always for some time with my tape recorder running to capture their thoughts in their own words. (In my text, all direct quotations not otherwise identified originated in this fashion.) Their wholehearted and friendly cooperation in these and many other ways made my task not only possible but highly enjoyable.

Beyond this, I must gratefully acknowledge a very personal debt to these eight conductors and the orchestras or opera companies I heard them conduct. I cannot cite every occasion, but must mention a few unforgettable experiences encountered in writing this book: performances with three orchestras, plus several rehearsals, in which Claudio Abbado plumbed depths of the Mahler Fourth Symphony in ways I have seldom known in music. Hearing the Verdi Requiem, conducted by Riccardo Muti, in Brunelleschi's incomparable basilica of San Lorenzo in Florence. Revelation of the previously unappreciated (by me, at least) greatness of the Bruckner Fifth Symphony in rehearsals and a performance by Daniel Barenboim and the Chicago Symphony Orchestra. The shattering impact of the final slow movement of Mahler's Third Symphony in Zubin Mehta's reading one Sunday afternoon in Los Angeles. My utter delight in several extraordinary performances of *Falstaff* at the Santa Fe Opera that Edo de Waart conducted in two different seasons. The chamber-music luminescence of the Metropolitan Opera orchestra in *Lulu* and *Pelléas et Mélisande* as conducted by James Levine.

Only after I had finally chosen the eight subjects of this book did I detect some other common elements among them that were not used as criteria. Though I leave most of these to the reader, I believe that I can pinpoint the emergence of a new generation rather precisely on the night of January 19, 1961, when Zubin Mehta made his debut with the Los Angeles Philharmonic. Other events preceded that one—the meeting of Abbado, Barenboim, and Mehta at Siena in 1956, for instance—but Mehta's Los Angeles debut was the first really dramatic emergence of any of these conductors before the public.

Tar and feathers probably await me for not including more than one American conductor and for completely omitting women or blacks. Let me anticipate that criticism with assurances that these considerations were always in my mind during the screening process. In fact, I might well have leaned over backward to rectify these neglects had even a reasonable borderline case arisen. If I had not limited myself to eight conductors, actually more than I originally planned, more Americans might have been included. Had my age bracket been wider and this book twice as long, one or two women might have been covered. Among the young black conductors there are several promising talents, but none has reached the international stature and accumulated the variety of experience that met my basic criteria. My parameters were not fixed nor my criteria established with any intention of excluding women or blacks or to reduce the coverage of Americans. I personally view all three as important elements in our total conducting scene, but this book is not about that larger subject.

Nevertheless, the matter of national origin in the broader context does deserve comment. Of the eight conductors I cover here, two are from Italy and one each from Japan, India, the Netherlands, Great Britain, Israel, and the United States. Yet there is none from France, the Soviet Union, or that traditional Central European breeding-ground of musicians comprising Germany and what was once the Austro-Hungarian Empire. That circumstance was no more intentional than my omission of women and blacks.

P.H.

Santa Fe, March 1979

CONDUCTORS
A NEW GENERATION

DANIEL BARENBOIM

As a child prodigy grown up to protean maturity, Daniel Barenboim has combined the careers of a major concert pianist and a conductor at the very top of the orchestral world. While his God-given talent has been shaped by the best possible training, in musicianship and technique, Barenboim has come to think broadly and deeply about the art of music and about his own role in serving it—thoughts that he expresses articulately and fervently. With this mastery of performance and persuasive command of ideas he combines an outgoing magnetism and facility for managing people that are typical of gifted men of short stature.

At the simplest level of the public's view of him, Barenboim has many of the characteristics of a typical celebrity—a fondness for Havana cigars, Italian handmade shoes, and, as his occasional and only alcoholic drink, Krug champagne, often supplied by solicitous recording companies. He speaks six languages fluently: English, Hebrew, Spanish, French, Italian, and German. His friends and admirers around the world fall into two quite distinct groups. The acquaintances and fans that gather about musical celebrities provide a sort of fleeting company for someone who has devoted a major portion of the last two decades to the life of an itinerant musician. More satisfying indeed are those close friends, most of them congenial musicians, who form what the media have dubbed the Barenboim gang. With either group, he is usually at the center, guiding the conversation or the making of chamber music in his own positively authoritative way.

A woman journalist from London, in a dispatch to the *New York Times,* once described him as a "dark, powerful, compact, small man with curly hair and curly sideburns. He looks very young. His features are curiously concentrated to the center of his face, giving it an intensity that matches the impression of controlled vigor and sexuality often given by men of his shape. He has the soothing quality of voice that veils the authority of a born teacher. There is nothing aggressive or flamboyant about him, just a certainty about how music should sound, how things should be done. . . . His energy is demoniac, his ability apparently unlimited, his confidence Olympian."

The concentration of his features has its psychological counterpart in the intense concentration with which he thinks and works. Midway in a rehearsal of a difficult Bruckner symphony, he will spend the intermission on the long-distance phone, conferring with a manager thousands of miles away on the logistic minutiae of an engagement two years hence, and then return to the podium and resume rehearsing exactly where he left off and command the full attention of one hundred musicians as completely as he had before the break.

Like some, but by no means all, musical geniuses, he has a prodigious memory. It is his standard practice to memorize a work as the initial step in his study of it. He is extremely intelligent and highly articulate in expressing his thoughts. Unlike such "instinctive" musicians as his wife, Jacqueline du Pré, he thinks logically about music, analyzes what he is studying, and expresses his views on art, whether on specific compositions and performances or on generalities, with a persuasive eloquence.

The driving force behind this protean talent is love for music—not an abstract or intellectualized feeling but a love of making music for the pleasure it gives him. "Music is alive," he told interviewers from *L'Express* in 1977. "It is emotional because it is in motion. Essentially it is something that is endlessly changing, if only because you yourself receive it differently each time. But feeling in music goes beyond transient subjective experience. To serve music it is not necessary to become abstract, but one must go beyond one's transient feelings and seek a deeper and more sincere truth. The less one depends on his own emotional states, the closer he comes to his own truth. . . . The power of music is precisely that of expressing the eternity of feeling, not transient or subjective emotion. While the duration of a human life is seventy years, that of a symphony by Beethoven is forty minutes. Yet, in the space of that time, Beethoven has expressed the intensity, richness, and diversity of an entire lifetime.

"There is nothing static in this world. When one is aware of having attained something, one appreciates the fluidity of things. I believe that many frustrations in life arise from not having had the chance to experiment. In my case, I have had that—the opportunity of constantly developing in music. . . ."

"My parents had a very small flat in Buenos Aires where they both taught piano," says Barenboim. "My mother taught beginners; my father taught more advanced students. And, therefore, until I was old enough to go out in the street really, I didn't meet people who did not actually play music, because during my waking hours everybody who came into the house was obviously either family or students who came to study with my mother or with my father. Therefore, it was absolutely normal and natural for me to think that everybody in the world played piano until I actually went out in the street, as it were."

Of Russian Jewish extraction, Ernesto and Aida (Schuster) Barenboim were natives of Argentina. Their only child, Daniel, was born November 15, 1942. Although he first studied the violin at the age of four, he soon changed to piano, at which he could, on occasion, play duets with one of his parents. His first lessons were with his mother before he joined the advanced students taught by Ernesto, who was the only formal instructor he ever had in piano. Looking back, Barenboim sees this as a distinct advantage for him, noting that most talented young pianists study with a succession of teachers who often have different approaches to the instrument and to music.

Barenboim, who remains close to his parents, has an affectionate respect for his father's intelligence: "He's not the usual type of over-possessive father of a talented child, and he was, and is, an excellent teacher. He was able to show me that basically the one thing that one can learn is the curiosity and the wish to go on finding out more and more things. I know this sounds terribly oversimplified, but it really isn't because in the end that is the main thing that keeps us going as human beings, musicians and nonmusicians—the fact that one has, and never exhausts, his thirst for knowledge. The mistake so many teachers make is that they feed the student information instead of education. To educate someone means to give them, of course, the basic principles of whatever the subject is, but more basic is to instill in them this never-ending thirst for knowledge and curiosity. Of course, that is something which you can do at home very much more than if you have to go outside once or twice a week for your lessons."

Just as Barenboim's own London apartment was later to become a musical and social center, his parents' in Buenos Aires was the scene of much chamber music and talk about music. He vividly recalls the sheer physical sensation of Artur Rubinstein's performance of Schumann's *Carnaval* and the first time he heard the Beethoven Violin Concerto, with Adolf Busch playing the solo *and* conducting. Busch also performed with chamber orchestra in the Bach Brandenburg Concertos and some Handel works. Some of the international celebrities visiting Buenos Aires were also guests at the apartment. Among these was the conductor Igor Markevitch, who urged the Barenboims to bring their son to his summer conducting class in Salzburg. When he was seven, Danny gave his first public recital. He recalls the great pleasure he had from this first contact with the public, for he had no experience of "nerves" on this occasion. After a program including the music of Bach, Beethoven, and Debussy, he played seven encores before apologizing to the audience that he had run out of music to play. The critic of one Buenos Aires newspaper hailed young Barenboim as Mozart reborn; another denounced the criminality of thrusting such an untalented child on the public.

In 1952, the Barenboim family moved to Israel, feeling that their talented son would be better brought up in a nation where he and his family were not part of a minority. En route, the family spent the summer and fall in Salzburg and Vienna, arriving in Israel in December. Although Barenboim nowadays recalls what he regards as a "normal childhood," it is obvious that his musical training commanded highest priority. He may very well have enjoyed some of the childhood pleasures he recalls—skipping school and the like—but he also had a daily routine of intensive practice that few of his fellows knew. Moreover, the family's later trips to Europe for Danny's special training undoubtedly deprived him of the vacations enjoyed by "normal" Israeli children in their early teens. From the very beginning of his father's instruction, Barenboim established basic work methods that have persisted to this day. Although he likes to say that he hates to practice or does not practice much, he will explain somewhat more seriously that his father insisted on intense concentration and piano practice, to the point that more was accomplished in a shorter time than many others devoted to practice. He strongly disapproves of a colleague who said that he could practice his scales with the morning paper propped on his piano's music rack. This extraordinary ability to concentrate—partly innate but partly implanted by his father's training—remains with Barenboim to this day. Yet a distinction should be drawn here between intensive piano practice and the study of music in a broader sense. Barenboim recalls, for instance, how in his early youth, he would spend hours with opera scores, singing every role as he played through the operatic repertory.

The Barenboims spent the summers of 1954 and 1955 at Salzburg, originally at Markevitch's behest, so that Daniel could study conducting with him. In addition to this conducting class, Barenboim worked with Enrico Mainardi in chamber music and with the noted Swiss pianist Edwin Fischer. From each he gained much of lasting value. Mainardi's classes strengthened and broadened his early exposure to chamber music at home; Barenboim remains an avid ensemble musician. Fischer not only coached Barenboim in the piano literature but was the first pianist whom the youth saw conduct a chamber orchestra from the keyboard, an impression to have important consequences later. Markevitch's conducting class not only gave young Barenboim basic instruction in baton technique and score-reading but had the important advantage of actually working with an orchestra six days a week for two months each summer.

Beyond this classwork in Salzburg, the most important impact on young Barenboim was his meeting in the first summer with the great German conductor Wilhelm Furtwängler, who was to make a deep and lasting impression on him. Furtwängler invited the young pianist to appear with his Berlin Philharmonic the following season. The Barenboims felt that it was too soon after the Holocaust for a Jewish musician to play in Berlin, but Furtwängler's glowing recommendation of Daniel elsewhere opened many doors for him in the next few years: "Daniel Barenboim is a phenomenon; his musical and technical capacities are amazing." This great German musician has exerted a powerful influence on many of the younger generation of conductors, especially those trained in Europe. In Barenboim's case, his encounter with Furtwängler in the last year before the older man's death made an extraordinary impression on the youth, an impression that has been maintained by intensive listening to his published recordings and to privately made records and tapes supplied by the conductor's widow and others. As he matured and drew about him a circle of friendly colleagues, Barenboim became a fervent advocate of the Furtwänglerian approach to music.

Barenboim's first summer at Salzburg came at the beginning of an important period of international study and performance extending from his twelfth to fifteenth years. Between 1954 and 1956 he studied theory and composition in Paris with Nadia Boulanger on a scholarship from the America-Israel Cultural Foundation, the first granted to a young Israeli for musical study in Europe. He also received a master's degree from the Accademia di Santa Cecilia in Rome in 1956. In the spring of that year he entered the Alfredo Casella Piano Competition in Naples; although he was under the minimum age for contestants, he was awarded a special prize. That summer he enrolled at the Accademia Chigiana in Siena to study conducting with Carlo Zecchi, with whom he had worked in Rome. There he met as fellow students Zubin Mehta and Claudio Abbado, his seniors by six and eight years, respectively.

"With Zubin I was very struck, because you see, although I was younger, I was actually much more experienced musically speaking than he was. I had been playing concerts, you know, for quite a few years, and he had just come to Europe. The reason I say this is that although he had no experience to speak of at the time, the force of his musical personality was so incredible that he took us all completely by storm."

During these years of intensive study, Barenboim continued to play in public. He made his Paris debut in 1955 with the orchestra of the Paris Conservatoire, with André Cluytens conducting. The following year, the London audience first heard him with the Philharmonia Orchestra under Josef Krips. Before that concert, Artur Rubinstein introduced him to the impresario Sol Hurok, who arranged Barenboim's American debut in New York for January 1957 with the Symphony of the Air under Leopold Stokowski; on that occasion the fourteen-year-old pianist made a strong impression playing the First Piano Concerto of Prokofiev. Later, he returned to the United States, giving his first solo recital in New York, and appeared elsewhere in recital and in concert. This began a long association with the Hurok management and its successors, which has only recently ended simply because he has so little time for extensive American touring. "Nowadays," says Barenboim, "Zubin is my manager, and I am his."

When the fourteen-year-old Barenboim won the special prize at the Casella Competition, it was reported that he had a repertory of over two hundred compositions and knew all thirty-two Beethoven sonatas by heart. One reason for this was his father's encouragement to explore and develop his curiosity. He urged Daniel to avoid playing any one piece more than two or three times in concert. For this reason, Barenboim's piano repertory in his mid-teens was considerably more catholic than it was to become a few years later. In addition to playing a Prokofiev concerto in his New York debut, he gave the first performance outside the Soviet Union of that composer's Ninth Sonata at a concert in Paris in 1955.

Moreover, he created something of a sensation when he was fourteen by playing the Beethoven *Hammerklavier* Sonata, a work usually reserved for pianists two or three times his age. Years later, in an interview with Robert Jacobson, he recalled his early performances of this sonata, which he has now recorded three times: "People questioned me when I played the *Hammerklavier* Sonata at fourteen—'too young,' they said. Of course, I couldn't probe it all, but neither can some sixty-year-olds! There are those who say some music is only for maturity, but it only matures when you play and study and repeat it. Maturity is to realize that it is never finished. I'll never forget how the score of the *Hammerklavier* shocked me the first time I looked at it. Every time I play it now, I have that same shock." Yet, when he performed this sonata in London at the age of fifteen, the critic of *The Times* of London hailed his performance as one of the best heard in this century.

In his late teens, Barenboim recalls, he experienced a crisis in his career: "As a child, I did not make the sort of sensation and success that some other children have made. I had a sort of reasonable success, and then when I was sixteen, seventeen—around that time—I was not a child anymore, nor grown up yet. Nobody really wanted to engage me; nobody wanted to give me opportunities to have a professional existence."

That crisis was resolved when the city of Tel Aviv invited him to perform the complete cycle of Beethoven sonatas there in 1960 and to return the following year for a comprehensive series of Mozart recitals. Then, in 1962, he toured Australia, where he had had a great success four years earlier. On this occasion, however, he not only played piano recitals but also conducted orchestras in Sydney and Melbourne. He regards these latter appearances as his first with full-scale professional orchestras. These engagements, coming between his eighteenth and twentieth years, marked his transition to youthful maturity, in which he was to concentrate on the Austro-German classical repertory, especially as piano soloist, for the next few years. On the other hand, his emergence as a symphonic conductor was not to be followed with other similar engagements for several more years.

From the time he was sixteen, Barenboim's parents allowed him to travel alone, often for extended periods of time and over great international distances, as the orbit of his career expanded. He developed rather early what has been termed the conviviality of the solitary, establishing cordial but fleeting acquaintanceships literally around the world and acquiring a self-sufficiency in coping with the itinerant life of the touring musician. He also formed the habit of running up substantial long-distance telephone bills, as he assuaged his loneliness by keeping in touch with his family and close, but faraway, friends.

By his early twenties, Barenboim was becoming established. No longer a *Wunderkind,* he had become an artist of surprising maturity. At the very outset of his career as a mature pianist, Barenboim decided to build his repertory around music that was, as Artur Schnabel often remarked, better than it could be performed. His first records, made while still in his teens, with the American Westminster firm, were of sonatas and concertos by Beethoven and Mozart. Moreover, when he resumed recording in 1966 for British EMI, it was to begin a series of Beethoven sonatas, some released separately during the next few years and finally published as a complete set in the Beethoven centennial year of 1970. In 1968 he gave a series of "master classes" on the Beethoven sonatas for BBC television. To many, it seemed presumptuous for a pianist still in his twenties to tackle the most monumental and complex musical challenges in the piano literature—a challenge accepted by the great masters of earlier generations only when they were twice Barenboim's age.

The English critic Edward Greenfield, now a strong admirer of Barenboim, recalled, "Indeed I was dead against him. It seemed so cavalier to rush through the Beethoven cycle like that, so brash, another of those get-along-quick young men. But by the end of the cycle I was kneeling at his feet. In his recording of the great C-minor Sonata that I listened to the other day, I could compare with Schnabel and Kempff, and if you are honest you had to admit that it was more interesting than either. It was even more breathtaking when he did it in the flesh. To a degree that I find almost disconcerting, Barenboim already matches the two great Beethoven masters in their strongest suits: Schnabel in power and vitality and Kempff in range of tone color and intensity."

In 1965, a year before he began recording for EMI, Barenboim began a long association with the English Chamber Orchestra (ECO). A cooperative, player-governed group of top British instrumentalists, the ECO was the orchestra for Benjamin Britten's English Opera Group and has long been very active under various conductors, both in England and on international tours and on records.

From the beginning of his association with the ECO, Barenboim conducted both from the podium and at the keyboard. The latter position, of course, has long historic precedent, going back to the time when ensemble music required harmonic filling-in by the keyboard continuo, whose player was the obvious one to give at least a minimum of essential cues to the rest of the players. Even as late as Haydn's visit to London in the 1790s, the composer played along with Salomon's orchestra in fully scored symphonies. These performances by Haydn were quite different from Mozart's a decade earlier when he played the predominant solo in concertos of his own composition at public concerts. Although the nineteenth century saw divergent specialization between pianism and conducting, a number of musicians—von Bülow a century ago and Bruno Walter, Dimitri Mitropoulos, and Leonard Bernstein more recently, among others—occasionally conducted from the keyboard. Barenboim's mentor at Salzburg, Edwin Fischer, although primarily a pianist, frequently led a chamber orchestra in concert or on records, sometimes in Mozart concertos, sometimes as continuo player, and sometimes without piano at all.

Given his own conducting ambitions, Barenboim would inevitably be drawn to the soloist-conductor role with a chamber orchestra, but his encounters with Fischer unquestionably shaped Barenboim's standards at an early point in his training. From the older pianist-conductor, Barenboim learned the necessity of complete preparation of his own part before the first rehearsal: he had to have full command of both the piano part and the orchestra score, not as separate elements of solo and accompaniment but as the integrated conception of the composer. One advantage of this method was the psychological pressure that being conducted from the keyboard puts on orchestra players who must concentrate more intensely on such less expansive gestures from the conductor as a special nod of his head or a signal from his eyes.

Although Barenboim conducted the ECO in a broader concert rep-

ertory from the outset, his first records with it were Mozart piano concertos; and as in the case of the Beethoven sonatas, the success of early
releases led to a complete series between 1970 and 1975 of the twenty-
seven Mozart concertos. Again Barenboim was taking on a repertory
previously associated with the great German master pianists, but he
carried it off as successfully as he did the Beethoven sonatas. In fact,
Barenboim's appearances with the ECO as conductor and soloist greatly
contributed to its international success on records and on tour. In 1973,
Allen Hughes reviewed for the *New York Times* an all-Mozart program played by Barenboim and the ECO:

> His conducting of the Divertimento for Two Horns and Strings (K. 334)
> was characterized by the same felicitous blending of liveliness and lyricism
> that made his playing of the Piano Concerto no. 27 in B-flat (K. 595)
> so enjoyable. . . . However he has done it, Mr. Barenboim has ar-
> rived at an understanding of Mozart given to few musicians of any age
> or at any stage of artistic maturity. There may have been one or two in-
> stances in which he veered slightly toward affectation of phrase or effect,
> but on the whole his interpretations flowed smoothly and with brilliant
> naturalness that spoke directly to the listener.

This critic's caveat concerning "affectation of phrase or effect" was
often expressed by other reviewers, not only about Barenboim's piano
playing but also about his conducting. Such misgivings seem to be expressed more freely in America than in England, where Barenboim has
become, in the last decade or so, something of a national musical treasure
and where a certain expressive spontaneity and individuality are more
highly regarded than they are in many American circles. There relative
consistency of tempo and avoidance of rubato in the classics of Mozart
and Beethoven—ideals attributed with varying justification to Toscanini and his disciples—are more admired. In the last analysis, Barenboim's artistic roots go deep into the German tradition. Both of his
parents were musicians steeped in Austro-German music, and their approach to music, implicitly and explicitly, laid the groundwork for their
son's response to Furtwängler at Salzburg and to the eventual develop-

ment of his understanding of the elder conductor's contribution to musical performance.

Although he also studied in Italy and France, Barenboim's deepest affinity, as he matured, was for the classic Austro-German tradition. The outward manifestation of the resolution of the young Barenboim's career crisis in his late teens was a highly specialized repertory of Beethoven and Mozart in his Tel Aviv cycles. Another manifestation of this affinity for the Austro-German tradition is the fact that, apart from his Mozart piano concerto recordings, the few others he made of the standard repertory were with such conductors as Otto Klemperer, Dietrich Fischer-Dieskau, and Sir John Barbirolli—all of them artists steeped in that idiom.

As his international career as a young pianist developed, Barenboim was most warmly received in England, though he performed extensively elsewhere. In fact, he has found the musical atmosphere so congenial in London that he has lived there for a good number of years, making it more or less his headquarters since about 1960, when he was establishing himself on the international music circuit. Barenboim endeared himself to English musical circles when, after he had begun to conduct extensively, he became a missionary for the music of Sir Edward Elgar, which he programmed not only in London but abroad. It is hardly accidental that the Edwardian Elgar was the most German of English composers in this century.

Barenboim's London "digs" became the social center for an international group of congenial musicians variously referred to as the Israeli Mafia, the Stern gang, or the Barenboim gang. The composition of this group was rather like a planetary system, the pianist-conductor himself at the center, with the closer orbit occupied by musicians like Zubin Mehta, the Israeli violinists Itzhak Perlman and Pinchas Zukerman, the Russian exile pianist Vladimir Ashkenazy, and, of course, Jacqueline du Pré. Somewhat farther out from the center, and more occasional in their participation, are such older musical luminaries as Isaac Stern, Artur Rubinstein, and Dietrich Fischer-Dieskau.

As Barenboim and other members of his circle became international musical celebrities, their activities together and separately received devoted attention from the media. Barenboim's and Mehta's shared addiction to the long-distance telephone has been fully reported. They have played Furtwängler tapes to one another over the telephone. When both were preparing for the premiere of a new Israeli piano concerto, they explored its problems over the telephone by actually playing the music to one another. The phone is, in fact, an important bond within this group of internationally active artists who seldom have an opportunity to be together for any length of time. The phone is also an extension of their humor: they will call one another, imitating the voices of mutual friends or business associates, to carry out elaborate and preposterous practical jokes. It was, in the early seventies, a sort of musical Camelot, the long-distance phone replacing the Round Table, with Danny its King Arthur. However, these friendships often have deeper expressions. Not long ago, Barenboim used his only two days off during a New York Philharmonic engagement to fly to Los Angeles and play the Beethoven *Emperor* Concerto with a youth orchestra conducted by Zubin Mehta's father, Mehli.

Moreover, this circle was not merely social in function: with Barenboim as the catalytic force, it entered upon a variety of chamber-music ventures. For three years beginning in 1968 Barenboim was director of the South Bank Music Festival, based on London's complex of auditoriums including the Purcell Room and Queen Elizabeth Hall as well as Royal Festival Hall. The repertory for these summer festivals was primarily chamber music and works within the means of the ECO, with the core of participants drawn from the Barenboim circle. Even Zubin Mehta was enlisted to play double bass in the Schubert *Trout* Quintet, an event covered in a BBC television program devoted to Barenboim and his friends.

To varying degrees and in different ways, the musicians in Barenboim's circle shared basic musical principles and approaches despite considerable artistic individuality and freedom. Several of the group participated regularly in the annual Casals Festivals in Puerto Rico and were sympathetic to Don Pablo's intensely romantic approach. Jacqueline du Pré had studied with Mstislav Rostropovich, whose freely expressive style had great appeal to the group. But the dominant influence on Mehta, Barenboim, and others undoubtedly was that of Wilhelm Furtwängler. Both Barenboim and Mehta were allowed by Frau Elisabeth Furtwängler to study her late husband's marked scores and to listen to private recordings that she had. (Barenboim has played the Furtwängler Piano Concerto with the Berlin Philharmonic, conducted by Mehta.) Interest in Furtwängler was by no means confined to the conductors in the group: it was equally strong on such instrumentalists as Ashkenazy. At gatherings of the Barenboim circle, Furtwängler performances were played and compared with one another and with those of other conductors. Since Barenboim was the only one of the younger members of this group who had actually heard Furtwängler "live," he had a special authority in such discussions.

Another strong bond of ·most, though not all, of the Barenboim circle is that they are Jewish and share a strong commitment to Israel. The most prominent non-Jewish colleague, Zubin Mehta, is musical director of the Israel Philharmonic Orchestra. The fact that Barenboim is a Jew unquestionably affected the course of his career. Music has long been one of the vocations that enabled a talented and ambitious Jew to emerge from the ghetto. Earlier generations applauded a Heifetz or a Rubinstein, not only as exemplars of Jewish talent but as objects of gentile admiration as well. Barenboim's status in the international Jewish community is, however, somewhat different: he is an Israeli as well as a Jew. Though born in South America, he is an Israeli citizen; though he lives in London, his "home" is Israel. This is true of such other young Israeli musicians as Perlman and Zukerman, who were trained abroad and still live most of the time away from Israel. In this respect, Barenboim is the archtypical Israeli artist of our time. The older type of admiration remains, but to it is added a strong element of Zionism, of pride in Israel, and of the Israeli artist's responsibility to Israel.

On each occasion when Israel was attacked by the Arabs, her musicians rallied to her cause. From their homes abroad or from tours, they returned to play for the soldiers and civilians of Israel, often canceling lucrative engagements in Europe or the United States. A focal point of such activity is the Israel Philharmonic Orchestra, with whom Barenboim has appeared in time of crisis, as well as in time of peace. And then, when the crisis at home passes, the Philharmonic takes off to tour abroad, playing benefit concerts to which Barenboim, like his colleagues Jewish and gentile, contributes his services for return far below what he would normally receive and frequently for nothing at all. The support that Barenboim gives to Israel, morally and financially, is reciprocated by music-lovers in the Jewish community in Europe and America. They not only flock to the concerts of the Israel Philharmonic and other Israeli artists that are given as direct benefits or to promote the sale of bonds but are also faithful patrons at other Barenboim appearances.

The best media copy to come from Barenboim's circle stemmed from his marriage to Jacqueline du Pré, the whirlwind international courtship that preceded their wedding during the Six-Day War in 1967, their storybook domestic and artistic union during the next few years, and the tragic turn their marriage took in 1973.

Although their paths might have crossed earlier in the social activity of London musical circles, neither was conscious of the other personally—only distantly as emerging celebrities in the musical world. Barenboim apparently first heard of Du Pré when he was confined to bed at the Westbury Hotel in London with glandular fever, and mutual friends consoled him with tales of Du Pré's similar ailment at the same time. Although they exchanged symptoms over the phone then, they actually first met at a London party early in 1967 at the home of pianist Fou Ts'ong. As Du Pré later told London journalist Maureen McCleave, "I was shy, more or less—until I met Danny, that is. I was shy except when I played, and then it never bothered me what happened. . . . When I met him, I was very huge; I weighed one hundred and eighty pounds and I felt like a great lump. I had been in Russia for five months eating potatoes and studying with Rostropovich. We were all drinking coffee when this small dynamic young thing burst into the room. Being a very shy and somewhat insecure person at the time, the only thing I could do was to get up and play."

Within two weeks Barenboim determined to marry her; rearranged his performance schedule; and, if that was impossible, ran up his long-distance phone bills to astronomic heights while he conducted a courtship on two continents and behind the Iron Curtain. In the spring of 1967, they announced their engagement to be married the following September, the earliest that their respective schedules would allow.

However, when the Six-Day War broke out in Israel in June 1967, Barenboim and Du Pré canceled their previous schedules and hastened to Israel to play for the troops and civilians. On June 15, after Du Pré had received full ritual conversion to Judaism, they were married in Jerusalem. That night they appeared in Tel Aviv with the Israel Philharmonic. The bride played the Schumann Cello Concerto conducted by the groom. He played a Mozart concerto, conducted by Zubin Mehta, who gave the bride a fur hat to match the mink coat from her husband.

Jacqueline du Pré was born in Oxford, the first of her family since the Norman Conquest to be born away from the island of Jersey. Like Barenboim, she grew up in a musical household: her mother was a musician—a pianist, conductor, and composer at the Royal Academy. For her fifth birthday, she received a small cello, having been captivated by the sound of the instrument on a BBC broadcast. In London her principal teacher was William Pleeth, but she also worked with Paul Tortelier in Paris and with Rostropovich in Moscow. She was twenty-three when she married Barenboim, already launched on a distinguished career with encouragement from such musicians as Sir John Barbirolli.

The courtship and marriage of the Barenboims captured the fancy of musicians and public alike. They were hailed as the most touching musical couple since Clara and Robert Schumann. The "musical romance of the century" became the focal point of media interest that far outstripped previous coverage of the partying, practical jokes, international phone calls and public avowals of friendship and affection on the part of "Pear-tree" (an anglicization of Barenboim), Jackie (or, as her husband dubbed her, "Smiley"), Zubin and Nancy Mehta, Vladimir (Volodya) Ashkenazy, Pinky and Genie Zukerman, Itzhak and Toby Perlman, and their friends. Defending Danny's fondness for inviting thirty or forty friends to impromptu postconcert parties, Smiley pointed out, "It's really nothing. Zubin takes the whole symphony and that's a hundred people." On such occasions, Barenboim's organizing talents were given full play: if Smiley looked tired during supper at a restaurant, one of the guests was ordered to take her home so that she could rest a while before the group rejoined her there. The guest list was also checked to make sure that it included proper personnel for late-hour chamber music.

Although Du Pré and Barenboim continued to pursue their individual careers—he at the piano and increasingly on the podium and she with her cello—they tried to coordinate their schedules, not necessarily for joint appearances in chamber music or concertos but just to be together. Their friends have described Barenboim's attitude during these years as one of intense solicitude and protectiveness. Nevertheless, he did not dominate her musically: her own way of playing the cello, very like that of her much admired teacher Rostropovich, was passionate and broadly conceived. "Playing lifts you out of yourself into a delirious plane, where you feel abandoned and very happy—like being drunk," she once said. And Barenboim has admitted that she was not always easy to conduct with in a concerto: "Sometimes we mortals have difficulty in following her." When someone marveled that two such diverse and forceful characters could get on so well, Du Pré replied, "Music is the spine through it all."

Early in 1973, one began to hear in Du Pré's playing technical problems that were not necessarily a manifestation of musical exuberance. A joint recital with Barenboim in New York received an unfavorable review, and her appearance in March at a Philharmonic pension fund concert was canceled, on account of "arm trouble." The medical diagnosis was multiple sclerosis, a devastating disease of neural deterioration that is virtually incurable and frequently fatal. The best medical advice on two continents was sought, but nothing could be done to arrest the progress of the disease. New living quarters were found in London with the help of Margot Fonteyn, whose husband is a paraplegic, and Du Pré progressed under therapy and expert medical care to the point where, in the fall of 1977, she began to teach. "I tried to put my energy into teaching, which isn't easy because most teachers teach by demonstration. Since I learned music instinctively, I never think about it. Now I am forced to be totally articulate because I cannot demonstrate. I try to remember what I loved, and I have learned how to put those thoughts into words." It is the nature of her illness that Jacqueline du Pré alternates between periods of improvement and serious setbacks: during the former it is possible for her to resume her teaching, but during the latter, Barenboim cancels his appearances to be at her side and summons the best doctors he and his friends can find.

Because of his wife's illness, Barenboim tries to spend as much time as possible with her at their home in London. Since taking over the Orchestre de Paris in 1975, he commutes between London and Paris during the weeks he is working in the French capital, spending virtually every weekend at home with her. If she feels up to seeing visitors, she arranges for them to drop in then. But they also spend much time together alone. Deprived of their former means of communication through playing music together, they have learned to talk about music. When he is away from London, they talk constantly by phone. In America, Barenboim keeps in mind the difference in time in London, planning his calls when she is least tired or likely to be resting and avoiding in his own schedule any commitments that might interfere with his calls to his wife. Barenboim conducts and plays much less in the United States than he did prior to Du Pré's illness and his taking on the Orchestre de Paris. On a number of occasions he has canceled or curtailed engagements away from London. In the spring of 1978, when Du Pré suffered a relapse, Barenboim canceled everything, including participation in Mehta's "farewell" concerts in Los Angeles and the thirtieth anniversary celebration of Israel's nationhood.

Du Pré's illness has been deeply felt by the Barenboim circle of friends. They have organized a multiple sclerosis research foundation in her name, to which Barenboim and others contribute fees received from benefit concert performances.

When asked what recordings Barenboim considered his best—those that most completely represented his artistry—he replied with a laugh, "The two I am making next week!" Flippant as this may sound, this remark actually tells a lot about Barenboim's attitude about recording and music-making in general. He has probably made more recordings, at the keyboard and on the podium, than any other artist of like age. They include his own piano solos; chamber music in various combinations with his wife, Zukerman, and clarinettist Gervaise de Peyer; lieder with Janet Baker and Fischer-Dieskau; and, of course, conducting such orchestras as the ECO, the Chicago Symphony Orchestra, the New Philharmonia, the New York Philharmonic, the Philadelphia Orchestra, and the Orchestre de Paris. His repertory on records —by no means as wide as it is in concert—is still both catholic and intensive. With the ECO and larger orchestras he has explored the music of Elgar extensively. In addition to Mozart's piano concertos, he has also recorded most of that composer's important symphonies and some of his operas. Virtually all of Beethoven's piano music—solos, concertos, and chamber music—is included in his recorded repertory. Recently, he has begun an exploration of French orchestral music with the Orchestre de Paris and embarked on major Schumann and Bruckner cycles with the Chicago Symphony Orchestra. Given his dual role as pianist and conductor, his recorded repertory is unmatched by any other musician today, young or old.

He has, for instance, recorded twice as many Beethoven sonatas and Mozart concertos as has Rudolf Serkin, an artist twice his age, who specializes in the same repertory. Artur Schnabel was fifty when he began his historic recordings of the Beethoven sonatas, and he took five years to complete the series. A pioneering apostle in his time of the Mozart piano concertos, Schnabel recorded only six over a span of two decades. There are, of course, technical and economic reasons for these quantitative differences. Schnabel's Beethoven sonata series involved a great financial risk that could be undertaken during the 1930s only through initial release as a limited "Beethoven Society" edition; in the vastly expanded international record market of today, the long-play reissues of the series as historic documents have sold many more copies than the original 78-rpm discs did. Moreover, recording in the prewar era was a much more arduous task than it became after the advent of magnetic recording tape. Schnabel worked under great strain to avoid technical slips that would require repeating an entire four-minute side and risking another error in correcting the first. Nowadays, it is possible to splice corrections into the original tape or to combine sections of various "takes" to obtain an optimum performance, a practice Barenboim, like many others, deplores.

Beyond these technical and economic factors, there is also a difference in Barenboim's attitude toward recording. To musicians of an earlier generation, a recording was a major and singular event, an opportunity to create a definitive statement, not only for the present but for posterity. But, for Barenboim, a recording is a document of a given moment, a reflection of how he played or conducted a given piece of music at a given time and place. Although he never approaches a recording session lightly, he does not seek a letter-perfect reading at the expense of spontaneity or expressive involvement. Nor will he record a work in a succession of short takes, or "inserts," just to make his task easier. In the first movement of Beethoven's *Eroica*, a work he has not recorded, he cites a difficult passage in bars 96 and 97 what would "sound" more effectively if the conductor and orchestra began over again at bar 95. Such a practice in a recording session, he feels strongly, would completely violate his musical ideals by destroying the structure and continuity of the music. In fact, the very awkwardness of that brief passage is essential to the context of the music at this point.

Working as a soloist with another conductor can produce quite different results from Barenboim. His recordings of the Brahms piano concertos with Sir John Barbirolli have a mellowness and integrity that reflect the shared ideas of the conductor and soloist, especially their mutual admiration for Furtwängler. To judge from the concert performances in New York early in 1979, his new recordings of these same concertos with the New York Philharmonic under Mehta will be quite

different, reflecting both Barenboim's greater maturity and the interaction with a quite different conductor. Similarly there will unquestionably be differences between the recordings of the five Beethoven
concertos that he is scheduled to make with Leonard Bernstein and the
Vienna Philharmonic and the controversial ones he made many years
earlier with Otto Klemperer conducting.

Suvi Raj Grub, who produced Barenboim's early records for EMI,
has written, with pardonable lack of objectivity, of this collaboration
between two very dissimilar artists who were both his close friends and
colleagues: "At the age of twenty-two, Daniel Barenboim already had an
established reputation as a sensitive musician whose performances were
characterized by powerful imagination. . . . Here too was a pianist
whose music-making matches that of Klemperer's. There was the same
sense of style, of the feeling for architectural design and for the long-
breathed phrase, and with all attention to detail which revealed so much
more of the musical score than one normally hears. Above all there was
in Barenboim the same spontaneity and sense of adventure with which
Klemperer approached a familiar work, so that a listener felt that he
was hearing the work for the first time."

The result was a highly controversial series of performances. The
reviewer for *High Fidelity* noted "a yawning chasm that separates the
yielding, sensuously romantic Barenboim and the didactic, stiff-jointed
Klemperer." In England the editors of the *Penguin Stereo Record
Guide* were more sympathetic: "No more individual performances of
the Beethoven concertos have ever been put on record, and not everyone
will like them. . . . For every willfulness of the plodding Klemperer
there is a youthful spark from the spontaneously combusting Barenboim.
That may imply a lack of sympathy between conductor and soloist,
but plainly this is not so. These recordings were made much more
quickly than usual, with long 'takes' allowing a sense of continuity
rare on records."

Another Beethoven series, recorded for the 1970 Beethoven bicentennial in a relatively short time, is that of the piano trios with
Du Pré, Zukerman, and, in op. 11, de Peyer. This set, comprising seven
major works plus a number of shorter pieces (nearly four and a half

hours of actual playing time), was recorded in the space of a week, often in takes of more than one movement. Warts and all, this record documents the kind of spontaneity that Barenboim seeks in his music-making.

The maturing of Barenboim's artistry as a pianist in the late 1960s coincides with his emergence as a conductor of full-scale orchestras and of the ECO independently of the keyboard. He did some conducting in 1957 and 1958 in Haifa, but now dates his professional career as a conductor from 1962, when he led full-scale orchestras in Sydney and Melbourne. Although he began working with the ECO in 1965, he did not direct a symphony orchestra in Europe until the New Philharmonia in London in 1967. In that same year, he toured the United States with the Israel Philharmonic after the Six-Day War, playing concertos and occasionally conducting.

However, his New York debut in April 1968 as a symphonic conductor was, in the great tradition of "breaks," as a last-minute substitute for an ailing colleague. Istvan Kertesz had been scheduled to conduct the London Symphony in a series of four concerts at Carnegie Hall, featuring Barenboim's friend Vladimir Ashkenazy in one Rachmaninoff concerto on each program. Barenboim's contribution made a favorable impression on Harold C. Schonberg of the *New York Times*:

Mr. Barenboim is a born conductor, and doubtless will develop into a major one. He directed the London Symphony in Weber's *Oberon* Overture and the Beethoven *Eroica,* and his work was impressive. Technically, it was impeccable. Mr. Barenboim has a good ear, a fine feeling for balance, and the clearest, most incisive of beats. He is not one of those right-hand conductors whose left hand flaps symmetrically along. His left hand is independent, busy but not fussy, supplementing and not echoing the right. As an interpreter he leans toward the literalist school, but with a significant difference. That is, he observes every note value, every nuance, and is scrupulous in following the composer's intentions, but—unlike so many of the younger conductors today—he brings some personality to his work. It is far from anonymous conducting. It is spacious, rather leisurely, but not out to impress, and completely divorced from the hectic, neurotic quality so often heard. Indeed there is something of the old Middle European school in it. What it lacks, at present, is metrical variety. The phrases are a little too regular, the meters lack the deft delicate shifts and adjustments that more experienced conductors can bring. Nevertheless, the *Eroica* moved in a strong manner, and in the slow movement, there was a kind of intensity that speaks well for Mr. Barenboim's future.

These New York appearances with the London Symphony Orchestra led to a number of engagements with the most important orchestras in the United States. Within a few years following his appearance with the Boston Symphony Orchestra at Tanglewood in the summer of 1969, he also appeared as guest, either in the summer or during winter subscription series, with the orchestras of Los Angeles, New York, Philadelphia, Chicago, and Cleveland. He now spends several weeks a year guest-conducting American orchestras and invariably must decline requests for more time there. However, during the 1970–71 concert season, Barenboim appeared more in New York than he has ever done before or since—in fact probably more (thirty-one concerts) than any other visiting musician has and certainly in more varied capacities. In honor of the Beethoven bicentennial he played all thirty-two of the piano sonatas and, with Du Pré, the five cello sonatas. He conducted both the Philadelphia and the New York Philharmonic orchestras and collaborated in lieder recitals with Dietrich Fischer-Dieskau and Janet Baker. A highlight of this truly protean performer's season was an appearance in Carnegie Hall with the Philadelphia Orchestra in December 1970. (This was part of a two-week engagement with that orchestra, most of it in Philadelphia.) The program included the Elgar Cello Concerto, with Du Pré as soloist, and the Beethoven Second and Schumann Fourth symphonies. Following this concert, Schonberg was especially glowing in his praise of Barenboim:

He has come up as a pianist and only recently has turned to the podium, but it is on the podium that he belongs. Certainly he conducts with much more freedom and authority than he plays the piano. His conducting may not be to everybody's taste. He favors slow, deliberate tempos, and he uses a great deal of rhythmic fluctuation. His personality is so strong, his style so naturally big, his control over the players so powerful, that he is able to be his own man. At the age of twenty-eight, he has arrived at the point where agreement or disagreement with his interpretation is immaterial. This is a musician with something to say, and what he has to say is important. Thus one might argue over fine points—a tempo here, an accentuation there, but not with the basic strength of his ideas. Mr. Barenboim's rhythm is flawless. There are no accented upbeats in his work, nor is there ever a slackening of tension. Even when, in the slow movement of the Beethoven, and throughout the Schumann, Mr. Barenboim used tempo fluctuations, the basic meter remained intact. This kind of rhythmic control is unusual. It is seldom practiced today, though it goes back to the line from Wagner to Furtwängler. Conductors of the more objective Toscanini school generally avoid it. . . . The Schumann Fourth is a Romantic work that needs a Romantic interpretation. Traditions of performance practiced in Romantic music have all but vanished, and musicians today have much more feeling for the Classic style. It may be that Mr. Barenboim has the ability to restore some of that tradition. What he did was to conduct in a manner that combined unity and variety. Avoiding the spasmodic stop and change-gear rhythms that many musicians consider "Romantic," Mr. Barenboim took the D-minor Symphony in one grand sweep, changing details within the line. He left plenty of breathing space, and he had enough confidence in his instincts to insert ritards where the meaning of the music so indicated (and never mind whether they were marked in the score), and his alert rhythm kept the music in constant flow.

There are moments when he could have taken faster tempos and other moments where the markings were a shade too emphatic. But the important thing is that the symphony moved, and the Schumann Fourth, with its constant violin diddling and repeated sections (not all of which Mr. Barenboim took) is a hard work to make move. This was ardent conducting—big, bold and soaring, with a perfectly gauged sprint in the last few measures. With such control and vitality of music-making, it is rather silly to call Mr. Barenboim a major talent. He already has arrived. He is here.

A few weeks later, when Barenboim was beginning his debut engagement with the New York Philharmonic, Schonberg was less enthusiastic:

It may be that Daniel Barenboim tried too hard at his Saturday night Philharmonic concert, but whatever the reason, he did not conduct with the flair and authority demonstrated last month with the Philadelphia Orchestra.

However, later in the same engagement, Schonberg found more merit in Barenboim's work:

His conducting—very different from his piano playing, by the way—is based on constant fluctuation of tempo, without losing what Richard Wagner in his essay on conducting called "Melos"—the underlying rhythm of the entire work. Mr. Barenboim applies his ideas not indiscriminately, but in relation to the specific piece of music. . . . In the Tchaikovsky Fourth Symphony, his fluctuations were wild. This was a most unusual reading, even eccentric at moments. One could see where Mr. Barenboim was heading, and even approve, but there were some tinkerings in the first movement that were awkward and hindered the natural flow of the music. The conductor was confident enough to insert ritards where none were indicated in the score, but at times he threw them out to a point that was almost ludicrous.

Barenboim has spent more time with the Chicago Symphony than with any other American orchestra. A brief tour of eastern Michigan in November 1970 preceded his first appearances in Orchestra Hall. In the first concert, on the campus of Michigan State University at East Lansing, Jacqueline du Pré was soloist in the Dvořák Cello Concerto, which was recorded a week later. He then appeared in Chicago in six out of the next eight seasons. From the outset, Barenboim has received a mixed critical reception in Chicago. On the occasion of his debut, Bernard Jacobson wrote in the *Daily News*:

Barenboim is twenty-eight now, and he has been conducting regularly for only four years, but he will one day be spoken of in the terms we now reserve for conductors like Weingartner, Nikisch, and Furtwängler. With an economical and infallibly lucid baton he can make an orchestra play to the hilt of its capacity for precision, power, and eloquence—he has made music I know by heart come to life for me with the intensity of first acquaintance.

Another critic present at the same concert noted, however, that some subscribers walked out after each movement of the Bruckner Fourth Symphony. In 1977, Thomas Willis wrote of Barenboim in the *Chicago Tribune*:

> The analytic streak which at one time threatened to turn him into something of a pedant was muted. . . . His inevitably clean baton technique emphasized the free interplay of theme and tempo variations which are a part of musical understanding.

Other critics were less cordial, referring on various occasions to a Brahms *German Requiem* as "drenched with feeling but low on drama," a Haydn symphony characterized by "overabundance of sweetness though hardly much light," and Schumann's First Symphony played with "affectionate ritards and sentimental phrasing."

Despite mixed critical reception in his American appearances, he is extremely popular with two elements that influence a conductor's career —orchestra players and symphony managements. Barenboim's solid popularity at the box office is not the only reason why orchestras in the United States and Europe seek to engage him. He is easy to work with —demanding on artistic matters but not unreasonably temperamental. In fact, orchestra managements will go to great lengths to accommodate Barenboim's crowded schedule, not merely to keep his goodwill but out of genuine friendship. Nor is it by any means inconsequential to symphonic administrators that Barenboim gets on well with the players of the orchestras he conducts. Managers like conductors who do not create personnel problems, and music directors do not like to find their players displaying the ill-effects of several weeks of fighting a guest.

Rightly or wrongly, orchestra musicians are notoriously critical of conductors, and few reputations, even those of the most glamorous international stars, can survive the scathing candor of a musicians' bull session. Barenboim survives better than most. As Willis wrote in the *Tribune* in 1972,

> Of all the younger conductors at work with major symphony orchestras today, Daniel Barenboim is probably one of the most respected by players. In many ways he is a musician's musician. He programs mainstream masterworks whose substance symphony men understand inside out. He is an analyst whose interpretive ideas are musical and structural, not dramatic. And his conducting technique is far and away superior to that of most of his colleagues—clear, incisive, and to the point.

Thirty years ago no orchestra player would have dared to address Toscanini as "Arturo" or Reiner as "Fritz" but Barenboim is "Danny" to most of the players in the orchestras he conducts. But familiarity is generally kept backstage: when the players are in their seats and Barenboim on the podium, the atmosphere is more formal, businesslike but not strained. From the outset, he makes it clear to the players that he is there to give the music his best and that he expects the same of them. He knows that an orchestra can "play games" with a conductor if he is not completely straightforward with the musicians. Barenboim has a keen understanding of crucial aspects of orchestral-player psychology, particularly in his recognition that these musicians typically grew up with hopes of virtuoso careers only to find themselves taking orders from someone whom they often regard as their inferior artistically. Barenboim's attitude toward his own talent and career—his acceptance of the responsibilities that are entailed in his great gift and his own vision of his career as an evolutionary process—impress orchestra players as modest and realistic.

Although some deplore his spreading himself too thin in his schedule (a complaint by no means confined to Barenboim), virtually all players agree that "he knows his scores." One of the highest compliments that a jaded symphony player can bestow, this phrase concerns more than a mere memorization of the notes: it includes the players' recognition that a conductor is in full control of all aspects of harmony, structure, timbre, and stylistic ambience of a piece. It assumes, moreover, that a conductor has the ability to communicate his "knowing the score" to the players. Although Barenboim is an extremely articulate talker about music, he curbs his verbal facility on the podium. He communicates a great deal with gestures that are extremely "orchestral" for a musician so completely at home at the keyboard. Many orchestral musicians claim that they can immediately tell if the piano or a string instrument was the conductor's original medium. The right-arm gestures of Toscanini in his time or Ormandy today are said to reveal a grounding in the bowing of a string instrument. On the other hand, a conductor who started as a pianist may be less sensitive to absolute pitch because of his long grounding in the tempered scale of the piano, but may be firmer in his beat and a more critical listener to harmony and timbre. Whatever validity these distinctions may have, they are a very real part of the mythology of the orchestra.

In Barenboim's case, musicians regard it as a compliment to say that he does not conduct like a pianist. One reason for this observation may well be the attention that he gives, both in gesture and in working with the principal players, to string bowing, the very basis of expressive phrasing. In discussing bowings with the orchestra, Barenboim spontaneously uses gestures of his right arm as if he were playing a violin or cello. Without impairing his own authority or giving the impression of condescension, he frequently consults principal players—especially such elder statesmen of orchestral string-playing as cellist Frank Miller and violist Milton Preves of the Chicago Symphony Orchestra—on specific details, or asks an entire section, "Are you comfortable with this bowing?" On the other hand, when he believes that a certain technique is necessary for expressive reasons, he does not hesitate to impose his own approach. Although he usually supplies his own sets of marked orchestral parts, he can be flexible in changing his instructions when a more musical solution to a problem emerges from the interplay of conductor and orchestra. He seldom sings to the orchestra, as some other conductors do, but obtains the phrasing he wants by gestures and by the flexibility of his right-hand beat. He also has a way of cupping his left hand to his ear, a gesture that may indicate that someone is out of tune or may, in other contexts, be a signal to a musician to play louder. (When asked about this particular gesture, Barenboim expressed surprise about it and was not quite sure why he did it.)

Like other conductors of his generation, Barenboim belongs very definitely to the nondictatorial school of conducting, quite different from the generation of Toscanini, Koussevitzky, Reiner, and Szell. (The story is told of one violinist in Koussevitzky's Boston Symphony who accidentally dropped his bow but continued to go through the motions of playing for fear of arousing the ire of the conductor.) It is doubtful, in fact, whether any conductor, certainly one who wants to guest-conduct extensively, could discipline orchestras as ruthlessly as did many of the great conductors of an earlier generation. Yet no conductor can achieve the necessary discipline to make a hundred players perform one man's conception without authority of some sort. With Barenboim, that authority comes from what he brings to the podium before he ever raises his baton: his instinctive understanding of players as people and artists, a personal magnetism that makes discipline and authority acceptable to the orchestra, and, above all, that knowledge of the score.

Barenboim works in rehearsal with that great concentration for which he is famous. Since he does not conduct anything but the best orchestras, he need not waste time teaching the players a work, even one they may not be familiar with. He may precede going through a movement for the first time with a few verbal instructions as to how he wants specific passages played. However, he generally works in relatively long spans of time without stopping for correction, except at the beginning of a movement where he may make an extra effort to get the music started the right way. However, during the course of playing, he will make brief verbal corrections or comments of approval, sometimes simply by gestures. Most correcting is done bit by bit after the whole movement is played; Barenboim has obviously made mental note of each passage that requires attention, and his ability to recall every such passage is one way he arouses the players' respect for his command of the score. A conductor's failure to correct mistakes that may have been made in rehearsal is one sign to the players that he does not know the score; on the other hand, excessive attention to trivial errors that the players themselves already recognize is a serious black mark in orchestra players' eyes.

Once he has a given work in satisfactory condition, he sets it aside until the final rehearsal, at which he generally goes through the entire program with very few interruptions for correction. However, when he prepared the Bruckner Fifth Symphony with the Chicago Symphony Orchestra, he did not ask the orchestra to play the entire work at the last rehearsal on the day of the concert for fear of wearing out the lips of the brass players and tiring the string players with long stretches of cramping tremolos. He agreed, however, that he could take such a chance only with an orchestra of Chicago's caliber. (The players' recognition of such consideration is another reason why they admire Barenboim.)

Barenboim's baton technique is not flamboyant; he does not put on a choreographic exhibition either in rehearsal or in concert, although his gestures may be more fluid in the latter, especially when he and the orchestra get caught up in the music. Players sitting in front of him all agree that he communicates a great deal with his eyes, an observation that will surprise no one who has talked face to face with him. At a concert, he enters briskly, acknowledges applause politely but almost as a matter of fact. He turns quickly to the orchestra, pauses briefly to focus his concentration, and starts conducting almost immediately. His demeanor is reserved and businesslike; his whole attention is focused on the orchestra, apparently unconcerned with how his back may appear to the audience. When a piece is finished, he bows, smiles slightly and generously shares the applause with the orchestra. In his attitude toward the audience when face to face with it, as opposed to when he is conducting, he is far more reserved than he is offstage with people in his dressing room following a concert.

Just as he has always memorized a piano work before touching the keyboard, Barenboim starts his study of an orchestral work by memorizing it. This is the first step in what he sometimes refers to as a process of "de-composing" the music at hand. This is analogous to the way in which a tailor copies a jacket: before he can make a new one, he must unstitch the old one to be copied. With a piece of music, Barenboim must re-create for himself the process whereby the composer himself created it. This is something quite different from interpreting the notes printed on a sheet of score, for Barenboim seeks to get behind the notes, between them, to what he regards as the flesh and blood of a truly biological creation.

"The process of the interpreter in the best sense of the word is the exact opposite of the one who composes. A composer starts out with some idea, maybe a motif or a melodic idea, or just a group of notes that have whatever characteristics or whatever binding material there is. It's like an atom. Then he develops that and builds on that and adds to that and subtracts from that and does all sorts of things, each according to his own method and personality, so that in the end he arrives at a complete piece. Now, when we as interpreters get the piece, we are in the opposite situation. We don't have all these little cells, these little atoms, that have been really at the genesis of his creation. We have the complete picture, as it were, and we have to 'de-compose' it—in other words, to go backward and try and find what the cells or these little atoms were, in order to understand how it was put together.

"I am not for one minute trying to suggest that the way I analyze a piece is the way the composer analyzed it. Not at all. What I am saying is that it is absolutely essential for an interpreter to be able to analyze and de-compose something in order then to re-create it. Sometimes the composer may have written something from a subconscious point of view; when we must re-create this subconscious state, we can only do it through our conscious means."

This, he believes, was the method of Furtwängler, who had, in Barenboim's opinion, a remarkable sense of the balance between the emotional and the rational. He recalls seeing in George Szell's studio in Cleveland an affectionately inscribed photograph of Furtwängler. Though no two conductors have been more different superficially in temperament or in the final results they achieved, both were masters, in Barenboim's opinion, of musical structure. The structure of music is for Barenboim far more than the succession or repetition of melodies. It is rooted as well in tempo and in harmonic progression. In his view, tempo fluctuations—in his own performances as well as in Furtwängler's —are not arbitrarily chosen for effect: the second subject slower than the first or a ritard for the transition from development to recapitulation in a sonata-form movement. Such changes may or may not be valid, depending on the total structure of the music. For Barenboim, tempo is not an absolute: it is the relation between tempos that clarifies the structure of a work, especially when that relation is coordinated with harmonic progression. He recognizes, too, that tempo is very much an expression of the conductor's own temperament: Toscanini's intensity at a slower tempo would be a travesty.

Long regarded as a leading spokesman in his generation for the Furtwänglerian approach as opposed to that of Toscanini, Barenboim recognizes the cultural forces that underlie the quite different musicality of these two conductors: "If Toscanini had grown up in Berlin or Vienna, you know, he would not have been the same. Furtwängler grew up in the mecca of Western orchestral music—Berlin, Munich, Leipzig, Vienna—where everything he heard and did was related to that tradition. He heard Wagner operas where they had been first performed, done by people who remembered that. But Toscanini started out in Parma—an absolutely uncultivated, backward, musical territory. When he fought for rhythm and intonation, he was working in an atmosphere where people, if there was a nice high note, would sit on it for a while. So, when he fought for the actual interpretation of music, he fought for fidelity to the score."

Wagner's music was radically new to Italy when Toscanini crusaded for it in his youth. Although the *Ring* cycle had been introduced to Italy by a German touring company, Toscanini inaugurated his first post as music director—in Turin in 1895—with the premiere performance by an Italian company of *Götterdämmerung*. He went on to give similar Italian premieres of three more Wagner operas—*Siegfried, Die Meistersinger,* and *Tristan und Isolde.* Moreover, he sought completely new standards in the performance of German symphonic music, another instance of what many Italians of his day regarded as Teutonic radicalism.

If Barenboim views Toscanini as standing somewhat apart from the mainstream of Austro-German music, he finds Furtwängler at its very center. The particular sonority Furtwängler evoked from the orchestra—warm, mellow, and harmonically colored, the very antithesis of Toscanini's tight intensity—Barenboim deems the most perfectly suited to this music: "Furtwängler's was a conception of sound based very much on harmonic tension and on a tremendous feeling for the structure of a piece. There was something organic in everything he did, where every detail was very much related to the whole unity, in the same way that the waves are related to the sea or the trees to the forest. Structurally he knew exactly how to build a movement so that it had a climactic point, that it had a feeling of growth, a gradual mounting of tension."

Strict fidelity to the score is an ambiguous concept to Barenboim: "The composer gives you a guide to the dynamics, he tells you where he wants a crescendo or where he wants a diminuendo, but he doesn't give you a guide to the degree or a guide to the fluctuations. He doesn't tell you how far a crescendo goes, how much. These are things you have to really understand and feel yourself. And the same thing with tempo. He gives you a basic idea, but the fluctuations of tempo you have to understand and feel yourself."

In contrast to his programming as pianist or conductor of the ECO, Barenboim's repertory with full orchestra is much more centered on mid- and late-nineteenth-century music, with Schumann, Bruckner, Mahler, Berlioz, Elgar, and Saint-Saëns added to his earlier interest in Brahms. His great zeal for the music of Bruckner, which he shares with his friend Zubin Mehta, is popularly and correctly associated with Furtwängler's influence. In 1972 he conducted the Cleveland Orchestra in New York City in a performance of the Bruckner Seventh Symphony that Donal Henahan of the *New York Times* reviewed:

The age of musical controversy is not dead. Daniel Barenboim stirred a mild tremor or two at Carnegie Hall on Monday by conducting the Cleveland Orchestra in a remarkably luxuriant and elastically phrased performance of Bruckner's no. 7 in E. At the close of the Adagio, which

(35)

Mr. Barenboim chose to punctuate with a questionably authentic cymbals and triangle crash at the famous triple forte climax, a voice from the balcony called out in the hushed silence: "Beautiful—just like Wilhelm Furtwängler!" The remark had a sarcastic ring although admittedly it is difficult to judge such subjective matters.

London, the center of Barenboim's professional life as well as his home, enjoys the services of five first-class orchestras, four of them player-managed and therefore extremely sensitive both to the conductor's relations with players and to his ability to draw good audiences. Competition is keen between London orchestras, both for audiences and conductors, the more so because subscription systems of the American type are less of a factor in the operations of London orchestras. It is not surprising, therefore, that Barenboim is much sought after as a conductor by all of the London orchestras. However, each orchestra likes to establish something like a long-term relationship with its important guests. They are selected by representatives of the players themselves, who in turn rely financially on the takings from their performances and recordings. Barenboim's favored status with one of London's best orchestras, the London Philharmonic, reflects both its players' esteem and their knowledge that he will be a "good draw" in Royal Festival Hall for the few appearances he can make with them each season. However, Barenboim now appears less frequently as a conductor in London than he does in the United States or in France.

For several years, Barenboim was very active at the annual Edinburgh Festival, both as pianist and as conductor. It was there that he made his operatic debut, in Mozart's *Don Giovanni* in 1973, repeated in 1974, and followed by *Le Nozze di Figaro* in 1975 and 1976. Given the precosity of his pianistic and conducting activities, Barenboim came late to opera, being thirty-one at the time.

To judge from firsthand reports as well as the recording, Barenboim's *Don Giovanni* emphasized its *dramma* at the expense of the *giocoso*. Even ardent English admirers felt that, in his operatic debut, Barenboim went too far in slavish Furtwänglerism, and they tend to agree, in principle if not in outrage, with the *New York Times* critic Peter G. Davis who wrote of the recording of this *Don Giovanni,*

> This performance goes several leagues past Furtwängler in its subjectivity, misplaced sentimentality, and melodramatic breast beating. . . . The pacing is awful, painstakingly slow and deliberate, the orchestral sound is thick and turgid, dynamic accents are leaned upon heavily as each aria, duet, and ensemble heaves, groans, and grinds to the double bar line. Mozart called Don Giovanni a *dramma giocoso* and in his music evolved a delicate balance between comedy and drama that gives the opera its fascinating ambiguity. Barenboim, however, inflates every phrase with a ponderous sense of tragedy and gloom.

Whether or not Barenboim was consciously imitating Furtwängler's *Don,* his reading may well go back to that fountainhead of one school of German interpretation of *Don Giovanni,* E. T. A. Hoffmann's "A Tale of Don Juan." Furtwängler, like Mahler (as reported) before him, belonged to that school, as such colleagues as Richard Strauss, Fritz Busch, and Erich Kleiber did not. In any case, whether or not the Hoffmannesque *Don Giovanni* can be brought off, Barenboim did not do so. He was considerably more successful with his next Mozart production for Edinburgh, *Le Nozze di Figaro,* also recorded by EMI but not, understandably after the American reception of *Don Giovanni,* released in the United States.

Since conducting the Mozart operas in Edinburgh, he has given concert performances with the Orchestre de Paris of Berlioz's *Béatrice et Bénédict* and Saint-Saëns's *Samson et Dalila,* both of them recorded, as has been Cimarosa's *Il Matrimonio Segreto.* Early in 1979 he made his debut at the Berlin State Opera with *Le Nozze di Figaro*; whereas his previous Mozart opera performances had been criticized as being too slow in tempo much of the time, this one was condemned by the critic of *Opera News* as generally too fast. Wrote James Helme Sutcliffe of Barenboim's part in this new Berlin production,

> It all left me cold, mostly because of the perfect but bloodless playing of the orchestra, slick as a Madison Avenue commercial, lacking in every-

thing ingratiating and setting only one accent, the overemphasized for-
zando at "Almeno io per loro otterro" in the fourth act finale. Indeed,
Barenboim seemed so determined to break every speed record that the
final Allegro assai became a prestissimo and just avoided coming apart
at the seams.

At the same time that Barenboim was establishing himself as a
major conductor in the United States and the United Kingdom, he made
similar headway in Europe: he first conducted the Berlin Philharmonic
Orchestra in 1969 and the Orchestre de Paris in 1971. His success with
the latter led eventually to his becoming its director in 1975.

The Orchestre de Paris was conceived as a French effort to achieve
international grandeur in the symphonic field. Traditionally the Parisian orchestra scene had been chaotic, to say the least. The only firmly
established orchestra activity offering its players stable income under
contract was that of the government's National Orchestra of French
Radio and Television, known simply as the ORTF. There were other
orchestras, often player-managed as in London but, unlike London's,
notoriously unstable. There were also several "vanity" orchestras financed by friends or wealthy relatives of its specific conductors. In the
international music world, horror stories have long been rife about the
use of substitutes in French orchestras, most typically of the player who
announced that he could make all of the rehearsals, but not the concert
itself. The custom of sending substitutes to rehearsals and performances
was also the rule at the Opéra, where the orchestra players were under
salaried contracts. As a counterpart to Charles de Gaulle's national and
international effort to restore France to its historic position of political
grandeur, André Malraux and, after him, Georges Pompidou, set out
to achieve a similar rehabilitation of French art. The collection at the
Louvre was completely restored; the Opéra was totally reorganized
beginning in 1973 by the German impresario Rolf Liebermann; the
controversial center of contemporary art, visual and musical, at the
Beaubourg was planned and completed; and a new orchestra of international stature was decreed, for, wherever the French looked abroad,
they saw the great symphony orchestra as a symbol of national cultural

glory. London had five orchestras of world renown; the United States had at least six or seven; and Amsterdam and Vienna, capitals of nations smaller than France and less significant as international powers, had orchestras of great fame. Most galling of all, the Berlin Philharmonic, since 1954 under the direction of Herbert von Karajan, was the brightest gem in the cultural crown of an isolated, once devastated city. The solution was to build a new French orchestra on the American or Berlin model rather than that of London, with players contracted at good salaries to devote full time to their jobs. As in Berlin, but not in America, the major financing was to come from government, in this case both the city of Paris and the national government.

Obviously for such a venture to succeed, a conductor of international stature was required, and fortunately in 1967, a native French artist was available in the person of Charles Munch. A pupil and disciple of Furtwängler, for whom he had played as concertmaster of the Leipzig Gewandhaus, he had a distinguished career as a conductor in Paris before becoming Koussevitzky's successor in Boston from 1949 to 1962. Munch was a conductor of the inspirational, rather than disciplinary, school. At the age of seventy-six and already in poor health, he accepted the task of organizing the Orchestre de Paris and took it on a tour to the United States in 1968. During the course of that tour, in Richmond, Virginia, he died.

For its next conductor the Orchestre de Paris went abroad; through the efforts of Michel Glotz, a power in French musical and recording activities, the orchestra secured the services of Herbert von Karajan, then at the height of his myriad activities as "general music director of Europe." Unfortunately for Paris, these were not to include close attention to building another orchestra there as he had in Berlin. Karajan appeared in too few concerts with the Orchestre de Paris, made too few records with it, and won too few supporters in Parisian musical circles to be accounted a success. In 1971, another central European, Sir Georg Solti, added the Orchestre de Paris to his duties with the Chicago Symphony, having just left Covent Garden; while still with the Orchestre de Paris, he began in 1973 a close association with the Paris Opéra that was generally more successful than his orchestral role in the

French capital. (More recently, he has become principal conductor of the London Philharmonic Orchestra.) Shortly after Solti resigned from the Orchestre de Paris in 1974, it was announced that, effective in the fall of 1975, the orchestra's new director would be Daniel Barenboim, a choice generally welcomed because it was understood that the Orchestre de Paris would be Barenboim's major post and that the French orchestra would not have to share its conductor with other organizations at home and abroad, as had been the case with Karajan and Solti. Barenboim's fluent command of the French language was equally welcome.

For Barenboim the Orchestre de Paris was a very desirable post. His conducting career had reached the point where he needed a regular orchestra, not a succession of guest-conducting engagements. That was impossible in London, by the nature of the orchestras there, nor was there in Britain the challenge of orchestra-building that Paris offered. And, although several American orchestras were reported to be interested in involving Barenboim in something more than guest-conducting, Paris was closer to his home in London, which he had no intention of giving up, and to his sick wife, with whom he could spend more time if his work was in Paris.

From the outset, Barenboim has looked upon his post with the Orchestre de Paris as more than just another conducting stint. He has worked assiduously to build the quality of its personnel, joining himself with the management in dealing with the intricacies of Parisian musical habits and labor relations. He paid special attention to the brass section of the orchestra, for French brass instruments themselves and their players' technique and style of playing were quite different from that of other countries and quite inappropriate for the sonority that Barenboim desired for performances of Bruckner and other German music. For several years, the principal horn player of the Orchestre de Paris has been Myron Bloom, an American who long held the same position in the Cleveland Orchestra under George Szell. The Orchestre de Paris now uses German bassoons and trumpets but retains French flutes, clarinets, and oboes. Although he recognizes the dangers of depriving

(40)

this orchestra of its characteristic timbre, he finds these changes necessary if he is to achieve the Furtwänglerian sonority and harmonic richness that he desires, not just for Bruckner but for most of the non-French repertory.

Barenboim recognizes that the French audience has found some of his repertory hard to take—Bruckner more so than Mahler, he says. And he defends his programming from critics who say that he neglects French music, traditional and modern, to find room for his Teutonic favorites, by pointing out that he is merely bringing the French orchestra's repertory into the international mainstream. He has embarked on a complete Mahler cycle conducted by himself and guests spread over several years. He plans to cover all the orchestral music of Arnold Schoenberg, plus some of his chamber music in recitals under the orchestra's auspices. He has worked closely with Pierre Boulez since the latter's return to direct the center for new music at the Institute for Research and Acoustic/Musical Coordination (IRCAM). He participated in IRCAM's inaugural season as piano soloist, in chamber music, and as conductor of the Orchestre de Paris. He also commissioned a new orchestral work by Boulez. Furthermore, he is deeply concerned with completely reviewing the music of Debussy, which French musicians have come to take for granted.

Barenboim devotes at least twenty weeks a year to the Orchestre de Paris and more if there is an extensive tour. He actually conducts about half the subscription season in Paris. However, his responsibilities and interests extend well beyond simply conducting concerts. At his urging the Orchestre de Paris sponsors an extensive season of chamber music, in which he, orchestra members, and guests participate. There is also a fine professional chorus, directed by Arthur Oldham, with whom Barenboim worked at Edinburgh. Another Barenboim-instigated project is a youth orchestra, which he sees as a "feeder" of young personnel trained in the international style he seeks for the Orchestre de Paris.

Much of what Barenboim has been doing with the Orchestre de Paris since 1975 is based on the model of American rather than London practice. He has conceived and implemented the role of the orchestra's director as being more far-reaching than any of his three predecessors, at least two of whom had heavy administrative responsibilities elsewhere. Although management matters lie outside of his direct responsibility, he has urged the promotion of a scheme of regular subscription series on the American model and has worked to establish a regular schedule of concerts and rehearsals. Teaching commitments for the orchestra members, long a reason for excuses from rehearsal, are concentrated on Wednesday, to leave other days free for rehearsals and concerts.

There has been, however, a rumble of criticism in Paris of both Barenboim and the Orchestre de Paris. Much of the complaint about the orchestra arises from the resentment of its bigness: despite a great deal of musical activity in other French cities, many feel that the Orchestre de Paris and the Opéra receive a disproportionate amount of national government support. In Paris itself many feel that undue emphasis has been put on such nationally symbolic organizations as the Orchestre de Paris, the Opéra, and Boulez's IRCAM at the expense of a more balanced support by the government of a greater variety of activities and services in the nation's capital. There is resentment, as well, of Barenboim himself, partly because he is not a Frenchman (a criticism leveled even more strongly against his two immediate predecessors) and partly because of his effort to overcome French provincialism in repertory and orchestral style. Nevertheless, officials of the Orchestre de Paris report a steady growth of subscriptions and of attendance generally. Although other noted conductors appear as guests in the subscription season, Barenboim holds his own as a draw. All agree that a major problem is the halls in which the orchestra must play its concerts. Every program is played, and all rehearsals are held, in a vast and acoustically imperfect auditorium in the Palais des Congrès designed more for conventions than for music. It is located in a mammoth modern building at the Porte Maillot, which is more of a shopping mall than a center for performance arts. Its one advantage is a large seating capacity (3,700). Much smaller (1,700) is the old Théâtre des Champs-Elysées, where most of the subscription programs are repeated in more congenial surroundings. Barenboim is outspoken in his belief that a new concert hall is one of the highest cultural priorities of Paris.

Despite his intensive commitment to the Orchestre de Paris, which involves both conducting concerts and playing chamber music, Barenboim now conducts about fifty concerts a year elsewhere—in Berlin, London, Israel, and the United States. At one time, he mixed his conducting and piano playing on an almost day-to-day basis but more recently has tried to concentrate his respective activities into mutually exclusive periods. For one thing, there is the sheer physical problem of adjusting his arms and hands from the conducting gestures to playing the piano. For another, there is the matter of the different kinds of mental concentration required by two quite different ways of making music. Although he would now like to have as much as a month in which to "switch gears," this is not always possible. During his first two weeks in New York in 1979, however, he played and recorded both Brahms piano concertos with the Philharmonic under Mehta and then conducted the orchestra in a difficult program, including a Bruckner symphony. In fact, he was rehearsing the orchestra one day and playing the piano that evening. But he views this as a very exceptional kind of scheduling nowadays, occasioned only by very special circumstances—the desire to play and record with Mehta.

Barenboim's professional life is now considerably less hectic than it was a few years ago. This is unquestionably caused in part by his wife's illness, for the long-distance phone is never a satisfactory substitute for immediate companionship. For this reason he now tends to schedule his touring in tight blocks so that he will be away from London as little as possible. Moreover, because of the up-and-down nature of Du Pré's illness, Barenboim does not hesitate to cancel engagements if her sudden relapse requires his presence at home.

Those encountering Barenboim nowadays for the first time are somewhat surprised to encounter an artist who is in many ways, superficially at least, quite different from the youthful prankster of the Barenboim legend. The wit and warmth for which he has long been famed, the articulate brilliance of his conversation, and the deep seriousness of his artistic commitment are, if anything, more dominant in Barenboim today than when they were diluted, in media reports at least, with tales of practical jokes and the antics of his "gang." Friends who have known him for a long time attribute the emergence of a more serious Barenboim both to the impact of his wife's illness and to the natural process of his maturing. Despite continuing complaints that he spreads himself too thin in his work schedule, Barenboim is managing more time off from actual performance, whether to be more with his wife or to devote himself to study, nonmusical reading, and socializing.

But, if he is maturing and broadening, Barenboim has lost none of the dedicated ambition that has fueled his phenomenal career so far. In 1977, he affirmed this in an interview with *L'Express*: "When I tell you that it is not necessary to be obsessed by a career, I do not want you to get the impression that I am not ambitious. . . . I believe that ambition can be a very constructive feeling, very creative, provided it remains in perspective with talent and devotion to art. Talent, to be sure, is something that you were given when you were born; we cannot take credit for that. Much more important is the way one uses his talent. Please understand that I am not indifferent to the public side of a career. But I believe that one must choose, at any given moment, between being an entertainer or an interpreter. That is a question of conscience. If one chooses to be an entertainer, one will never become a great artist. But if one chooses to be an artist, it is quite possible to become a celebrity as well."

However, Barenboim's sense of responsibility is by no means a recent development. More than a decade earlier, when Maureen McCleave interviewed the Barenboims jointly for the *New York Times Magazine*, he declared, "I feel very strongly that we have a responsibility toward talent, to nourish it. It must never become stale or die away. Most people's lives begin after they retire—people who work in an office. Our great fortune is that our life and work are one."

ANDREW DAVIS

To an interviewer from *Opera News* who inquired whether it would be possible for an excellent conductor or singer to remain unknown on the music scene of our time, Claudio Abbado replied, "No. If he is excellent he is already known, or soon will be. There is such a demand for excellent performers that it is impossible to hide a great talent. No—if he is unknown, he is not excellent." He is certainly correct insofar as he is concerned with the recognition of major talent by the international professional music world—conductors, soloists, managers, record producers, critics, and the more avid portion of the audience known as "fans."

The process by which a young conductor of exceptional talent advances his career may follow many courses. Competitions sometimes bring him to the attention of the profession, just as some young conductors have skyrocketed to fame as a last-minute substitution for an ailing colleague. Nevertheless, the music world is often aware of major promise before a sensational event brings it to public attention: Leonard Bernstein's extraordinary talent was known to such older conductors as Fritz Reiner, Artur Rodzinski, and Serge Koussevitzky and to such managers as Arthur Judson well before he burst into public view by substituting for the ailing Bruno Walter at a New York Philharmonic concert in 1943. The career of Andrew Davis, brief as it is, offers a good example of how this system works at its best. It has progressed, not through any one sensational event like winning a competition, but rather because the international musical grapevine carried the message of his growing achievement with increasing frequency. "Breaks" are important in the career of any young conductor. Davis enjoyed the respect that led those in authority to propose him in such situations, and he rose to these occasions with a display of real talent. For that reason, his reputation in musical circles, at first in England and then in America, grew rapidly among the musicians and music administrators. By the time he took over the Toronto Symphony Orchestra in 1975, it was impossible to discuss young conductors with music professionals in London or the principal cities of the United States without Andrew Davis being mentioned immediately as one of the major talents of his generation. Whenever major conducting posts in the United States or abroad have become vacant, the name of Andrew Davis has invariably been on the "short list" of prospects to fill it.

Andrew Davis is the product of a system that has done a remarkable job of integrating music into elementary and secondary education. Foreign musicians, including conductors, who work with professional British musicians are amazed at the quantity and quality of involvement of young people in Britain in music—school orchestras, bands, and youth orchestras. It is no wonder that London boasts more fine symphony orchestras than any other city and that the country as a whole supports so many orchestras of quality.

Born at Ashridge, Hertfordshire, in 1944, the son of a printer, Davis was first exposed to music at Watford Grammar School, where he sang treble in a highly regarded children's choir. Later, having begun to study the piano, he was dragooned by fellow students and some teachers into conducting their orchestra. But piano remained his consuming interest, and his talent was such that in 1963 he was awarded the King's College Organ Fellowship at Cambridge University.

This fellowship has been described by one commentator as ranking in the hierarchy of choral church music as the equivalent to taking choir practice with the heavenly host. King's College Chapel itself is a masterpiece of British ecclesiastical architecture, and the college's organ scholar has specific duties in assisting with the musical services there. "I worked with the choir every day, getting up at seven o'clock in the morning to go down to rehearse the little boys before breakfast," says Davis. David Willcocks was organist at King's College and director of its renowned choir. Davis worked closely with him, both as student and as assistant, and thus strengthened his already deep fondness for choral music.

There has always been in England a close relation between the academic musicians of the "Oxbridge" and other universities and the performing musicians of London. There appears to be less of the dichotomy that seems to prevail in the United States between the "academic" and the "practical" musician. One of England's major musicologists of the postwar era, Thurston Dart, was equally at home at Cambridge, and later at the University of London, and in the concert halls and recording studios of London. A specialist in baroque music, Dart was an excellent keyboard player and worked closely with such groups as the Academy of St. Martin-in-the-Fields in playing and recording baroque music in authentic style.

Davis knew Dart, both at Cambridge and later in London: "I had some lessons with him. He was generally very helpful. In my last year at Cambridge—by that time he was already at London University but kept a house at Cambridge—I bumped into him at King's, and he said, 'Mr. Davis, what are you going to do with your life?' in that wonderfully pompous way he had. Unbearably pompous, but underneath it all very sweet and musicological. And I said to him, 'Oh, I am going to be a conductor.' So he said, 'Come and have sherry.' So I went to his house, and we drank a lot of gin, and he proceeded to talk to me for hours, telling me I should specialize—in contemporary music, in baroque, or early classical, or something. I listened to him, but I knew that was absolutely the wrong thing for me to do."

Although, as Davis later recalled, he had gone to Cambridge assuming that he would end up a church organist, the conducting bug—orchestral as well as choral—had already bitten him. Very soon he was leading small chamber groups of students informally and eventually became Willcocks's assistant conductor of the Cambridge University Music Society.

His first public performance with its orchestra of a major work was Schoenberg's *Five Pieces for Orchestra,* an enterprising choice for an organ scholar. Conducting was for him "something that I obviously had some special talent for. It's hard to analyze why, except that I was communicating and obviously expressing myself in a way that I had never felt before as a musician. So then I went to Rome."

Once again his talent was recognized with a scholarship, this time to spend a year studying with Franco Ferrara in Rome: "When I arrived in Rome, I realized what a sheltered life I had been leading. Rome and Milan were very exciting, but for the first time I came into contact with opera, which strongly appealed to me.

"Ferrara as a teacher was very interesting. He was more of an inspirer than anything else. Sometimes I would be conducting the orchestra in class, and I would feel that it wasn't going right but didn't know why. He would never say, 'Put your elbow lower,' or anything like that. But if you pestered him, then he would say, 'Oh, yes—that's because your upbeat's not clear.' He would analyze things but only if he were pushed to do so. He was very strict about all kinds of details. We worked with a terrible kids' orchestra, and he would say, 'Why do you let the second clarinet play so loud?' Little things like that which developed the habit of not letting people get away with anything.

"What I learned more from him was, well, the way he communicates with special intensity. He's one of the most extraordinary men, and I learned most from the very, very few occasions when he got up and conducted himself. He'd conduct twenty or thirty bars occasionally, and that was when one really learned. His career—this neurological problem that means he can't actually conduct much himself—is one of the greatest tragedies of our times, because he's a fantastic musician."

Returning to London in 1968, Davis faced the task of getting a conducting job: "After I came back from Rome, I was mainly playing harpsichord and organ continuo and things like that. I did a little proofreading for Schott when I was running out of it. That first year, I conducted only one concert, an amateur orchestra which I had conducted a while before I went away."

Then he was one of four in a young conductors' seminar at the Royal Liverpool Philharmonic Orchestra, spending two weeks working with the Philharmonic and a student orchestra. This led to guest engagements in Liverpool and eventually to his being designated as principal guest conductor.

Meanwhile, he was also establishing himself with the ECO and the Academy of St. Martin-in-the-Fields. He had worked with both as continuo player when they played with the King's College Choir, and he kept up that association after he returned to London. Although he never conducted the Academy, he eventually worked with its conductor, Neville Marriner, on an orchestration of Bach's *Art of the Fugue,* in which he played both harpsichord and organ in performances and recording.

From the Liverpool seminar and concerts, word of Davis spread to other parts of the United Kingdom, and he had a chance to audition for the assistant conductorship of the BBC Scottish Symphony in Glasgow. This turned out to be a very valuable experience for the young conductor. "I did fifty concerts a year there for two years, with very little duplication of repertoire, so I was going crazy learning scores. Of course, a lot of them I learned superficially, I'll be the first to admit that, but I got through a lot of the standard repertoire and quite a lot of the nonstandard too, so it stood me in good stead."

In October 1970, Davis got one of those "breaks" that was to have important consequences later. A colleague who was to have conducted the BBC Symphony in London's Royal Festival Hall fell ill and a last-minute substitute was needed for a program that included the *Glagolitic Mass* of Janáček. "That was just after I had been appointed Scotland but before I moved up there; my belongings were somewhere in transit. And the big piece on the program was the Janáček." He had never conducted the piece, although he knew and liked it from a record, by then packed in his luggage. With intensive study, he learned the rather complex score and enjoyed a great success with it, earning lavish praise from critics who had no idea that Davis had learned the piece on short notice for the occasion. This success in 1970 was to have important consequences a few years later.

His work with the BBC Symphony Orchestra in London greatly impressed Sir William Glock, then controller of music for the BBC, whose subsequent recommendations of Davis played an important role in the young conductor's career. This success and his work in Scotland led to engagements with the other major London orchestras; eventually he conducted all four of the player-governed orchestras and was re-engaged by the BBC Symphony. By 1973, he was appointed associate conductor of the New Philharmonia, a post he held for three years. During that time he made three tours to the Continent with that orchestra. In 1974, he spent ten days working with the London Schools Symphony, made up of school children from all over London, "a very enjoyable experience."

His work with the ECO led in 1973 to his joining Daniel Barenboim with the group on a tour of the Far East—Bombay, Singapore, Bangkok, Hong Kong, Manila, and Japan. Returning to England via North America, the ECO played a concert in Anchorage under Davis's direction, his U.S. debut. It was in Tokyo that Barenboim had a phone call from Zubin Mehta asking him to recommend an assistant for an American tour with the Israel Philharmonic. Mehta took Barenboim's recommendation of Davis, who has since become a regular guest conductor with the Israel orchestra.

Thus, in a few years after returning from Rome, Davis was firmly established in London as a conductor to reckon with. When he conducted the BBC Symphony at the closing concert of the Proms in the summer of 1974, Edward Greenfield said of his performance of Schoenberg's *Verklärte Nacht,* "It was really a case of the night being transfigured. Andrew Davis drew from the strings the most passionate, the most committed, yet one of the most clean textured performances I have ever heard." Elsewhere, Greenfield, a great admirer of Davis, has noted that the young conductor's recordings do not show him to the advantage that his live performances do.

Andrew Davis is slender, of medium height, and by his body language, on or off the podium, exudes a sense of almost naive enthusiasm. He wears his light brown hair in a full air-blown "bob" that can become unruly when he is conducting energetically. When he first conducted in Toronto, his face was thin almost to the point of emaciation; women in his audiences were said to want to take him home and feed him. Even extremely thick glasses cannot obscure the penetration of his commanding light blue eyes. ("I tried contact lenses, but they are too damned uncomfortable.") There is a perkiness in his eyes and general demeanor that reminds one at times of an alert and friendly chipmunk.

Yet for all this apparent immaturity, there is a vein of steel determination in the young man. "It is very difficult for a young conductor [in England]. There just aren't enough opportunities, but I think one of the qualities a conductor needs is determination." He has the self-confidence typical of a conductor; were it not backed up by talent, one might call him arrogant. His voice is that of a much older, more experienced man—resonant and authoritative, both in what he says and how he says it. There is also something rather donnish about Davis—an interest in foreign languages for their own sake and his hobby of studying stained glass. Were he to abandon his worldly conducting career, he could probably blend right back into the scene at Cambridge, directing the choir or playing the organ at King's College.

The donnish strain comes out at times in rehearsing the orchestra: calling for an A from the oboe, he obliquely asks, "Could you oblige us?" He sometimes concludes instructions to the orchestra with something like "and we hope that that should put us all to rights." He dresses for rehearsal as though he were going for a stroll in the countryside—baggy slacks, a bulky pullover, and a nondescript tweed sport jacket which he sheds before settling down to work. One British writer found Davis a bit Beechamesque in his courtliness, then realized that Davis belonged to a generation that had never heard or seen Sir Thomas "live." Yet, like the noted baronet, he works with an orchestra, not on it; even if his humor is not as outrageous or his manner as imperious, Davis belongs to a new generation that controls an orchestra by demonstrating from the outset his command of the score with courtesy and consideration for the players as people rather than as a mean to his ends.

Technically, Davis's is an impeccable baton. Says one player, "It is picturebook conducting. It's clear and consistent without being routine. That's a pretty thin line to tread." Davis does not talk a great deal to the players in rehearsal but sings a lot—somewhat off key to be sure but graphically. His ear for balance and intonation—good and bad—is uncannily accurate; as he learned from Ferrara, he lets no one get away with bad playing if he can help it. He prefers to work in long stretches of music, going back a considerable distance with corrections, but he will, when the occasion requires, go through a passage phrase by phrase until he is satisfied that he has conveyed his desires to the orchestra. The sound he seeks is impressive but clear; in late romantic music or that of Shostakovich, he evokes the kind of committed, passionate tone that Greenfield described, without sacrificing clarity and balance. His rhythm is very precise, fluctuating somewhat for expressive purposes but always in relation to a solid underpinning. Despite his exuberance, he is not an acrobatic conductor, nor does he lose his firm control of the flow and texture of the music.

Among conductors of earlier generations, he feels the closest affinity with Sir John Barbirolli, through whom much of the Furtwängler ideal was transmitted. Asked where he might fall within the Toscanini–Furtwängler spectrum, he replies, "Well, in the middle but closer to the Furtwängler end, I think. Toscanini always produced a terrific clarity, which I like to aim for, particularly in certain repertoire. But I wouldn't emulate Furtwängler in Stravinsky, for instance. I don't think Furtwängler did much Stravinsky, but as far as the classical and romantic composers go, I am very much on the Furtwängler side. But my Beethoven hero is still Klemperer, and I think he always will be. I don't say that mine comes out like Klemperer but. . . .

"Furtwängler, of course, I have heard on recordings. Barbirolli is actually my number-one hero, but he had a very distinct personality of his own. The kind of sound that Barbirolli went for is very much on my list of aims. He was fond of the string sound, always. Terrific warmth and richness and love."

For Davis the performance itself is the culmination of a long and detailed process of preparation. Although he seldom depends on recordings during his study of a score, he does refer to them for special purposes—Richard Strauss's or Stravinsky's of their own music. Even so, that must be preceded by thorough study "at the table" so that he becomes involved in the score before hearing another's view of it. Similarly, he plays the score on the piano only after he has studied it thoroughly: "When I am in the middle of preparing a piece and I am in sort of a mood for it, I'll sit down at the piano and crash through the whole thing just to give myself some kind of sonic picture of it."

The overall shape of a piece is very important to Davis, and his understanding of that shape must be transmitted in musical terms rather than verbal analysis to the orchestra in rehearsal. Yet Davis's conception is realized fully only in performance. He sees a danger in "peaking" too early, during rehearsals. His own preparation and then the rehearsals should be a crescendo leading toward the performance.

Davis's repertory is very broad, having been shaped by two intensive years with the BBC Scottish Symphony and relatively extended seasons in Toronto. As he says, he plays everything from Bach to Shostakovich and beyond. Despite his early solid grounding in baroque music, he has come to prefer the richer sonority of music for full orchestra. He recently seems most at home with such late romantics as Bruckner, Richard Strauss, and Elgar and in such neoromantics as Shostakovich and Prokofiev. In March 1979, he conducted the Philharmonia Orchestra in what he called "a mini-festival" of Elgar's music—four concerts including all the major orchestral pieces. Both in England and abroad he also conducts the music of Michael Tippett and such younger British composers as Peter Maxwell Davies and Harrison Birtwhistle. He also admires the work of Hugh Wood, which he has conducted in England but not abroad. He had been scheduled to conduct the Orchestre de Paris in a program of Debussy, Berg, Ives, and Mahler as a part of Pierre Boulez's IRCAM series but was forced to cancel the appearance—not because he was unsympathetic to the repertory, but because he was too exhausted after a long and hectic season.

An important phase of Davis's career in the United Kingdom has been his association with the Glyndebourne Festival since 1973, when he conducted a highly successful production there of Richard Strauss's *Capriccio.* He has returned to the beautiful Sussex estate annually, conducting Tchaikovsky's *Eugene Onegin, Die Schweigsame Frau* of Strauss, and *Die Zauberflöte* in 1978. Reviewing the 1975 production of

Eugene Onegin, Rodney Milnes of *Opera* magazine was especially enthusiastic about Davis's contribution to the production:

> That this was one of the best performances to date was mostly because of the incandescent conducting of Andrew Davis. He gave the impulsive score its head, made no apologies for the romantic passions contained therein, and from a carefully controlled crescendo in the prelude right through to the agony of the final scene, he never let tension sag for a moment.

The 1978 production of *Die Zauberflöte* drew a mixed reaction. Much interest centered on the visual production designed by the young British painter David Hockney. Writing in the *International Herald-Tribune* shortly after the premiere, Henry Pleasants reported:

> This is a production of visual rather than aural wonder . . . nor is it a matter of singing alone. There is a consistent lack of character projection, a lack of animation and involvement. Some of the responsibility may fall on Andrew Davis, the conductor. He draws a lovely, clean texture from the London Philharmonic, but without achieving a requisite sense of urgency and pace.

John Rockwell of the *New York Times,* hearing another performance later in the season, was considerably more favorable to Davis:

> Mr. Davis has struck this listener as one of the most promising members of his generation in previous encounters; his *Schweigsame Frau* here last summer was a masterly account of Strauss's deceptively tricky score. Mr. Davis's *Flute* was faulted in several reviews of the first performance on May 28 as too slow, but by June 23, it seemed superb—which is not to say that this writer might not have found it superb in May. Mr. Davis' tempos were indeed measured in spots. But they were lively elsewhere, and throughout, his phrasing and the playing of the London Philharmonic Orchestra were full of the most delightfully pointed, exquisitely executed subtleties: the delicately disjointed yet idiomatic opening of

Papageno's first act aria was just one early case in point. Glyndebourne has extremely dry acoustics, and partly because of that, no doubt, Mr. Davis avoided the grand and magisterial account. But his chamber approach suited the production and the circumstances, and provided considerable musical pleasure even when the singing was not the best.

So far, Andrew Davis's operatic work has been confined to Glyndebourne. With a new production of *Salome* in 1981, Davis will make his debut at the Metropolitan Opera. The same year, he is scheduled for *Der Rosenkavalier* at the Paris Opéra. Nevertheless, he hopes to continue his summertime affiliation with Glyndebourne, where he has become very popular. Two operas that he would like to do, he says, are Berg's *Lulu* and *Wozzeck,* but so far no concrete prospect has developed for them.

Within five years of completing his studies with Franco Ferrara in Rome, Andrew Davis, still under thirty, had laid a firm foundation for the next step in his career—the music directorship of the Toronto Symphony Orchestra, the largest and best in Canada and one comparable to such second-rank American orchestras as San Francisco, Cincinnati, and Minnesota.

Founded in 1921 as a part-time "community" orchestra by Dr. Luigi von Kunits, the Toronto Symphony had grown into a professional orchestra of considerable stature under the leadership of Sir Ernest MacMillan from 1931 to 1956. Until the mid-1960s, its players were also employed by the Canadian Broadcasting Corporation, an arrangement that offered substantial financial security to the orchestra's members.

The orchestra continued to grow, paralleling its counterparts south of the border, under the successive leadership of Walter Susskind (1956–65), Seiji Ozawa (1965–69), and Karel Ančerl (1969–73). Toronto was Ozawa's first major post, although he was already director of the Chicago Symphony's Ravinia Festival. Ančerl, an older and highly experienced Czech conductor, was in sharp contrast to the charismatic Ozawa. As one Toronto critic put it, "For the orchestra the fun and games had ended. . . . Ančerl didn't want to dilute any of the orchestra's playing. Instead he wanted to remove some of its rawness and replace it with a sonority that marks great orchestras with long lives. Ančerl wanted a solid marriage instead of a tempestuous love affair, but he died before he could lead the orchestra to the altar."

Actually, Ančerl conducted the Toronto Symphony Orchestra for four years before his death in July 1973, a time that made planning for the next season extremely difficult. Walter Homburger, the orchestra's managing director, not only tackled the problem of filling in his schedule of conductors on extremely short notice, but also succeeded in retaining much of the repertory that Ančerl had promised his subscribers.

It was Homburger's determination to retain Ančerl's programming that actually led him to Andrew Davis, although he might have arrived there in any event, for the young Englishman was now being recommended widely in London. One of the highlights of the Czech Ančerl's season was to have been the first performance in Toronto of the Janáček *Glagolitic Mass,* with which young Davis had scored a real success with the BBC Symphony Orchestra on short notice a few years earlier. Although Davis's commitments with the ECO, the Israel Philharmonic, and other engagements prevented his appearing in Toronto earlier, he finally conducted the Janáček *Mass* there in May 1974, toward the end of a season that had included several other conductors who were obvious candidates to succeed Ančerl. However, when Davis appeared, as one player recalled, "We all knew very early that Davis was the one. The talent was obviously there at the first rehearsal. I now think he is potentially a great conductor, and we will all be lucky if we can retain him." Within two months, negotiations were completed for him to become music director in Toronto at the beginning of the 1975–76 season, a delay of one year to allow him to meet commitments he had already made. He did, however, give as much time as he could to the Toronto Symphony with the cumbersome title of "Conductor Designate." His original three-year contract has been extended to the summer of 1981, seven years after his first appearance in Toronto.

For Davis, the Toronto post has been a very successful step in his career. A conductor in his early thirties needs a solid affiliation for a considerable part of each year and extending over several years, where he can develop an intensive repertory, including experimentation with new music, and gain an insight into his own strengths and weaknesses. Except for the BBC, there are few such positions in the United Kingdom, and Davis had derived what benefit he could from his two intensive years in a secondary position with the BBC Scottish Orchestra. Moreover, the designation of Riccardo Muti as principal conductor of the Philharmonia Orchestra, the London orchestra to which Davis was closest as an assistant conductor, rather barred his advancement there. His commitment to Toronto, some five months a year, left him ample time to guest-conduct elsewhere but still gave him a firm base of operations.

To Toronto, Davis offered youth and enthusiasm—traits for which many Torontonians still hankered after Ozawa's brief tenure. He also brought a CBS recording contract, originally drawn up for work in London but shortly altered to include the Toronto Symphony Orchestra once its women's committee came forth with some subsidy to compensate for the more expensive payroll in Toronto. The management of the Toronto Symphony greeted Davis's arrival as music director with a saturation publicity campaign, including Andrew Davis T-shirts. Using the by now familiar brochure mailing technique developed by Danny Newman for many U.S. orchestras and opera companies, the orchestra mailed 850,000 gaudy brochures hailing Andrew Davis as "our brightest new superstar." Davis was quite shocked and a little offended by what he saw as a promotion of himself in something less than good taste: "When I first went to Toronto I was frankly rather horrified by this kind of approach to marketing, which is something that we don't experience in England. In fact, eventually I had a bit of a dust-up with management about the 1977–78 season's brochure, which was, I thought, done in an extremely vulgar way. So, in fact, next season's brochure is more classical and has much more emphasis on the music rather than personalities. So far, it has been selling better than ever; so, you know, I think I've made a point there."

However, the 1975 mailing of 850,000 brochures resulted in 23,000 subscribers, one of the largest such lists in North America.

Moreover, as Davis points out, a change to a less flamboyant promotion has also been successful, no doubt because the new audiences attracted by the earlier mailing liked what they heard and kept coming back.

While Torontonians gave Davis a warm welcome, he has also been well received on tour with the Toronto Symphony in Canada and in the United States. Indicative of the fruit of his first three years as the orchestra's musical director is the reaction of Peter G. Davis in the *New York Times* in April 1978, when the orchestra appeared at Carnegie Hall:

> There were many fine qualities to the performance [of Bruckner's Seventh Symphony]—clarity, balance, precision and a true Brucknerian sound that, despite some thin tone in the strings and an occasional hole in the brass section, had real weight and grandeur. If Mr. Davis's reading did not quite come off, this was partly because of his inability to make the fluctuating tempos cohere convincingly and to a rather crew-cut objectivity that never really came to grips with the symphony's rapturous mystical fervor. Still, it was an impressive technical achievement as well as being an interpretation that showed much promise for the future.

Of its total operating budget of close to $4 million, the Toronto Symphony Orchestra receives grants of $1.2 million from the Canadian government's Ministry of Culture, the Province of Ontario, and the City of Toronto. All of these are direct subsidies, and not dependent on rendering specific services.

The only conditions are set by the Ministry of Culture, which requires evidence of sound and honest management of its grantees and, in the case of symphony orchestras, stipulates that at least 10 percent of the repertory played be by Canadian composers and that 10 percent of the soloists with the orchestra be Canadians. One result of the Canadian composition condition is that there tends to be less non-Canadian contemporary music played by the orchestra. Davis does not find this requirement restrictive: "After all, if you don't let contemporary composers ever hear their work performed, how can they improve? And it could be very useful to give preconcert talks about unknown or difficult pieces of music." Moreover, there is nothing in the ministry's policy forbidding repetitions of Canadian-composed pieces that are successful. Nor does the Canadian component necessarily have to be contemporary: the Toronto Orchestra frequently plays rather conservative music by its beloved former conductor, the late Sir Ernest MacMillan.

The Toronto Symphony Orchestra has toured abroad on a number of occasions, not just in the United States but in Europe with Susskind, Ozawa, Kazimierz Kord (replacing Ančerl) and to the Far East with Ozawa in 1969 and Davis early in 1978. All of these tours received substantial financial assistance from the Canadian government, and the 1978 tour to the People's Republic of China was part of a cultural exchange that had brought a Chinese theatrical company to Canada earlier.

Although three other major Western orchestras—the London Philharmonic, the Vienna Philharmonic, and the Philadelphia—had visited the People's Republic previously, the last nearly five years earlier, the Toronto Symphony was the first to tour there after the cultural "thaw" that followed the death of Mao Tse-tung. The Chinese government asked the orchestra to submit four suggested programs along with biographical information, scores, and records; from these they selected two programs. Although Beethoven's music had been denounced in the Chinese press after the Philadelphia Orchestra had played the *Pastoral* Symphony in 1973, no objection was raised to the inclusion of the Fifth Symphony in Davis's programs. It included, in addition to the Beethoven, music by Berlioz, Mahler, Liszt, Brahms, and Tchaikovsky, together with two Canadian compositions—MacMillan's *Two Sketches on French-Canadian Folk Songs* and *Boréal,* by the contemporary Canadian composer François Morel. Two Canadian soloists, contralto Maureen Forrester and the young pianist Louis Lortie, performed with the orchestra throughout the Far East tour. The Toronto played three concerts in Peking, and two each in Shanghai and Canton; on the way to China, the orchestra stopped in Tokyo for two concerts.

When the chartered plane carrying the orchestra personnel landed in Peking, Davis descended the ramp wearing a bright red shirt and socks to match. During his stay he met Li Teh-lun, conductor of Peking's Capital Orchestra, who told him that his orchestra had been allowed to perform only three pieces of music—the *Yellow River* Concerto and two cantatas—for eleven years. Only recently were they allowed to play music of such Western composers as Beethoven, Mozart, and Haydn. Two members of the orchestra who had been with the Philadelphia on its 1973 tour were impressed with how much more relaxed relations were between the Chinese and their visitors.

Davis was particularly delighted with two meetings in Peking: "One was with about twelve of our players and twelve of theirs, and also some people from the conservatory in Peking and some management people, for a very interesting morning of discussion. But the most fascinating morning was when the two orchestras got together. They played a string piece, a rather beautiful arrangement of traditional Chinese music, which we are actually going to play this summer. Then they played a horrible piano concerto, composed by four people—shades of Rachmaninoff, Tchaikovsky, and Liszt—called *Fighting the Hurricane*. Then I conducted the Peking orchestra in the first movement of the *Eroica*. Their conductor conducted our orchestra in the first movement of the Beethoven Fifth, and then all the players got together in little groups. All the flutes playing flute quartets, like that. It was a wonderful morning, one of the most remarkable things about the trip."

There was no music criticism in the Western sense in the Chinese press. Instead, reporters mingled with the audience, getting comments from prominent Chinese officials and musicians about the performance. Everyone was, of course, very polite in his comments, as for example: "Our famous conductor Li Teh-lun said of Andrew Davis that he was a famed, deeply trained artist. He conducted the orchestra in a light and natural manner and in a clear precise way. Under his baton, the performance resounded with beautifully elegant sounds, and the style and harmony were rejoicing to the ear."

When the orchestra returned to Toronto, Davis remarked in an interview, "It started with tremendous formality, but by the time we left, they were hugging us and behaving with a kind of warmth we would have never dreamed possible."

Davis likes Toronto and its orchestra. Despite the dust-up over the promotional brochures, he has found no reason to modify some comments he made to the *Manchester Guardian* soon after he was hired: "Toronto is a great city, and the Symphony has such a fine reputation that it has attracted excellent players from some of the world's most famous orchestras, such as Leningrad and the Philadelphia. Having one's own orchestra is a marvelous experience, because you can plan programs to help both yourself and the players to develop as you build up an interesting repertory. . . . I look forward to my contract there, because it gives me time to find out whether my work is going along the right lines. Naturally, I want to expand my repertoire as well as my other activities, and being director of an orchestra on a permanent basis means that I can develop at a pace within my own control."

One project that involves Davis greatly in Toronto is the design and construction of a new Massey Hall. The old hall on Victoria Street is one of the monstrosities of late nineteenth-century architecture. Its lobby and backstage are abominably cramped and its boxlike auditorium, with exposed girders and drab decor, is unattractive acoustically and visually. Somehow Torontonians have endured this building since 1894, but the end is in sight. The Massey Foundation hopes to open a new concert hall by the fall of 1981, and Davis has been consulted on its general design, as well as on its organ. However, the new hall will not be designed to accommodate opera, much to Davis's regret. The present Toronto Opera Company, a good one directed by Lotfi Mansouri, must perform in the cavernous O'Keefe Center. Although Davis has had some discussions with this group concerning his appearing with them, it is, all things considered, a remote possibility. For the present, conducting the orchestra remains his Toronto function, while he pursues his operatic activities elsewhere.

Outside of Toronto, Davis has done extensive orchestra conducting elsewhere in North America. Thanks to the recommendation by Sir William Glock at the BBC to his friend Pierre Boulez and to his serving as Zubin Mehta's assistant on the 1973 U.S. tour by the Israel Philharmonic, Davis was already getting bookings in the United States when the Toronto appearance materialized. In fact, he was guest-conducting in the States before making his Toronto debut. Originally he was to have appeared first with the New York Philharmonic, at Boulez's invitation, in the spring of 1974, but the Detroit Symphony was actually the first U.S. orchestra he conducted, in February of that year. Within eighteen months, he had conducted all of the most important orchestras in the United States, plus several of the second rank.

When Andrew Davis made his New York debut in 1974 with the Philharmonic, Allen Hughes described him in the *New York Times* as "born to the podium." Elaborating on this observation, he continued:

> He was so clearly at home there, so natural and so happy in his work, and the movements through which he accomplished it, that it would be difficult imagining him doing anything else.
>
> And this positive visual expression was reinforced by the quality and spirit he elicited from the orchestra. It was vigorous, buoyant, and vital. Even slow, introspective music had an air of urgency about it that compelled active listening attention.

The following August, Davis appeared for the first time with the Los Angeles Philharmonic Orchestra in Hollywood Bowl, a debut that one critic referred to as "sensational." When he played the Berlioz *Symphonie Fantastique* later that week, Bernard Soll of the *Herald Examiner* said,

> Again he demonstrated amazing maturity of both technique and expression in a symphony that has defeated interpreters twice his age. Davis's highly disciplined abrupt changes and gradual ascent to powerful climaxes achieved without stridency stand out in my memory.

Davis's debut with the Boston Symphony early in 1976 evoked high praise for both programs in his two-week appearance from Richard Dyer in the *Boston Globe*:

> At the end of last night's Boston Symphony concert, the orchestra was applauding as enthusiastically as the audience. That is not a regular occurrence. But neither is the immediate awareness that a major talent has

revealed itself. . . . Anyone can see, anyone can hear, that this is a man born to conduct, just as birds are born to fly and politicians are to lie.

On the evidence of this first concert, Davis is a superbly uncluttered talent; his mind and his instincts go right to valid musical points and his technique surely and fluently communicates them both to players and public. The effects he makes are ones the composers put there for someone to bring out. Davis sees no reason to parade them, to lecture about them, dance to them. . . . He didn't make it easy for himself. The program began with the rhythmic intricacies and textural transparencies of Stravinsky's *Divertimento*; it continued with accompanimental problems of the Chopin F-minor Piano Concerto (just where is the fourth beat going to fall?) ; at the end came the Third Schumann Symphony, the *Rhenish,* more suite than symphony, and the one of Schumann's Tovey thought the worst orchestrated, the one on which the native fog hangs most heavily.

To the difficulties of these pieces Davis found convincing solutions; to the character of each—and the several characters within each—Davis made responses; the Stravinsky, for example, always sounded like music made for dancing. . . . Like a dancer, a conductor has to find ways to make music visual—and the most successful conductors do it not simply for players but for the audience as well. But a conductor isn't the same kind of musical agent as a dancer: He shouldn't stop attention at himself. What Davis does on the podium invariably directs attention to features of the music.

That Davis is no nine-day wonder in the conducting world has been amply demonstrated by his continuing success: he is not only consistently reengaged but sustains his previous good impression when he returns. When he conducted the New York Philharmonic in April 1977 Donal Henahan of the *Times,* after noting that Davis "looks like a choirboy," said of the performance of Stravinsky's *Divertimento,*

It quickly became clear that he knows his business. He gave the *Divertimento* the poised performance that never lost impetus, and brought out an especially robust sound from the Philharmonic's string section. The brass voices were in balance, clear at all times, a tribute to his ear and orchestral sound.

(65)

Henahan said of Davis's reading of Elgar's *Enigma* Variations, something of a specialty with him,

> Mr. Davis fashioned a reading of the score that exuded ease and inevitability. There was less hearty humor than we sometimes hear . . . and more introspection, notably in the Romanza. The Philharmonic gave out red-plush sonorities for this eminently Victorian occasion, and Mr. Davis knew how to use them well.

Given the almost uniformly laudatory reception that Davis has had with the orchestras of the United States that he has conducted, it is no secret that he has received more than one offer to move southward and become music director of an orchestra there. Although he frankly admits that he has received such invitations, he politely refuses to name their source or to confirm or deny specific rumors. However, there is no doubt that serious efforts have been made to lure him away from Toronto and that he has declined them: "Its partly loyalty to Toronto. You know, I feel that I am building an orchestra in Toronto, and I think, well, in quite an impressive way. I think the orchestra's improved a lot since I have been there, and it sounds immodest of me, but I don't feel that I've finished that process by any means. I want to see how far I can take the orchestra, and I think it could be a long way.

"Also, I like the city. It's a city which is developing more and more into an important center and becoming more and more internationally recognized as a major city. It obviously has great commercial importance, and also is developing quite a strong reputation in the cultural field. It has one of the best theatrical lives of any city in North America, very good chamber music, a strong concert series. We get concerts that go in Toronto as well as happen anywhere, with the exception of New York, in terms of numbers."

Moreover, at this point in his career, Andrew Davis can afford to be in not too much of a hurry. In ten years of increasing conducting activity, he has showed more than promise. He has, to borrow Verdi's phrase, "served in the galleys," learning repertory, encountering a variety of orchestral situations, and generally handling them with success.

In Toronto he has what few colleagues of his age and standing have—a "permanent" post with a well-supported professionally administered orchestra. There he can not only build an orchestra but also ripen and deepen his own talent, his technique, and his special perception of how music should sound. He asserts, "A conductor's life is not so easy as outsiders imagine. People think that because you don't have to practice an instrument every day, you have an easy time. But you are always studying new scores, preparing all the scores you have in your repertory."

Lunching in a Sussex pub not far from Glyndebourne during his preparation for *Die Zauberflöte,* Davis expressed a desire to take more vacation; not necessarily because he felt exhausted or played out but because he needed more time to think, to read, and to study scores for the challenges he faced in a busy schedule already plotted for the next two years: "I am planning to take more vacation now. This is one of the problems about being a relatively successful young conductor. You find that you are completely booked out, and I have found both last season and this season were a little excessively so. I mean, it depends on the person. You know, there are some people who apparently can go on nonstop without suffering. I have found that I need to take a little time, and so, in fact, from this season onward I am taking more time off. But of course it is something that one has to plan two or three years ahead."

CLAUDIO ABBADO

LA SCALA.

To opera lovers the world over that name exerts a very special magic. There are other important lyric theaters in Italy, great opera houses elsewhere in Europe and America, but a special aura emanates from the Teatro alla Scala. If Italy is stage center for what is popularly regarded as the opera world, La Scala has played, for much of the past two centuries, a major role on it.

The present theater, designed by Giuseppe Piermarini though extensively renovated several times, dates from 1778, when it was called the Nuovo Regio Teatro Ducale. An earlier theater, built in 1717 but burned down in 1776, was on the site of a church, Santa Maria alla Scala, dating back to 1381. Thus, the name of the church eventually became associated with the theater. What we now know as Teatro alla Scala opened its doors on August 3, 1778. Unfortunately, the musicians of the present La Scala were on vacation on the actual day of the two-hundredth anniversary of this occasion, but the building was open, free to the public, from ten in the morning to midnight, for a continuous showing of sound films of opera and ballet productions from the La Scala archives. Thousands thronged to La Scala, causing traffic jams that closed the Piazza della Scala. Such was the success of this anniversary celebration that "La Scala Aperto," or "La Scala Open House," will become a regular summer event.

Today the Teatro alla Scala is a self-governing body—or *ente autonomo,* in modern Italian corporate terminology—that reaches an audience of more than 100,000 people with recitals, orchestral and ensemble concerts, and chamber music, in addition to its traditional opera and ballet. It performs in scores of theaters, factories, and community centers throughout the region of Lombardy as well as in Milan. Offering some seven hundred performances a year, it is a highly diversified producer of music, by no means restricted to opera, for which it is best known. Obviously, such diverse and complex production of music needs artistic direction. Years ago, long before La Scala proliferated and was still mainly a producer of opera and ballet, Arturo Toscanini is said to have declared that to be the *direttore artistico* of an Italian lyric theater, one must unlock the door in the morning and turn the key the last thing at night. Frequently Italian lyric theaters fill this post with musically experienced administrators rather than with outstanding performing artists.

The present artistic director of the Teatro alla Scala violates this rule: while actively exercising his authority at La Scala, Claudio Abbado is also a conductor of exceptional artistic stature who holds important positions with the London Symphony and the Vienna Philharmonic and appears regularly with the top American orchestras. Still in his forties, this disarmingly shy man, slender and modest of stature, appears at first to lack the drive, political guile, and the autocratic manner that one would expect in a musical figure of such exalted position. Yet his achievements, in status and artistic performance, mark him as a leader of first rank in his generation.

The Abbados of Milan take pride in a family tree extending back to the year 1200. One of their ancestors was the architect of the Alcazar at Seville; Claudio has found his name carved in the stone of that edifice. The present-day Abbado family has been deeply involved for three generations in the arts. Claudio's father, Michelangelo, born in 1899, is a noted concert violinist and teacher at the Giuseppe Verdi Conservatory in Milan. His mother, who came from Sicily, is the author of children's books and a good pianist. His older brother, Marcello, is a pianist and composer, now head of the conservatory. A sister works for Ricordi, and his younger brother is an architect. Abbado's own son, Daniele, barely out of the university, has already been involved in theater and film production, and many of his cousins in the third generation, numbering eleven, are following artistic pursuits.

Young Claudio grew up in a household where music was a matter of everyday life. There was much chamber music played by members of the family and professional friends. One friend of the family recalls that the sound of practicing could be heard from every room in the house. For his first lessons, Abbado did not have to leave home. He was no prodigy and did not start to study music until he was eight; after a brief exposure to the violin from his father, he turned to the piano, studying first with his mother and then with his older brother, Marcello. Along the way, he picked up the rudiments of theory and harmony.

Born in 1934, Claudio grew up under Italian fascism before and during World War II. The Abbado family, though strongly antifascist, did not suffer seriously from political retaliation until the very end of the war. Then, when the family took into its home a Jewish orphan child, Signora Abbado was briefly jailed. Abbado remains to this day a fervent antifascist, with strong sympathies for the political Left in Italian politics. Although he is not a Communist party member, he supports the Italian party as a politically effective and incorruptible counterforce to fascism. These views, often misunderstood in the United States, fit into the Milanese political scene and have unquestionably smoothed Abbado's rise to power and authority at La Scala, where labor unions and municipal government have a strong voice in the *ente autonomo*.

When he was ten, young Claudio heard a performance by Antonio Guarneri of Debussy's *Three Nocturnes for Orchestra* that so excited him that he resolved, with childish determination, to become a conductor so that he could himself play that music. (The composition is included in a record that he made years later with the Boston Symphony.) When Leonard Bernstein first visited Milan in 1949, Michelangelo Abbado played the violin solo with him in a Bach *Brandenburg* Concerto and brought the young American to visit the family home. Meeting the fifteen-year-old Claudio and hearing of his ambition to conduct, Bernstein encouraged him, remarking that he had the eyes of a conductor.

Even at that point, Abbado was not firmly set on a musical career. He was, he now recalls, very shy—perhaps overwhelmed by his talented family. Perhaps he was still taking music too much as a matter of everyday life. In any event, despite his early infatuation with the idea of conducting, Claudio did not become really serious about music until he was sixteen. He then enrolled at the conservatory, where he pursued a typically exacting course of study, including instruction in piano, theory, composition, and conducting, the latter with Antonino Votto, already something of an elder statesman at the conservatory and La Scala, having been Toscanini's assistant in the early 1920s. Although he did not teach conducting, Carlo Maria Giulini worked with the student orchestra, and Abbado recalls him with affectionate awe both as a great musician and, with more emphasis in Abbado's voice, an extraordinary human being.

The major musical event of Abbado's youth in Milan was, of course, the return of Arturo Toscanini from America. In the worst days of the war, when La Scala itself was a bombed-out shell, some patriot had scrawled on the wall *Vogliamo Toscanini* ("We want Toscanini"). Toscanini had been a hero of patriotic antifascists ever since, two decades earlier, he had defied Mussolini by refusing to play the party anthem at a concert. His return from the United States to Milan after the war was a very emotional occasion for the Milanese. When he conducted the concert with which the La Scala was rededicated, the chorus sang "Va pensiero," the lament of the repressed and exiled Israelites from Verdi's *Nabucco,* which had become, during the composer's lifetime, the rallying anthem of the Risorgimento and had made Verdi a hero of Italian nationalism. During one of Toscanini's later visits to Milan, the eighteen-year-old Abbado played and conducted a Bach clavier concerto in a program given in Toscanini's home by students from the conservatory. Toscanini's performances left an indelible impression on Abbado, an impression reinforced and expanded later by recordings.

But along with the impact of Toscanini's appearance in Milan, an equally lasting impression on young Abbado was made by Wilhelm Furtwängler, whom he heard conduct at La Scala. He especially recalls the legendary 1950 performances of Wagner's *Ring* with Kirsten Flagstad that Furtwängler conducted at La Scala.

Abbado spent the summer of 1955 in Salzburg, studying with Friedrich Gulda, the Viennese pianist with whom he has since recorded Mozart concertos. There he met, but only in passing, Daniel Barenboim, a student in Igor Markevich's conducting class. There he also heard for the first time Bruno Walter, whom he recalls with special admiration. The summers of 1956 and 1957 found Abbado at the Accademia Chigiana in Siena, first to study conducting with Carlo Zecchi and then to work with Alceo Galliera. In his first summer there, he formed close and lasting friendships with Zubin Mehta, then twenty, and the twelve-year-old Daniel Barenboim. Mehta had been studying with Hans Swarowsky at the Vienna Academy of Music and helped Abbado to decide to join him there in the fall of 1956.

Vienna was then recovering from the war. Austria had in 1955 regained its independence, and the military occupation, with its separate Western and Russian zones, had ended. Late in 1955, the Vienna State Opera had moved back, with great fanfare and no little emotion, into its completely rebuilt theater on the Opernring. Herbert von Karajan was about to displace Karl Böhm and begin his seven-year rule of the State Opera. Abbado and Mehta joined the Musikverein chorus in order to sing under such conductors as Karajan and Walter and, of course, to observe their conducting at close hand. At the Vienna Academy there was much chamber music, in addition to conducting classes, with a faculty steeped in the Viennese musical tradition stretching back through Mahler, Bruckner, and Brahms to Haydn, Mozart, and Beethoven.

Even in his student days, Abbado established contacts with Viennese musical circles that remained of great importance to him. The young Italian, already exposed to Austro-German music, was now steeped in it, both academically and in the personal contacts he made with all types of musicians. Like Mehta, his deep understanding of Bruckner and Mahler is rooted in his student days in Vienna, when that music was virtually absorbed through the pores of the skin. From the beginning, however, Abbado was not an admirer of the Vienna State Opera. Even today he takes a rather patronizing view of the Austrian theater and its lackadaisical way of doing business. Though he has been invited to conduct there, he has never done so. From time to time, there has been talk of a visit by La Scala to Vienna, but as Abbado points out, there has never been, so far at least, enough advance planning. Beyond these problems, however, there seems to lurk a basic Italian lack of sympathy with the Viennese ways of opera.

In the 1950s, Hans Swarowsky was the most renowned teacher of conducting in Europe. Hungarian-born and a pupil of Schoenberg, Swarowsky had a moderately successful conducting career in Germany, Poland, and Austria. He was not, in Abbado's opinion, a very good conductor, but he was an excellent teacher; he was also a caustic critic of other conductors. Through him, Abbado first encountered the music of the Second Viennese School—Schoenberg, Berg, and Webern—music then virtually unknown in Italy. Swarowsky was equally authoritative in his teaching of the basic Austro-German repertory from Haydn through Mahler. Although Abbado found him rather "mathematical" in his approach, he taught a rigorous analytical method that is the basis for Abbado's own preparatory work to this day. He also placed a great emphasis on projecting the characteristic style of the music, whether historical or peculiar to the composer.

Although Abbado does not recall some of the more extreme pedagogical methods attributed to Swarowsky, such as having a student conduct with one hand tied behind his back, he remembers his emphasis on good stick technique. One method of encouraging independence of manual gestures was to have a student conduct with one hand while playing from a piano reduction of the orchestra score with the other. He also regarded a conductor's eyes as an essential means of communicating with the orchestra. In general, he sought to instill in his students the idea of achieving maximum musical communication with the most economical means. Although some of the lessons were at the piano, Swarowsky's students had ample opportunity actually to conduct orchestras—the student orchestra at the academy itself and the professional Tonkünstler.

Following Swarowsky's death in 1975, Abbado conducted a performance of a Mozart mass in his memory with the Vienna Philharmonic, a chorus from the State Opera, and soloists. The performance was recorded by Deutsche Grammophon. On that occasion Abbado paid tribute to his teacher: "Unforgettable are his fanatical respect toward each score, and his profound knowledge, his perseverance and patience in explaining the works. He always tried to show new ways to analyze the score. He wanted everyone to understand him and was tireless in his search for new methods."

After two years in Vienna, Abbado and Mehta spent the summer of 1958 at the Berkshire Music Center at Tanglewood. There, in a conducting class taught mainly by Eleazar Carvalho, but with visits from Charles Munch and Pierre Monteux, Abbado and Mehta were friendly rivals for the annual Koussevitzky prize awarded each summer to the best young conductor. That prize, voted by both the student orchestra players and the instructors, was based not on any one audition but on the overall performance of the young conductors during the summer. In a close decision, Abbado won the Koussevitzky prize but declined an offer by an American manager to build a career for him in the United States that might lead to a resident post here.

Abbado has often denied a driving ambition for a "big career," and the next five years were a time of absorption and consolidation. So, while his friend Mehta was moving ahead rapidly, especially after 1960 in North America, Abbado, between twenty-five and thirty, kept a much lower profile. In the two years following Tanglewood, he made his symphonic and operatic debuts in Trieste and became instructor in chamber music at the Parma Conservatory. With his background in family ensemble playing, he was an ideal instructor, for he shares Bruno Walter's conviction that performing chamber music is basic to conducting. Although he has, even today, no great interest in teaching conducting, he retains fond memories of his work in Parma, from which, he says, he learned as much from the students as they probably did from him. Among the works he prepared with his students at Parma were Hindemith's *Hin und Zurück* and Stravinsky's *L'Histoire du Soldat*. In 1960, he made his debut in Milan conducting an Alessandro Scarlatti program at the Piccola Scala during the tricentennial celebration of that composer's birth. He also organized a chamber orchestra, the Soloisti di Milano, that played in Milan and elsewhere in northern Italy.

It was nearly five years before Abbado returned to the international music scene, having confined himself, after Vienna and Tanglewood, to Italy. In 1963 he entered the first Dimitri Mitropoulos Memorial International Competition for young conductors. This competition, sponsored by a group of Jewish women's charities in New York, had been first held a year earlier for pianists. In 1963, however, it offered young conductors cash prizes and, for the three co-winners, a season's engagement as assistants to Leonard Bernstein at the New York Philharmonic. During this trip to North America, Abbado also conducted in Montreal and Los Angeles at the invitation of Mehta, already firmly established as music director of the orchestras in both cities. Neither appearance generated much success, and one critic in Montreal went so far as to suggest that Abbado abandon conducting altogether, advice hardly conducive to encouraging him in the forthcoming competition.

Nor was the Mitropoulos Competition a pleasant experience for the shy young Italian. Sixty-five competitors went through a series of elimination rounds prior to even standing before an orchestra. "I remember the quarter finals. I thought I would be eliminated because I had conducted so badly. At the semifinals, I was even worse, terrible. But then at the finals I conducted like it was a regular concert, and it was good. I hated it so much, though, I knew it would be the last competition for me." According to the *Time* critic, of the three winners he had the most flair: "He stood with feet planted as on a rolling deck and with great sweeps of the arms drew a rich sound from the orchestra."

Some musicians regard an assistant conductorship at any orchestra as a competition prize as the equivalent of the old New York vaudeville joke about a weekend in Philadelphia. Abbado recalls his season as an assistant at the Philharmonic with mixed feelings. In the first place, there was the language problem, for he spoke virtually no English. Leonard Bernstein, an old acquaintance from Milan and Tanglewood, was kind and thoughtful, but the only chance Abbado had to conduct the Philharmonic in concert was when he shared one program with his two co-winners. Encountering George Szell for the first time as guest at the Philharmonic, Abbado was greatly impressed by his performances of Haydn, Mozart, and Schubert and recalls Szell's generous interest and counsel with continuing gratitude.

However, the Philharmonic was very flexible in giving Abbado leaves of absence to conduct elsewhere. The most important of these engagements was with the RIAS Orchestra in West Berlin. Karajan heard him there and immediately engaged him to conduct the Vienna Philharmonic in the Mahler Second Symphony at the 1965 Salzburg Festival and the Berlin Philharmonic Orchestra the following year. The Mahler performance, more than any of Abbado's previous appearances, established him as a young conductor of importance on the international scene. He was thirty-two at that time, rather old by comparison with many of his colleagues.

That Salzburg performance in 1965 was also the beginning of a steady association with the Vienna Philharmonic Orchestra, of which he became "permanent conductor" in 1971. Although one of the oldest of all symphony orchestras, having been founded a few days before the Philharmonic Society of New York in 1842, the Vienna Philharmonic is not a full-time symphony orchestra in the sense that its British and American counterparts are. Its players are drawn from a large pool of musicians employed full-time by the Vienna State Opera, which gives nearly three hundred opera and ballet performances a year, leaving relatively little time for extended symphonic activity. The Philharmonic plays a concert season of ten programs in pairs plus festivals in Vienna and Salzburg; tours; and makes recordings. Although they are state employees, the orchestral musicians at the Vienna State Opera are involved in the artistic policy of the company. Those who are also members of the Philharmonic manage that organization as a player-cooperative, electing a governing committee, determining who shall be admitted to membership in the Philharmonic, and selecting the orchestra's permanent conductor. They are, in fact, the elite members of the State Opera Orchestra and earn additional income from their Philharmonic membership.

Since a number of guest conductors are engaged for the Philharmonic concerts, the demands on the time of the permanent conductor are not very heavy. But he is expected to participate in major tours and festivals, and the prestige conferred by the position is by no means inconsiderable. With such predecessors as Mahler, Weingartner, Walter, Furtwängler, and Karajan, it was singular for a young Italian to be so honored.

As permanent conductor, Abbado has made a number of tours—almost annually—with the Vienna Philharmonic Orchestra. He especially treasures a tour to the Far East in 1973, to Australia for the opening of the new opera house in Sydney, and to the People's Republic of China not long before the visit there of the Philadelphia Orchestra. Unlike other visitors from abroad, Abbado did not sense the musical isolation of Chinese musicians working in the Western idiom. He encountered a number of Chinese players, some trained in Germany and others in Russia. He brought back an impression of the Chinese that he encountered as "very simple people" with a high sense of morality and recalls his visit as a most inspiring experience.

Thanks to the Mitropoulos Competition and the contacts he made then and the following year in New York, Abbado was invited eventually to conduct all of the major orchestras in the United States—Los Angeles and Pittsburgh in addition to the "Big Five." The critics found him less tense than in his earlier appearances. In 1970, with the Philadelphia and Boston orchestras, it was noted, Abbado conducted with "small ritards and relaxations [that] let the music breathe" and was "less stiff" than on previous visits. In these years, he played a great deal of Russian music—Tchaikovsky, Mussorgsky, Prokofiev, and Stravinsky—in which he was generally better received than in such composers as Brahms and Schumann. When George Szell came down with German measles in March 1970, Abbado stepped in to conduct the New York Philharmonic in a benefit concert at which he was described as a "perfect partner" for Jacqueline du Pré in a cello concerto.

Although he is too tactful to cite a favorite American orchestra, he is most enthusiastic, implicitly if not explicitly, about the Philadelphia and Chicago orchestras and the Cleveland under Szell. His opinion of the New York Philharmonic is unquestionably influenced by the environment in which it works. Comparing New York with Philadelphia, for instance, he says that New York musicians "have no time to enjoy life." In Philadelphia, "they try to help you make music. . . . [In New York] it's strange, because individually they are wonderful players. I remember Szell conducting the Philharmonic. They played well, but I heard him do the same pieces with Cleveland, and it was completely different. I liked New York for some weeks. But I could never live there. It's a crazy city, like a meat-grinding machine."

Generally, he finds American orchestras flexible, open to new ideas and suggestions. He is especially lavish in his praise of the Chicago Symphony Orchestra, with whom he first appeared in 1971. On that occasion Bernard Jacobson of the *Daily News* was ambivalent about Abbado: "That he can lead an orchestra with skill, discretion, and a good measure of generalized passion is not in doubt. What I have so far missed is a sense of really personal involvement in the music that he conducts, or for that matter a fine intellectual grasp of its broader structural implications." During that same engagement, Thomas Willis of the *Tribune* wrote: "Mr. Abbado is a virtuoso; Mr. Barenboim is a strategist. A Cleveland friend of mine told me that Mr. Abbado turned off many of that city's excellent orchestra men by 'trying to teach them the Brahms First,' and I can believe that." Nevertheless, Abbado eventually established himself with critics, public, and orchestra players in Chicago. His recording of the Mahler Second Symphony with the Chicago Orchestra followed performances that were received rapturously, and the record itself is regarded as one of the finest interpretations of this monumental work.

Less successful was Abbado's only appearance with an American opera company when he conducted Verdi's *Don Carlo* at the Metropolitan Opera in 1968. The production, which had inaugurated the Rudolf Bing regime in 1950, was already threadbare; even Verdi's own four-act version was cut in several essential places. Abbado recalls that Bing had promised him certain singers who did not turn up, that rehearsals were too short, and that cast substitutions were not to his liking. "It's a matter of principle. I don't like being promised something and then not getting it."

Before he actually arrived at the Met, there was talk of his returning to do an "original" *Boris Godunov,* but the circumstances of the
Don Carlo obviously prevented that. (In fact, that version of *Boris* was
not produced at the Met until the 1976–77 season.) There were later
discussions with Goeran Gentele to conduct his new production of *Un
Ballo in Maschera* and still later negotiations with James Levine to do
that work at the Met. At the moment, Abbado feels inclined to confine
his operatic activity to La Scala. That commitment and those to the London and Vienna orchestras have precluded his accepting, even on a
part-time basis, any of several American offers reported to have been
tendered him. For the time being at least, his American activity will be
confined to a few weeks each year as guest conductor of one or two top
orchestras and occasional visits with his European groups.

The celebration of the American bicentennial in 1976 at the Kennedy Center in Washington, D.C., was the occasion for one of Abbado's
most impressive successes in this country. After much·uncertainty·and
international complication, the entire La Scala company appeared at
the center in four operas, stopping enroute at Covent Garden, where
Harold Rosenthal wrote in *Opera* that *Simon Boccanegra* was "one of
the truly great experiences of the postwar era—a production that was
all of a piece, one that showed that La Scala truly had Verdi in its
blood." Abbado conducted *Macbeth* and *Simon Boccanegra,* as well as
the Requiem of Verdi, and Rossini's *La Cenerentola.* The occasion was
a triumph for all concerned, but Abbado's contribution was recognized
as crucial.

The Mitropoulos Competition and his eventual success with the
Mahler Second at Salzburg also launched Abbado's European career.
Within a very few years he was conducting extensively in Germany—
Berlin, Munich, Stuttgart, Dresden—as well as in Amsterdam, Paris,
and London. In the latter city, he first conducted two orchestras, the
New Philharmonia and the London Symphony, but has appeared only
with the London Symphony since 1971. He has been a regular visitor to
the Edinburgh Festival, first with the New Philharmonia and later with
the London Symphony, which he has conducted there in both concert

and opera performances. In 1968, he went to Covent Garden to direct a revival of the famous Luchino Visconti production of *Don Carlo,* this time in the so-called Modena version in five acts. Increasingly, his London activity has centered on the London Symphony Orchestra, which designated him one of its two principal guest conductors in 1971.

Late in 1977, the players of the London Symphony voted to engage Abbado as their principal conductor to succeed André Previn in 1979. (Previn had held this post since 1968 and has also been music director of the Pittsburgh Symphony since 1976.) London orchestras have a way of affiliating a number of conductors with themselves. The masthead of the London Symphony's program book late in the Previn regime included, in addition to him as principal conductor, Karl Böhm as president, Abbado and Colin Davis as principal guest conductors, and Eugen Jochum as conductor laureate. In this hierarchy, the principal conductor plays the most important role, similar structurally to that of the permanent conductor of the Vienna Philharmonic, but a much more active one, since the London Symphony is, unlike the Vienna Philharmonic, a full-time symphony orchestra, with only occasional excursions into the opera pit.

The London Symphony is governed by a committee of players elected by the members of the orchestra. This committee and its chairman (also a player) fill the roles played in American orchestras by the board of directors and, in matters of musical policy, by the musical director and manager. When the principal conductor and managing director join in committee deliberations, they act as highly valued and expert advisers to the players' committee that makes the final decision. Since this governing group consists of professional musicians, it has, in dealing with the principal conductor, considerably more artistic expertise than the usual American board of directors. On the other hand, as long as the members of such an orchestra depend for their living on income from concerts, tours, recordings, modest government support, and even more modest private and corporate support, their committee has a much deeper understanding of the problems of orchestra operation than the orchestra committees and unions generally do in the United States; in a player-governed orchestra there is no place for an adversary relation between musicians and management-board. At the same time, lacking a guaranteed salary, players have considerably less financial security, although an orchestra like the London Symphony has a long-standing record of producing a certain level of income for its players. There is, however, a great pressure to play as many concerts as possible, to hold rehearsals to the absolute minimum, and to develop such ancillary income as recordings. Because of the players' desire for work, recording rates are held low—less than one-third what they are in the United States—and work rules are less restrictive. Consequently, London is highly favored as a site for recordings of serious music, offering as it does several top orchestras at bargain prices.

In selecting its principal conductor, as well as the guests who will lead a majority of its concerts in Royal Festival Hall, the London Symphony committee looks for a combination of artistic distinction and box-office appeal. It also wants a principal conductor who will work cooperatively in the innumerable artistic decisions it must make—choice of guests, repertory, scheduling of rehearsals, tours, and recording plans. One factor that often influences the engagement of conductors is the interest of recording companies in them. The London Symphony itself has no exclusive contract with any company and records with many guest conductors for virtually every company working in London. This is by no means to say that the principal conductors of these player-governed orchestras do not play an important part in shaping their artistic quality. At the very end of his long career, before his death in 1964, Pierre Monteux contributed much to upgrading the London Symphony, and André Previn left his own stamp on it during the more than ten years of their association. Abbado will unquestionably leave his mark, especially through his participation in crucial personnel decisions—hiring new players, easing out older ones—decisions that are hard for players to make when they concern students or colleagues and are therefore easier with the help of an outside authority.

Despite his association with La Scala, Abbado made his first operatic recordings with the London Symphony, both of them Rossini operas in new editions prepared by Alberto Zedda. These versions removed tradition-encrusted additions and alterations to Rossini's original scores and restored the composer's brighter and more transparent orchestration. Following his great success conducting the Jean-Pierre Ponnelle production of *Il Barbiere di Siviglia* in Salzburg in 1968, Abbado in 1971 conducted *La Cenerentola* at the Edinburgh Festival, with several of the same singers, notably Teresa Berganza and Luigi Alva. At Edinburgh, the orchestra was the London Symphony. Both operas were recorded with the orchestra in conjunction with the Edinburgh production of *La Cenerentola*. Although there had been previous recordings of *Il Barbiere di Siviglia* with the role of Rosina sung in Rossini's original mezzo-soprano range, this was the first time that either opera had been recorded in the Zedda edition. Abbado places great emphasis on musicological correctness, both in these operas and elsewhere. His recording of *Carmen,* another Edinburgh production with the London Symphony, uses the Oeser edition with spoken dialogue rather than accompanied recitative and seeks in its musical text to restore Bizet's intentions. When Abbado deviates from the Oeser edition, he does so, he says, because of the uncertainty of Bizet's actual intentions, the composer having died so shortly after the premiere of the work that he never had a chance to make final decisions on its text.

London has also been the focal point of another Abbado international activity—the European Community Youth Orchestra (ECYO). Organized by Lionel Walter and Joy Bryer, who had been involved in the International Festival of Youth Orchestras and Performing Arts, the ECYO is made up of young—fourteen- to twenty-year-old—musicians from the nine nations of the European Economic Community. These young players, selected by audition in their respective countries and numbering 135, gathered in March 1978 at a center a few miles from Amsterdam for intensive rehearsal and instruction—eight hours a day— under Abbado and his assistant, James Judd. Abbado was both amazed and inspired when these youngsters, after a long workday, would organize their own ensembles to play chamber music at night. In addition to orchestra-playing under the two conductors, the various sections of the orchestra were coached by some of the best musicians of Europe. At the end of two weeks, the orchestra played its first public concert at the Concertgebouw in Amsterdam, performing Mahler's difficult Sixth Symphony—"really fantastic," says Abbado—under his direction. The orchestra played in ten other European cities. In Paris a critic hailed it as superior to many professional orchestras. Later, in Edinburgh, most of its players joined others from youth orchestras from Germany, Egypt, Israel, and England for a performance of Beethoven's Ninth Symphony under Giulini.

Originally it was hoped that the European Community Organization would itself underwrite the expenses of the ECYO, but it soon became apparent that this expectation was in fact an obstacle to official authorization by its parliament. Once the sponsors agreed to finance the venture by soliciting funds from private individuals, corporations, and various governments, the parliament quickly agreed in March 1976 to the orchestra's establishment. Mrs. Bryer and dedicated supporters organized international committees of leading political figures in the EEC. Edward Heath, an ardent amateur musician as well as former Conservative prime minister of Great Britain, accepted the presidency of the ECYO; he has also appeared as conductor of a short selection in most of the orchestra's public performances. With a prestigious roster of committees, the sponsors were able to finance the initial activities of the orchestra, but they and Abbado still hoped to enlist the direct support of the European Economic Community on an increasing scale if the ECYO is to become a permanent international activity.

The ECYO is one subject on which the usually reticent Abbado will show unrestrained enthusiasm. During his U.S. engagements, he has also worked occasionally with student orchestras. In Philadelphia, Eugene Ormandy has made a special effort to bring his guests to the Curtis Institute of Music for weekly sessions with its student orchestra, from which Abbado has gained much satisfaction. In Chicago, he has worked with the Civic Orchestra, the Chicago Symphony Orchestra's training program, in such repertory as the Mahler Third Symphony. In these student orchestras, as in the ECYO, Abbado finds an enthusiasm and dedication that appeal to his own idealistic approach to music. He now hopes to organize a purely Italian youth orchestra, having been impressed by the fact that he had over two hundred applications from

Italy (from whom fifteen or sixteen were chosen) when the ECYO was auditioning.

Just as he says it would be impossible for him to teach conducting, Abbado finds it very hard to discuss his own conducting. He is much more articulate in discussing conductors whose work he admires—especially conductors from the past, for he is very tactful about his contemporaries. Toscanini made a great impact on him, both when he heard him after the war in Milan and from his records. Abbado had a first-hand chance, as a student in Milan, to hear Toscanini rehearse and conduct important orchestral programs of Verdi, Wagner, Beethoven, and other composers. He was especially impressed by Toscanini's discipline, his technical control over the musicians. Strictly as a conductor, Toscanini was for him the greatest. Unquestionably, Abbado also responds to Toscanini's typically Italianate insistence on the singing line.

Nevertheless, Abbado cites Furtwängler as the "greatest model of a musician." He recognizes Furtwängler's purely technical shortcomings but then points out that there was something about the conductor's physical presence, his charisma, that inspired his players and through them his audiences, and this in a way that had nothing to do with baton technique. He senses this very special communication even in Furtwängler's recordings, more so in those of actual performances than in those made in the studio. He especially cites the records of the live performances of Wagner, Beethoven, Brahms, and Bruckner as being among "the best you can hear." He told Alan Blyth in a *Gramophone* interview, "I think the La Scala performances of the *Ring* now available, in spite of the mistakes, are the most vital *Ring* ever heard. The live Beethoven Ninth too."

Abbado obviously has spent a lot of time listening to the records of conductors of the past, both commercially released and pirated. For instance, he much prefers a privately circulated Bruno Walter performance of the Mahler Fourth Symphony from a broadcast to the commercial version. Both from his observation of that conductor and from recordings, he especially admires Walter's performances of the major Mozart symphonies and of much of Mahler's music. Walter's readings of the Mahler Second, Fourth, Fifth, and Ninth share Abbado's affection with Mitropoulos's Third and Sixth, underground recordings which he regards as superior to any current commercially released versions.

Another conductor who stands high in Abbado's pantheon, especially for his Beethoven and Schubert, is Erich Kleiber, whom he knows only from recordings and secondhand through his children—Carlos, who conducts regularly at La Scala, and Veronica, who is Abbado's administrative assistant there. Among Italians, he has great admiration for Victor de Sabata and, of course, Guido Cantelli. Abbado's father was violin soloist when Cantelli made his debut in Milan, and Claudio attended those and other rehearsals. He regards Cantelli's early death in 1956 and Franco Ferrara's illness as major losses to Italian music.

Abbado's own conducting, especially as he has matured in recent years, seems to combine the sharply etched singing line of his Italian heritage with the broad sweep and melos of Furtwängler. He is not afraid to vary tempo, with or without explicit direction in the score, and he is keenly sensitive to the coloristic implications of harmonic tensions. He is also very responsive to the ambience in which he is performing. His performances of the Mahler Fourth, for instance, can be quite different according to the orchestra he is leading, the hall acoustics, or the setting of the concert. In Vienna, Abbado's Mahler Fourth was notable for the richness of the strings and the full sonority of Mahler's writing; much of this can be heard in his recording of the Mahler Fourth, but then Abbado says quietly that they played the piece better several times during a tour of Germany. When Abbado conducted the Philadelphia Orchestra in the same symphony in New York's Carnegie Hall, Andrew Porter was enthusiastic in his *New Yorker* review:

He is the most picturesque and most lyrical of Mahler interpreters, and supreme at making the picturesqueness precise, the lyricism lucid. . . . His use of rubato was bold. He is not afraid to pause for an instant of delicious expectation before launching into some heart-easing melody, to press forward within a phrase towards its climax, to dwell tenderly on a sweet cadence. The Philadelphians played for him like angels. The sensuous beauty of their sound was extraordinary. Every color was clear and full, every line lovingly drawn. And always in balance. The counterpoints were limpid. There was unusual depth to the sonic picture; some music seemed to come from far, far away, to spring up under one's feet, and everything conspired to create a world of marvels among which the listener was not lost but let to live an intenser life. . . . Abbado showed that a Mahler Symphony—even Mahler's best-known symphony—can still provide a transcendental experience.

That same transcendental communication was also to be heard in a later performance in Royal Festival Hall with the London Symphony Orchestra, but the texture was much lighter, the phrasing and interplay of the instruments often approaching that of chamber music. When asked about the differences between these performances, Abbado was at first puzzled, then attributed them to the differences in orchestras and acoustic ambience, and finally recognized that he himself was responding to the music differently each time.

When Abbado first conducted in the United States, his gestures were inclined to be stiff and his style rather flamboyant. He also played a great deal of gaudy Russian music; he was a notable exponent of such out-of-the-way Prokofiev scores as the Third Symphony and the *Chout* Suite. However, as time passed, he loosened up. His gestures are now more fluid, more appropriate to the singing line and dramatic climaxes he now so effectively achieves in Tchaikovsky, Mahler, and Verdi. In rehearsal he works in great detail with an orchestra, especially when first tackling a piece. At times he is almost painfully exacting as he keeps the players going over a passage again and again until they respond with the desired balance and inflection. Bowing, the basis of all orchestral phrasing, is very important to him, and he confers frequently with the concertmaster on this matter. Unlike some other visiting conductors, he does not provide his own orchestra parts but sends his working scores ahead so that the local librarian can mark his special bowings and phrasings in the orchestra parts.

Though he talks relatively little—"After all, I can't tell them how to play in concert"—his verbal instructions rely on the lingua franca of orchestra playing: "More legato, up-bow here. Start in the middle of the bow. A *Luftpause* after the F-sharp. Stronger horn on that C." Frequently, he will sing a phrase, not necessarily in tune, but always conveying the expression he wants. However, he communicates mostly through his hands and eyes; his gestures are clear and expressive, controlling the basic pattern of the larger rhythms as well as the bar-by-bar meter. Although he uses a score in rehearsal, he does not do so in concert except for very difficult modern works. With a score, he diminishes his visual rapport with the players; in opera he would lose contact with the singers. He feels that he can get deeper into the music in performance without a score. As predicted by Bernstein and confirmed by players sitting in front of him, he meets Swarowsky's admonition to convey his directions with his eyes, always watching what is going on, fixing the attention of players as they glance up from their scores, and conveying by their expressivity the melos that he feels in the music.

On the podium during rehearsal he is patient, either with players slow to catch on to his ideas or with the talking or "noodling" in which orchestra players indulge when the conductor is correcting someone else. When the latter gets out of hand on occasion, he can betray his irritation. Generally, though, he is extremely polite to the players, encouraging rather than demanding. Despite his frequently piecemeal way of beginning work on a section, it gradually comes together in something like the total conception that was always in his mind while he was attending to detail.

As Abbado has gained more control over the situations in which he works, he has become increasingly conscientious about seeking out authentic musical texts. Part of the success of the *Il Barbiere di Siviglia* in Salzburg and *La Cenerentola* in Edinburgh stemmed from his use of the Zedda editions. Abbado is deeply concerned with this kind of *Werktreue*. One of these days, in recording his Mahler cycle, he will have to decide whether to include the *Blumine* movement in the First Symphony, which he has not yet played. He gives a lot of thought to the problem of Bruckner, reviewing each symphony on the musical merits of various editions as well as taking documentary evidence into account.

Here the precedent of such performers as Furtwängler is also important; although he himself plays the Novak edition of Bruckner's Eighth Symphony, he is fascinated by Furtwängler's combination of the Haas and the "original" editions.

In 1967, Abbado made his operatic debut at La Scala in a new production of Bellini's *I Capuleti ed i Montecchi,* with which he toured to Montreal during the Olympic Games. In that production the role of Romeo, scored by Bellini for mezzo-soprano, was sung in transposition by a tenor. Abbado admits that this was a regrettable expedient at the time and hopes someday to produce this opera with a mezzo Romeo, possibly Frederica von Stade.

His most significant effort to restore a major work to its original form was his production in 1977 of Verdi's *Don Carlo* to open the bicentennial celebration of La Scala. *Don Carlo* is the most problematic work of Verdi: written for the Paris Opéra, it was revised during production there and later issued by Verdi himself in two different Italian versions, one in four acts and the other in five. Recent investigations by Andrew Porter, David Rosen, and Ursula Günther have brought to light other music that Verdi wrote for this opera, some even on pages in the original orchestra parts that had been pasted together. Although there had been performances of an urtext *Don Carlo* in a BBC studio presentation in the original French and a staging by Sarah Caldwell in Boston, both in 1973, the La Scala production was the first by a major company in truly "grand opera" style. This restored Verdi's original music, notably the chorus that opens the Fontainebleau scene (Act I) and the extension of the duet in Act IV for Carlo and King Philip with material later used in the Manzoni Requiem. The production was conceived by Luca Ronconi, one of the more innovative opera directors of our time.

Abbado is very enthusiastic about this production of *Don Carlo,* although he admits that the first performances were not quite as good as he wished. The revival in 1978–79 tightened up some of Ronconi's pageantry, although it did not modify his basic conception of the opera as one long funeral procession. In a dispatch from Milan in December 1977, Lon Tuck wrote in the *Washington Post*:

Don Carlo is a sprawling, five-act opera that can seem to go on forever when placed in the wrong hands. Wednesday night the elements necessary to prevent this were present—discipline, imagination, and momentum. Abbado was the key. As Washingtonians learned last year with his performances at the Kennedy Center of Verdi's *Macbeth* and *Simon Boccanegra*, Abbado has fashioned a way of performing Verdi that is so cohesive that the whole adds up to more than the sum of its parts. Nothing lags, nothing is rushed. This new production was by Luca Ronconi, a controversial figure with Milan audiences. Several times production details that displeased certain patrons were greeted with shouts of "stupido" and during the curtain calls Ronconi came in for his share of boos and heckling, some of which continued after the applause was over. Wednesday night, there were fifteen curtain calls, and when Abbado came on stage, bouquets of flowers started flying in all directions from La Scala's six steep tiers.

Andrew Porter, who has written extensively on this opera, reported on the La Scala production in the *New Yorker* (January 23, 1978) at some length:

[Abbado's] conducting was magnificent, and so was the playing of the Scala orchestra, a body that seemed to unite the virtues of his two other orchestras—the Vienna Philharmonic's richness and warmth of tone, especially the string tone, and the London Symphony's vigor and precision. His reading was highly colored and very theatrical but not showy. The music gleamed with brighter lights and the contrasts were fiercer than those of Giulini's performance; the phrasing was more natural, less self-consciously exquisite than Karajan's. And when—as in Posa's "C'est mon jour suprême"—Verdi wrote "Pianissimo" and "Très doux," the singing *was* very soft and very sweet. The small, correct details printed for the first time in the Günther-Petazzoni score seem, taken singly, to be minutiae such as make little difference to the run of the whole performance; but I feel sure that their cumulative contribution to the musical excellence of this execution was large.

The production of *Don Carlo* was also the occasion for controversy in international television. The RAI (Italian Government Radio and

Television) wanted to present the opening night of *Don Carlo,* also the beginning of the La Scala bicentennial, on worldwide television, including the Soviet Union, because two important Bolshoi singers, Elena Obrastzova and Evgeny Nesterenko, were singing important roles. However, four other members of the cast—Mirella Freni, José Carreras, Piero Cappuccilli, and Nicolai Ghiaurov—had sung in Karajan's abbreviated production of *Don Carlo* at Salzburg and were still under contract to record the opera for Deutsche Grammophon and to film it for Unitel, a producer of television programs. When it became impossible to resolve these contractual problems, the telecast was postponed for a month and other singers (Placido Domingo, Margaret Price, Renato Bruson, and Evgeny Nesterenko) were engaged for the occasion.

Abbado's next venture into an authentic production was the original *Boris Godunov,* about which the Metropolitan Opera had approached him at the time of his unhappy experience with *Don Carlo* in 1968. From his description of his intentions regarding *Boris,* it would seem that he uses basically the same performing version that the Metropolitan eventually produced under the late Thomas Schippers and that was recorded in Poland for EMI-Angel.

Abbado's concern with textual fidelity to the music of the past has its counterpart in his deep personal interest in certain contemporary music. During his studies with Swarowsky, he was exposed to the music of Schoenberg, Berg, and Webern by a teacher who himself had studied with Schoenberg and was an advocate of the music of the Second Viennese School. Abbado has frequently included their orchestral music in his own programs, and a highlight of the La Scala bicentennial was a presentation of Schoenberg's *Pierrot Lunaire* at the Piccola Scala. Although Alban Berg's *Wozzeck* was a scandalous failure with the public when Dimitri Mitropoulos introduced it to La Scala in 1955, Abbado revived the opera with great success in 1971 and conducted a new Ronconi production of it in 1977. The latter was to be repeated during an Alban Berg festival centered on the new three-act *Lulu,* brought to Milan by the Paris Opéra.

In addition to the Second Viennese School, Abbado programs a variety of contemporary composers—Luciano Berio, György Ligeti, Krzy-sztof Penderecki, Goffredo Petrassi, Pierre Boulez, Luigi Dallapiccola, and Giacomo Manzoni. But his closest association, as an interpreter and friend, is with Luigi Nono. Nono is radical both musically and politi-cally; his music employs dodecaphonic and electronic techniques and his subject matter usually has a strong political content of antifascism and pro-Communism, for Nono is an active member of the Italian Com-munist Party and writes music to express his political views.

Nono was born in Venice in 1924 and, after studies in Italy and Germany, worked closely with avant-garde centers in Darmstadt, Dart-ington, and Gravesano. He established the electroacoustic music studio of the RAI in Milan in 1960. Abbado has played in concert and re-corded Nono's *"Come una ola de fuera y luz"* ("Like a Wave of Strength and Light"), a large-scale work employing full orchestra, piano solo (their long-time friend Maurizio Pollini), a soprano soloist, and pre-recorded electronic tape in which the performances by the singer and pianist were altered electronically. The soloists also perform along with the tape and orchestra. The text of the piece is by the Chilean poet Julio Hausi and is an elegy for the young revolutionary Luciano Cruz. Abbado first conducted this work at a concert at La Scala in 1972 and has re-peated it elsewhere in Europe. In 1975 Nono's opera *Al Gran Sole Carico d'Amore*—its text drawn from the revolutionary writings of Marx, Lenin, and others—was first produced by La Scala under Abbado's di-rection. It was repeated in 1978 as a part of the bicentennial observance.

In performing the music of such avant-garde composers as Nono and Stockhausen, Abbado finds no difficulty in adjusting himself to the special requirements of conducting music that combines live perform-ance by an orchestra and soloists with prerecorded tape. Although he recognizes that the tape can fix certain tempos, he points out that Nono has indicated that certain passages need not be precisely coordinated. One of Abbado's early successes in Milan was Goffredo Manzoni's *Atomtod*, which was produced at the Piccola Scala in complete darkness. Recalling the popular failure of *Wozzeck* at its La Scala premiere, Abbado is convinced that the Milanese audience today is much more receptive to advanced contemporary music. Abbado himself feels at ease in this idiom; his attitude is neither patronizingly apologetic nor crusading. He sees it as simply a part of his own work in music and finds special satisfaction in working directly with the composer, as he does with Nono and others.

Although the range of his symphonic programming in the standard repertory is quite catholic—broader than his recordings might indicate —he has certain specialties. He has long been a colorful interpreter of Russian music, adapting himself with equal ease to the passionate emotion of Tchaikovsky and the more acid idiom of Prokofiev and Stravinsky. His performances of the Bruckner First Symphony in concert and on record were regarded as revealing a previously unappreciated quality in this work, and his other performances of Bruckner and Mahler show a strong affinity for the late-romantic style.

In addition to Bizet's *Carmen,* from the non-Italian repertory he has also conducted at La Scala Mozart's *Le Nozze di Figaro.* However, in discussing his long-range plans as La Scala's artistic director, he hopes to do Mozart productions with such guest conductors as Karl Böhm. He has never conducted any Wagner operas, although he told an interviewer in 1973 that he hoped to do *Tristan und Isolde* in 1975. For the time being, Wagner at La Scala is in the hands of Carlos Kleiber, and in 1979–80, Zubin Mehta will do the *Ring.* Sir Georg Solti is scheduled to conduct *Die Meistersinger* in 1980.

Abbado's operatic repertory is, not surprisingly, rooted in Rossini, Donizetti, Bellini, and, especially, Verdi; he has conducted little, if any, Puccini. His Verdi performances at La Scala and elsewhere have been an important force in the current reevaluation of that composer's total creative output. In addition to rethinking *Don Carlo,* he has conducted stimulating performances of *Simon Boccanegra, Macbeth, Un Ballo in Maschera,* and, in 1972, a Scala production of *Aida* that was visually very austere. If his recorded representation of Verdi is comparatively meager—*Macbeth* and *Simon Boccanegra*—it is partly because it takes a long time and effort to assemble the casts he wants and partly because, as in his Mahler symphony series, he insists that his conception "ripen" in actual performance for some time before he commits it to records.

Claudio Abbado is, first and foremost, a musician of Milan, with deep family and professional roots in that city's culture. Inevitably, the Teatro alla Scala has become the focal center of his career despite his international activities. He devotes at least half of his time to La Scala and unquestionably more than that proportion in his thoughts and interest. He has been associated in various capacities with La Scala ever since he conducted the Alessandro Scarlatti tricentennial program in the Piccola Scala. The 1965 premiere of Manzoni's *Atomtod,* again in the Piccola Scala, was followed two years later by his debut in the Teatro itself, a new production of Bellini's *I Capuleti ed i Montecchi.* In 1968, he was designated principal conductor, a position that gave him the authority with which to rebuild the orchestra. In 1972, a reorganization of La Scala administration produced the team of Paolo Grassi as general manager, Massimo Bogianckino as artistic director, and Abbado as music director. Much was made in announcements by Grassi and interviews with Abbado about La Scala's reducing the influence of the well-heeled industrial class of Milan, working with trade unions to bring workers into the Teatro, and taking the artistry of La Scala out into the factories and outlying areas of Lombardy.

In 1976, amidst much-publicized trouble with unions, strikes, and financial difficulties, there was another administrative upheaval at La Scala. Bogianckino having left to become superintendent at the Teatro Comunale in Florence and Grassi to head the RAI (he was succeeded by Carlo Maria Badini), Abbado became artistic director. None of this was accomplished without highly publicized crises and personal conflicts. For many weeks, Abbado himself withdrew from the La Scala administration, although he conducted the company on its tour to London and Washington. Abbado is typically reticent about this and other crises in which he has been involved at La Scala. But it is difficult not to credit him with considerable expertise in the Byzantine intricacies of Italian musical politics. To have survived, to say nothing of having steadily risen, in the complicated atmosphere of La Scala since the mid-sixties is no small feat. Nor was it because he had no opportunities elsewhere: Abbado has stuck with extraordinary persistence to building his role at La Scala.

Administrative titles at Italian lyric theaters have a meaning that varies from city to city or will become completely different according to who occupies the position. The *direttore artistico* of one theater may be little more than an administrator of schedules, contracts, and other operating routines, referred to by a somewhat inferior title of *dottore,* as opposed to *professore,* or, at the very top, *maestro.* Or he may be, as Toscanini and de Sabata were in earlier times at La Scala, truly responsible for the artistic work of the theater. In this light, Abbado is *direttore artistico* in the Toscanini tradition but with responsibility for a vastly more diverse program and working in an infinitely more complicated administrative and political situation than prevailed in the 1920s.

Like most corporate business in Italy today, the La Scala *ente autonomo* is run as a tripartite enterprise involving private, labor, and government elements—a syndicalist structure rooted in the Mussolini regime. Where the lyric theaters of Italy are concerned, the government is a partner, not only in financial support but in formulating management policy and in the choice of top administrative staff. Furthermore, both the national and municipal governments are involved in this, as are the national and local unions. Given the multiparty government in Italy, plus the fact that a municipality may be dominated by a party other than that of the national government, the situation becomes quite complicated. It is said, for instance, that the appointments of the top administrators of certain opera houses are parcelled out as patronage among the various political parties. Moreover, the basic working arrangements of the unionized staffs for all Italian theaters are decided in tripartite negotiations in Rome. Local unions representing the actual workers involved in a given theater have nothing to do with the basic pay and working conditions in a manner comparable to the unions in the United States vis-à-vis their actual employers.

The production of opera in Italy is further complicated by laws that, were they really enforced, would make the operation of lyric theaters of international stature virtually impossible. For instance, because national subsidies are voted annually, the law forbids administrators to make contractual commitments beyond the period of the appropriation itself. Yet the best singers, conductors, and other artistic personnel are in such international demand that they plan their schedules as much as three and four years in advance. When Abbado wished to schedule a new production of *Die Meistersinger* at La Scala with Sir Georg Solti conducting in 1980, he had to start planning and, most important, committing the conductor in 1977 or earlier. Every lyric theater in Europe or America faces this problem, but only those in Italy must develop legal subterfuges to make their planning secure within the law.

During the summer of 1978, some thirty administrative officials in Italian lyric theaters were arrested for violating another law affecting all opera houses. Passed in 1968, this categorically prohibited dealing with agents or managers of artists and required that every theater negotiate directly with each and every singer, conductor, director, and other individually engaged personnel. The law was aimed at the unscrupulous practices of some Italian agents who were charging their artist clients excessive commissions; allegedly bribing theater officials or taking bribes from them; and keeping worthy artists from appearing in state-supported theaters. According to some, the law was also designed to make it more difficult to hire non-Italian artists. Obviously, this created great problems in hiring artists, especially those of international stature. The sponsors of the law in 1968 had recognized this and promised to set up a government-operated booking service. Ten years later, nothing had been done to implement this intention and opera administrators were quietly conducting business as usual with agents when- suddenly, in the summer of 1978, a government official in Rome, quite without warning, ordered the arrest of many of the top administrators of Italy's most renowned lyric theaters. Timed just after the World Cup Soccer matches in Argentina, the incident easily garnered big headlines throughout Italy for several days. Nevertheless, long after the arrests, little had been done to bring the law into conformity with actual practice.

An even greater and more nagging problem arises from the incredibly slow process of getting money from Rome into the coffers of the theaters once it has been appropriated. This not only involves a mass of paperwork but can also be hindered if the political orientation of a theater is out of sympathy with the national government in Rome. The only way a company can stay in business in Italy is to borrow heavily from banks at high interest rates. Since the national subsidies have been as much as two years late in arriving, the interest cost can be staggering; technically it is not an expense that qualifies for reimbursement from Rome, although there was, in 1972, a special appropriation of $20 million to pay off the bank debts and interest that Italian opera houses had accumulated. Even so, the national subsidy still arrives late and theaters are still forced to choose between bank borrowing or curtailment of their activities.

During the 1977–78 season, the first year of the La Scala bicentennial celebration, the operating budget of the *ente autonomo* was 20 billion lire, approximately $25 million. In very rough terms, about 75 percent of its income comes from government sources, all but 5 percent from the national government, and the remainder from the City of Milan, the Province of Milan, and the Region of Lombardy. Private contributions and other miscellaneous sources, including radio and television, cover about 8 percent of La Scala's budget, and the box office produces 17 percent.

Under such circumstances, it seems to outsiders a miracle that any lyric theater manages to produce opera at all in Italy; opera obviously shares the economic malaise of the entire Italian economy. Yet, for all this, the lyric theaters of Italy manage to produce opera and, in the case of La Scala, opera of which Robert Jacobson could write in *Opera News*:

> La Scala is one of the few theatres left to us that maintain a gold standard, and this despite a political and social atmosphere that would seem uncongenial to opera today. While standards in most world houses shift and dip, those of La Scala hold to an admirably high level. With Abbado at the helm and the world's leading singers passing through the portals to work with some of the bright lights in direction and design, its standards are to be envied.

CONDUCTORS

The special bicentennial celebration aside, the usual opera season at La Scala includes eight to ten opera productions, one or two of them in the Piccola Scala. Abbado usually prepares and conducts three or four of these, although he may delegate some of the later performances in *stagione* to an assistant conductor, in much the same way that the casts change in a *stagione* to allow "covers" to appear. (*Stagione* is the presentation of several performances of one work in a relatively short period, not in alternation with several other works, as in the repertory system.) Each opera is given a *stagione* scheduling over a relatively limited period; from first rehearsals through last performance may take only two months. Therefore, with other activities such as ballet, recitals, and orchestral concerts also being given in the theater, only two or three operas may be given in rotation in any one period. Depending on the popularity of a work, an opera may be given anywhere from five to twelve performances.

Usually, one of Abbado's productions is a completely new one, sometimes the premiere of a new work. Other productions are conducted either by guest conductors or those on the La Scala staff; Georges Prêtre frequently conducts French opera; Carlos Kleiber has had great success with *Tristan und Isolde* and *La Bohème*; and the "house" conductors include Giovanni Gavazzeni and Riccardo Chailly. The season at La Scala customarily opens in December, either with a premiere or the revival of an important opera production, and extends into early summer. The concert season of the La Scala Orchestra does not begin until spring and includes ten programs, each given several times in the Teatro and sometimes repeated elsewhere. Performances resume early in the fall after a summer vacation when the orchestra series is completed and operas given earlier are continued until the new season opens.

Although visits by foreign orchestras and opera companies were scheduled more frequently during the bicentennial, they also occur in normal seasons. Moreover, exchanges of productions—including scenery, costumes, leading singers, and direction, but not including orchestra and chorus—play an increasingly important role in the La Scala schedule. Abbado hopes to expand this way of introducing variety into the schedule at a cost lower than mounting completely new productions.

In the fall of 1978, Abbado conducted such a production of *Simon Boccanegra* at the Paris Opéra, and there are plans for similar exchanges or borrowings with Glyndebourne, Hamburg, and the Chicago Lyric Opera. The latter was to send its production of Penderecki's *Paradise Lost,* an opera commissioned there, to La Scala for its European premiere in 1979.

Compared with the season of the Metropolitan Opera in New York, the La Scala season seems relatively modest. Whereas the Metropolitan usually offers twenty-four different productions in a season of thirty weeks, La Scala offers less than half that number spread over a somewhat longer period. Moreover, the Metropolitan performs seven times a week in repertory, whereas La Scala presents only two or three operas a week in *stagione.* The disparity is even greater when the Metropolitan spring tour and opera-in-concert programs in New York City parks are considered. On the other hand, it must be noted that La Scala not only presents opera in other theaters but is also offering extensive seasons of orchestral concerts, ballets, recitals, and chamber music.

For some time, with Abbado's enthusiastic support, there has been an effort to "democratize" La Scala, once the theater of the nobility described by Stendhal and later a center of ostentatious display where corporate moguls mingled with the remnants of a petty aristocracy. Democratization is being accomplished in two ways. During the *stagione* run of an opera, there is a varying price scale and different methods of selling tickets. The opening of a new opera production or a visit by a foreign company may be priced very high, but prices are much lower for subsequent performances of operas in a *stagione.* Moreover, certain performances are sold as a whole directly to labor unions, schools, or musical organizations. In addition, although taking opera productions out of the theater raises logistical problems, a few productions of opera and ballet play such nearby cities as Brescia and Bergamo. The La Scala Orchestra is often divided into a variety of groups—chamber orchestras, string quartets, and wind ensembles—which play in schools, factories, and small halls in Milan and surrounding communities.

During the two-year bicentennial celebration, which included a seven-month exhibition at the Palazzo Reale devoted to the history of

La Scala, the central operatic activity of La Scala expanded somewhat. The celebration opened in December 1977 with the new *Don Carlo,* which was repeated the following season. Other Verdi operas and works by Puccini, Wagner, and Mozart were also included in the repertory offered in the Teatro alla Scala, and there were several important ballet productions, including *The Sleeping Beauty* with Carla Fracci of the La Scala company and guest artist Rudolf Nureyev. Luigi Nono's opera *Al Gran Sole Carico d'Amore* was revived under Abbado's direction at the Teatro Lirico. At the Piccola Scala there was a new production of Benjamin Britten's arrangement of *The Beggar's Opera.* Three foreign opera companies planned visits to honor La Scala: the Vienna State Opera with *Fidelio,* conducted by Leonard Bernstein; the Zurich Opera with Nikolaus Harnoncourt's productions of three Monteverdi stage works; and the Paris Opéra, with the Patrice Chéreau production of the new three-act version of *Lulu,* conducted by Pierre Boulez. Coincident with the Vienna State Opera visit, there were two concerts by the Vienna Philharmonic, one conducted by Bernstein, the other by Abbado. Another visiting orchestra, in the late spring of 1978, was the Leningrad Philharmonic. The visit of the Paris Opéra was also the occasion for an extensive mini-festival built around the music of Alban Berg. Ronconi's 1977 production of *Wozzeck* was revived under Abbado's direction, to be taken later to Paris. In addition, Abbado programmed the La Scala orchestra in Berg's music, and there were seminars on the composer and performances of his chamber music.

Abbado has a voice in planning all of this activity, as *direttore artistico* of the La Scala *ente autonomo,* not just of the opera and orchestra. Although he scarcely plans each event, he must approve all that he does not initiate, and in setting the overall pattern of who plays what and where, he has important policy responsibility.

How then, to return to the question raised earlier, does he manage to discharge such awesome duties and at the same time perform as extensively as he does? To all such questions, he replies with his characteristic modesty, "Of course, one must have good collaborators." And there is no question that Abbado tries to administer the affairs of

La Scala as skillfully as he runs his own career. Like most conductors, he claims to hate administration. But, when he talks of the quality and variety of La Scala's manifold performance, his limpid brown eyes open wide and light up and there is a tone of enthusiasm as well as pride in his voice.

Although Abbado's disclaimers of ambition for career-building may sound hypocritical coming from a man who heads three of the most prestigious musical institutions in the world, there is an element of truth in that disclaimer. Abbado is a patient man—as patient in allowing his career to develop gradually as he is with orchestra players who noodle or talk during rehearsal. Nevertheless, beneath his almost boyish shyness and despite his patience, there must run a steely determination and a by no means inconsiderable talent for political intrigue. Musically knowledgeable Londoners regard the London Symphony as the "most difficult" of their orchestras and speak with admiring awe of Abbado's political skill in becoming its principal conductor. Patient and modest though he may be, once committed, he has been completely dedicated in his pursuit of what, for the lack of a better name, has become his career. Always prepared for whatever he has undertaken, he can be ruthlessly critical in a very modest way of some of the things he has done. But his persistence, artistic dedication, and political expertise, have guided a steady rise through the ruthless, and at times frustrating, world of Italian musical politics at La Scala.

The Abbado family's position in Milanese music unquestionably helped him, but the distinction he has brought to La Scala's performances is the work of a great and dedicated artist. Moreover, Abbado's growing power at La Scala was undoubtedly aided by his outspoken political views, which are more than acceptable in heavily industrialized Milan. When speaking with Americans, Abbado takes pains to explain his political views, as he did in an interview with *Opera News*: "In life every man has to take a position. When people say, 'Oh, he is a musician; why should he talk about politics?' This is stupid. I did a concert against fascism in Italy at La Scala. It was at the time of the election and the fascists were very strong. In Italy the opposition to fascism is Communism, but it is not like it is in America. I myself, however, belong to no party. I voted with the Communists simply because they were the opposition to the fascists. But I disagree with both Italian and Russian Communism on many things. My line is very clear. I am for freedom. Everything that is not for freedom I protest."

Believing that no artist can isolate himself from the human world about him, Abbado reads voraciously—not just in the arts but in such general literature as the writings of Kafka, Büchner, Musil, Chekhov, Dostoevski, Gogol, and Mann. For recreation he plays center forward on the La Scala soccer team—"Not very well," he says. At his vacation home in Sardinia, he studies his scores and reads intensively but finds relaxation in gardening and sailing. There the Abbados are often joined by the Nonos. Luigi's wife, Nuria, is the daughter of Schoenberg. Their daughter, Celia, is a close friend of Abbado's daughter, Alexandra. She and her older brother, Daniele, are children of Abbado's first marriage. He and his second wife, Gabrielle, have a second son, Sebastian. Their principal home is in Milan, but with his increasing duties with the London Symphony and recording, they have a small house in Chelsea.

In conversation Abbado combines modesty about himself and enthusiasm about his work, the latter being more vividly conveyed by body language than by the words themselves. He shuns categorical statements about himself and his work: asked to name the records that he has made that best represent his work, he deftly twists the reply to list those with which he is not satisfied and would like to remake. Sometimes he is most revealing when he speaks by indirection, again in his *Opera News* interview: "You know there was a great conductor named Hans Knappertsbusch. After a concert, he would leave and never come out for bows. Years ago I used to be somewhat like that. Now I take time to be polite. I like the reaction of the audience. I am not sincere if I don't say that. But it still embarrasses me to take bows."

"All my life I have hated to be closed in," he told the *Opera News* interviewer, and that feeling certainly determines his view of himself as an artist: "Many musicians believe that music is 'logic without concept,' that music can do without the ideologies and events of everyday life, without the world—that it can exist exclusively on absolute and eternal values. I do not. Like all human endeavors, music can be utilized for good and bad purposes, and for me the proper utilization of music is as important as its proper interpretation. My duty is not only to give the correct value to notes or to balance the sonority of an orchestra on the basis of certain criteria or taste. My duty consists of ascertaining that the best performances have the best destination."

RICCARDO MUTI

SUCCESSION—replacing a popular and successful director who leaves or dies—is an almost traumatic experience for an American symphony orchestra. For every success, such as Eugene Ormandy's following Leopold Stokowski in Philadelphia, there are many failures: Barbirolli after Toscanini, Defauw after Stock, Jorda after Monteux, or Martinon after Reiner, to name but a few. The problem is more pressing in the United States than it is in most European orchestras. To be sure, when Wilhelm Furtwängler died, Herbert von Karajan was his obvious successor with the Berlin Philharmonic, whose players themselves voted overwhelmingly to designate him as their music director in 1954. But in London, none of the player-managed orchestras wants or needs the kind of music director found in Berlin or the major orchestras of the United States: their tradition of player involvement in governing their affairs, of esprit de corps, and of musical responsibility for musical policy runs quite counter to the idea of artistic direction, as distinct from actually conducting, being centered in one authoritarian individual.

Philadelphia has been extremely fortunate in its conductor choices, partly because they were soundly made and partly because, in the case of Ormandy, everyone involved had the patience to wait out the difficult early years of a conductor's tenure. Ormandy's successor at the head of one of the world's undisputedly great orchestras will be only the third occupant of that position since 1912. For at least a decade, the choice of that successor has been a matter of concern, speculation, and endless gossip in Philadelphia and the musical world generally. Ormandy himself conducted an informal "educational process" in which he and other professionals candidly discussed with key trustees the merits and faults of possible candidates, either as they appeared as guest conductors in Philadelphia or as they were heard by trustees in their travels. Various favorites were rumored; some failed to satisfy Ormandy himself or the trustees; others encountered the hostility of the orchestra players; and some died or took other posts. It has been, in fact, the eye of a very small needle through which this particular camel must pass.

When the young Italian conductor Riccardo Muti first appeared with the Philadelphia Orchestra in 1972, he had the kind of success that set the wheels of the succession rumor mill in motion. Only thirty-one when he first conducted in Philadelphia, Muti was just beginning to build a European career and was making his first appearance in the United States. With regular return visits to Philadelphia, he consolidated his position there to the point where it was announced that, effective in 1977, he would be designated the first "principal guest conductor" of the Philadelphia Orchestra and would spend two months a year there each winter season.

That particular title, used on occasion by London orchestras, first appeared on the masthead of an American orchestra in 1969 when Carlo Maria Giulini was so designated at the same time as Sir Georg Solti became music director of the Chicago Symphony Orchestra. However, there have been many instances where a guest conductor's principal role was implied—Bruno Walter with the New York Philharmonic and Chicago Symphony and the elderly Pierre Monteux for a time in Boston, to cite but two examples—but these usually involved elder statesmen of conducting. Closer to the Giulini relationship is that of Colin Davis with the Boston Symphony Orchestra. Like Giulini, he is popular with the local audience and his musical style contrasts sharply with that of the music director, Seiji Ozawa. Unlike Giulini, Davis has another very demanding post, at the Royal Opera at Covent Garden. In both cases, the Chicago and Boston orchestras were able to contract for relatively extended services, exclusive in America, of conductors who could fill in a good portion of the orchestra's schedule not conducted by the music director.

In Philadelphia, however, the post of principal guest conductor served not only these purposes but also to groom a promising young conductor to succeed Ormandy. The entire arrangement had Ormandy's blessing, for he has long been concerned with the kind of conductor who would succeed him, as he told Herbert Kupferberg in 1968: "The conductor who comes here should be an outstanding, well-rounded musician, even if he is only thirty years old. By now conductors with great talent have great experience at thirty or thirty-five. He should remember that Philadelphia is a conservative city, but that it also likes to look forward. He should be able to present a variety of programs—classics, romantics, contemporaries. He should be prepared to stay—I don't think the board of directors would engage a man, even today, even with the fifty-two week season, who would want to conduct less than half the season. He should make up his mind that this is his home, this is where he belongs. He should be willing to become a leader in the community. All that combined would make the kind of conductor who should take over the Philadelphia Orchestra."

In this statement, Ormandy was prepared—as other, more ego-centered conductors might not have been—to discuss frankly and explicitly a problem that has continued to be reviewed and refined during the intervening years. If he was to a large extent describing his own role with the Philadelphia Orchestra, he was also echoing the views not only of the Philadelphia trustees but of those of many other major American orchestras. There remains even to this day, though less intensely than in 1968, a strong hankering for the old days, when a conductor of stature would devote a major part of his career to one orchestra—Stokowski in Philadelphia, Koussevitzky in Boston, Stock in Chicago, Szell in Cleveland, or Monteux in San Francisco. If these yearnings ignore the fact that the New York Philharmonic reached great heights under Arturo Toscanini, who sharply limited his time there as music director, they nonetheless carry the imprimatur of American symphonic tradition.

The continuation of that tradition has become increasingly threatened by a number of facts. The first is the obvious shortage of great conductors to match an international increase in great orchestras and opera companies. Moreover, the jet plane has made it possible for a conductor, like other celebrated musicians, to move easily from one engagement to the next, living artistically off a relatively limited current repertory, enough for a series of guest appearances but far short of what would be needed for an extended engagement of at least twenty weeks, such as Stock, Ormandy, and Koussevitzky once filled year after year. Another fact of American symphonic life is the extension of activity from a subscription season of less than thirty weeks to year-round activity that, even with time out for players' vacations, involves over forty weeks of actual performance. With a music director of international stature, touring is one way of filling those extra weeks, but that is in addition to his basic subscription weeks. Finally, there is the question of exposure: it may well be that, given comparison with the recordings and appearances of other visiting conductors, a resident music director could easily wear out his welcome with his subscription audience were he to appear too often.

If the realities of the American symphonic scene in the last quarter of this century no longer fit Ormandy's description of his successor, the appointment of Riccardo Muti as music director of the Philadelphia Orchestra, announced in May 1979 to take effect in mid-1980, will involve important adjustments by both parties.

Now in his late thirties, Riccardo Muti is an energetic, outgoing, obviously charismatic conductor. In conversation, he is articulate, even in heavily accented English, giving a natural impression of open frankness. He walks at a fast, springy pace, like a young man in a hurry, but he has the time to go out of his way to be helpful and courteous to a visitor. His lean body, of moderate height, has that animal grace frequently associated with the men of his land. Above the turtleneck shirts that he seems to favor, his head is dominated by a shock of black hair, combed back from a pronounced widow's peak that points down toward a nose that, in profile, is the counterpart of a more exaggerated version to be seen in Piero della Francesca's portrait of the Duke of Urbino in

Basic to Muti's training, as with all serious music students in Italy, was solfeggio, a music training based on vocalization, at proper pitch, of syllables rather than words or letters—*do, re, mi.* Serving for centuries in Italian music education as a basis for vocal instruction and for general ear-training, it has had much influence on the singing style of the purely instrumental performance of many Italian musicians. Muti's ability to sing, in tune and in tempo, solfeggio illustrations of how he wants a passage played has astounded even the most jaded players of the Philadelphia Orchestra.

When he was nineteen, Muti applied for admission to the Verdi Conservatory in Milan, where he studied conducting with Antonino Votto and composition with Bruno Bettinelli, a composer of the post-Stravinsky generation strongly influenced by him and by such French musicians as Honegger. Muti considers a thorough training in composition to be essential in conducting, and on graduation from the conservatory he received degrees in both arts. In the summer of 1965, he spent a month in Venice studying with Franco Ferrara, whom he considers "unique": "Not unique as a teacher but as a musician, as a conductor. He is an extraordinary musician when you see him working. From five minutes of his conducting and from what he says to the orchestra, you can understand everything. I remember once in Venice he took ten minutes to balance a pizzicato of the double-bass with the bassoon; that is a normal combination that you have all the time, but he spent ten minutes to have *this* sound and *that* sound and the second note not too fast. In the end this combination sounded like something really new. It was perfect, the ensemble with bassoon and bass, the timbre of the sound. The quality of the sound was completely new. From an experience like this you have an experience of a lifetime. He is a really great, great, great conductor, but especially a fantastic musician."

After leaving the Verdi Conservatory, Muti entered and won the Guido Cantelli Competition for young conductors in 1967. The following year, with help from friends in Milan, he made his first appearances outside Italy—sixteen concerts in Prague and the vicinity. In 1969, he conducted for the first time in Florence, at the Teatro Comunale with

Sviatoslav Richter as soloist. Such was Muti's success on this occasion that he was immediately scheduled for more concerts and was eventually engaged as principal conductor of the Teatro Comunale, a post that he has held since 1970. (The concert also marked the beginning of a close friendship with Richter, the latter being best man at the Muti wedding in Ravenna. Richter has since recorded the Beethoven Third Piano Concerto with Muti conducting.)

The Teatro Comunale is one of two lyric theaters in Florence, a strictly utilitarian facility built a century ago and fully modernized in 1960. More appropriate to the historical ambience of Florence is the Teatro alla Pergola, one of the first oval-shaped theaters of the Renaissance; although rebuilt several times since it opened in 1652, it retains its original form. Both theaters are under the same administration, but the Teatro Comunale, which houses major opera productions and orchestral concerts, is used much more frequently than the Pergola, where chamber opera and ensemble concerts are given. Most of the performances of the Maggio Musicale are offered in these two theaters. This festival, one of the most distinguished in Europe, was founded in 1933 by Vittorio Gui, a few years after he had established a permanent orchestra at the Teatro Comunale. A fine conductor, Gui also served for a time as Fritz Busch's successor at Glyndebourne. Although he had retired from the Teatro Comunale, he retained sufficient influence there to urge the engagement of Muti, whom he had heard when he was one of the judges of the Cantelli Competition. At the time of Muti's engagement as principal conductor, the Teatro Comunale was in something of a state of continuing crisis following Gui's retirement. Not until late 1974 was stability brought into the administration of the theater by the engagement as *soverintendente* of Massimo Bogianckino. A thoroughly trained musician, he had held important posts at Spoleto, Rome, and, most recently, La Scala, where he was a member of the triumvirate that also included Paolo Grassi and Claudio Abbado. He left La Scala, quite amicably, because he preferred a position that would give him more creative challenge. At La Scala, he had been a prime mover in engaging Luca Ronconi to direct a very controversial production of Wagner's

Ring, a project abandoned after Bogianckino moved to Florence. However, it has been revived as a joint effort of Milan and Florence, with Zubin Mehta conducting, beginning in 1979–80.

At the Teatro Comunale in Florence, Muti is principal conductor. He has no responsibilities beyond the specific productions or concerts he actually conducts, except for supervision of the orchestra. He is not artistic director of the theater, nor does he want to be. He honors Toscanini's admonition about unlocking the theater door the first thing in the morning and locking up at night. With a busy career in Philadelphia, London, and elsewhere on the Continent, he has no intention of becoming bogged down in the administrative details of running a full-time lyric theater. There appears to be a very clear understanding between Muti and Bogianckino as to how the former fits into the overall scheme of the Florentine *ente autonomo*.

Where his own responsibilities are concerned, Muti seeks fullest possible control. A major concern is improving the quality of the orchestra at the Teatro Comunale: "The unions in Italy are very different from the unions in England or in America. In Italy, the unions are political. The unions in America work mainly to get good contracts. Here, the musicians are paid by the state: if they work or if they don't work, at the end of the month they receive their salary. In London, if you don't play, no pay. English and American unions talk about concert and rehearsal hours, salary, but in Italy these things are in the hands of the office in Rome. In Rome they decide for all the workers how much to pay. So the unions here—they make noise. Until two years ago, if you had a player that was very, very bad, you couldn't touch him because the union said, 'No, he is a worker.' Now, they realize that in this way the quality of the orchestras is going down, so that they can't remain in this strong position. Also they are now more flexible in accepting foreign players in the orchestra. We now have a first trombone from Philadelphia, a pupil of the first trombone in the Philadelphia Orchestra. Also a tuba from Philadelphia. And we are thinking of others from America or from Japan. Until two years ago this was impossible."

Muti's duties in Florence include conducting several operas a year, among them at least one new production, and directing the orchestra in several concerts. Early in 1978, for instance, he conducted a new *Il Trovatore* that created something of a sensation. For one thing, the production was directed by the controversial Luca Ronconi, with a very bare nonrepresentational set in which the predominant visual motif was the constant flickering of flames. Somewhat less controversial was Muti's decision to present Verdi's score as written. Several cuts were restored so that the entire score was played. More important, Verdi's original notes were sung: even the Manrico was deprived of the customary interpolated high notes in "Di quella pira."

Recalling an earlier confrontation with a tenor's prerogatives in Italian opera, Muti told Dan Webster of the *Philadelphia Inquirer*: "When I was very young, we were doing *Pagliacci* in Florence. Richard Tucker came to me and said, 'Maestro, I will do the last words?' Since Caruso, the tenor has always said, 'La commedia e finita,' and I said, 'Of course.' It was only after the production that I looked up the manuscript and realized it should be the baritone. Leoncavallo was a sophisticated composer who knew that the opera should open and close with the baritone commenting on the drama, but, you see, the 'tradition' had changed that. I was at fault, but Tucker was doubly so because he knew but went ahead anyway. I think opera in [America] is different from opera in Europe. [In the United States] the singer is the star, but in Italy, at least, the composer is, and when you recognize that, you have already come a long way."

Nevertheless, he had some precurtain worries about how the audience would respond to this treatment of the tenor in *Il Trovatore*. Fortunately all went well, the audience's boos and catcalls being reserved for the decor and Ronconi's untraditional conception.

Both Muti and Bogianckino like working with Ronconi, who has mounted a number of productions in Florence, notably one of Gluck's *Orfeo ed Euridice* in the original Vienna version in Italian. Again Muti eliminated the accumulated additions and changes of tradition in presenting Gluck's score as written, as it was before Gluck adapted it for other cities, and ignoring the efforts of later producers to mix elements from several versions. "Marilyn Horne was to sing it," he told Webster, "but she wanted to do all of the ornaments and to add an aria by a little-known composer 'which was always done.' I said we were doing Gluck and we could not do a performance that way. We found another singer." Ronconi's concept of this opera was that, in going to Hades in search of Euridice, Orfeo was actually seeking his own self, and the costuming and the stage action reflected this concept. First given at the Maggio Musicale in 1977, this production was repeated the following winter by the Florentines in Bologna.

Like Mahler, Toscanini, and Karajan, Muti feels strongly that the conductor should have the basic artistic control of an opera. He does not believe in putting star singers under contract and then deciding what opera they should sing. Nor does he feel that the management should engage a director (or to use European terminology, a producer) and have him decide what opera to do, what singers to hire, and finally who is to conduct. The conductor has the best overall view of the artistic essence of the opera; he is best qualified in every respect to understand the supreme role of the composer. He should be the first choice of management and should have a voice in the selection of the director, decor, and cast. That, says Muti, is how he works with Bogianckino in Florence, how he has successfully worked on a number of productions with Ronconi, and how he likes to work in other opera houses he visits.

However, despite earlier announcements, Ronconi did not direct the new production of Verdi's *I Vespri Siciliani* during the 1978 festival. Although the actual production was quite conventional, Muti's musical performance was not. Again he insisted on playing the entire Verdi score as originally written except for the use of Italian rather than the original French. Muti does not regard it as completely impossible to produce Verdi's Paris operas in Italy in the language they were written; most soloists, he feels, would learn the French if they were given enough time, but training the chorus in French would present some difficulties. This was publicized as the first complete *Vespri* in many decades in Italy, and it not only included all of the vocal music Verdi wrote but also the long third-act ballet decreed by tradition at the Paris Opéra.

Muti has little use for a patronizing attitude toward *Vespri* as transitional in Verdi's development: "I believe it is a masterpiece. Some pages are not first class, but also in *Traviata* and *Trovatore* you have some parts that are a little routine, no? In *Vespri* you have this too, but *Vespri* is important because you find everything Verdi will write in the future—*Don Carlo, Aida, Otello,* and even *Falstaff* in the fifth act. So this opera is very important because it has everything Verdi wrote before and everything he will write after."

As for insisting on producing the complete score, Muti says, "I am against cuts, the traditional cuts, in opera, in symphony, because I believe that the conductor should give to the public the score exactly as the composer wrote it. We have no right to put our hands on the score and say this is good and this is not good. When you go in a museum to see all the pictures, you say, 'I like this' or 'I don't like this'; but in music, if you don't play everything, the public will never know what is good in a score and what is bad. Also I think that the line of the score will be clear only if the score is exactly as the composer felt about it."

For the Maggio Musicale, Muti has conducted complete and authentic versions of such operas as Rossini's *William Tell* and Spontini's *Agnes von Hohenstaufen.* When he performed Verdi's *Macbeth,* he adhered to the composer's revised text of 1865, without the traditional interpolation of Macbeth's dying aria from the earlier version; in his recording, however, this aria and other material were placed in an appendix. Someday, he hopes to conduct *Don Carlo,* an opera much discussed in Italy following the Abbado-Ronconi production at La Scala in 1977. However, he has no preconceptions as to how he will treat the text, which of the various versions he will use, and whether he will restore or delete specific passages in an effort to achieve an authentic *Don Carlo.* "I know all the differences, but I don't know which way I will follow. Surely I will follow the last idea of Verdi."

Muti generally schedules three periods each year in Florence—midwinter for opera, late spring for opera and concerts during the Maggio Musicale, and an orchestral season in the fall. His opera for the winter of 1978–79 was *Norma,* in a new Ronconi production, with Berlioz's *Damnation de Faust* scheduled for the Maggio Musicale the following spring in a concert version to avoid conflict on the stage with the new Mehta-Ronconi *Rheingold.*

In addition to conducting opera in Florence, Muti appears in several major opera houses in Europe. He has conducted several times at the Vienna State Opera, notably a revival of *Norma,* the first production there of this opera in fifty years. "For a strange reason, Bellini is still unloved and unknown in Vienna, and I try to explain to the Viennese how much Wagner loved Bellini. He always said that he would like to write one melody like Bellini, but, he said, he was never able to. For the Viennese it is very difficult to understand Bellini." He has also conducted *Aida* and *La Forza del Destino* in Vienna, *Don Pasquale* in Salzburg (where he has also conducted orchestra concerts), and *Aida* in Munich.

His schedule limits the amount of opera conducting he can do, as a new production and its run of performances, even in *stagione,* can absorb six to eight weeks. For this reason he has yet to find time to conduct at the Metropolitan Opera, although he has been approached. Another city where he does conduct opera regularly is London, which has seen his *Aida,* with *Andrea Chénier* scheduled for 1980 and *Ernani* for 1981. These engagements at Covent Garden can be coordinated with his concerts and recordings with the Philharmonia Orchestra, of which he has been principal conductor since 1973.

Founded by Walter Legge, head of the classical recording activities of the British electronic and entertainment conglomerate EMI, the original Philharmonia Orchestra was a fully employed orchestra supported by EMI. When it was abandoned by the recording company in 1964, it survived as a player-governed cooperative, thanks in large part to the loyalty of Otto Klemperer and Carlo Maria Giulini, who continued to conduct it as the New Philharmonia. However, as Klemperer grew older and Giulini's career took him farther afield, the fortunes of the orchestra declined, especially in the intense but polite competition between the four player-managed orchestras in London.

Fortunately, the New Philharmonia Orchestra had some loyal player-members and was eventually able to secure some corporate support. Muti arrived on the scene at the very end of Klemperer's career and immediately brought new life and hope to this orchestra. He first conducted the New Philharmonia late in 1972, shortly after his Philadelphia debut, and was elected principal conductor by its members in 1973. London sources say that his success with the orchestra was a major factor in obtaining crucial financial support from corporations. His engagement also provided EMI with an attractive new conductor who could bring fresh sound to their recordings of the orchestra. Moreover, although Muti was increasingly conducting opera in other centers, the orchestra provided a nucleus for EMI to record him in opera with it, especially in the increasingly popular Verdi repertory, with casts with whom he was working in Florence, Vienna, or Covent Garden. Muti's first records for EMI—Verdi's *Aida* and symphonies by Tchaikovsky and Mendelssohn—were released in 1974, and his most recent EMI contract extension runs through 1979. Under Muti, the Philharmonia, which legally reinstated its old name in 1977, has made substantial progress in rebuilding its following in London, attracting guest conductors, and making recordings under other conductors. Under the competitive orchestral conditions prevailing in London, it is not easy to rebuild an orchestra, but Muti has unquestionably been a good choice in this process.

Even before his engagement in London, Muti had opened the door to a potentially more important orchestral affiliation—with the Philadelphia Orchestra. During a European tour in 1971, Eugene Ormandy and the Philadelphia Orchestra played in Florence. As is customary in important cities on tour, the orchestra scheduled a brief rehearsal in the Teatro Comunale to adjust itself to the special ambience there. Several of the orchestra staff—including manager Boris Sokoloff; his assistant, Joseph Santarlasci; and the orchestra's personnel manager, Mason Jones —arrived early at the Teatro to plan for the concert. There was an orchestral rehearsal in progress on the stage, which gave the visitors a chance to hear how an orchestra sounded there and to plan adjustments of the Philadelphia's seating accordingly. Even more important, they were deeply impressed by the work in rehearsal of the thirty-year-old Muti. Arriving at the hall before his own rehearsal, Ormandy was equally impressed. Before leaving Florence, Ormandy and his colleagues met Muti at a small private lunch that included a few Florentines, among them Gui. The young Italian was engaged to appear as guest conductor in Philadelphia during the fall of 1972. As a result of Muti's "discovery" by Ormandy, his American manager, Ronald Wilford, secured engagements for him, during the next few years, with the orchestras of Boston, Cleveland, and Chicago. A scheduled appearance with the New York Philharmonic early in 1974 failed to materialize when Muti became ill in Italy; at the time, there was some confusion over this cancellation, because a breakdown in communication from Italy left the Philharmonic without any explanation of Muti's failure to arrive.

Muti's success in Philadelphia has been solid and widespread from the beginning. His youth and glamorous platform manner appeal greatly to the subscription audiences. The players in the orchestra, often hard to please in any orchestra, have taken a great liking to him. Friendly and considerate to them offstage as well as on, he treats the musicians as individuals, not as subordinates, displaying a personal interest in them and their offstage activities. Something of that informality prevails as Muti makes his way to the podium at a rehearsal; he will stop along his way for a brief word with players and will do the same after rehearsal. Once he settles down to work, he is quite relaxed and completely in control of the music, but not autocratically so. Players in Philadelphia and elsewhere stand in awe of his command of a score and of his ability to hear, and politely correct, errors in playing. His friendly warmth and authority are such that one player in the Chicago Symphony, where Muti has appeared as a guest, quite warmly suggested, "He may just be another Giulini." From that source, there can be no higher compliment.

To his orchestral conducting, Muti brings the same fresh and conscientious regard for the composer that he does in opera. When he conducted Mozart's *Linz* Symphony in Philadelphia, he brought with him the score of the new Bärenreiter edition, which has removed the accretion of editors' additions and "corrections." In rehearsal, he took great pains to restore Mozart's articulation and phrasing. "When you take the [old] Breitkopf edition, it's impossible. There are many mistakes—ligature and staccato, mezzoforte, mezzopiano, and some wrong notes." The result was a performance that one critic called "well scrubbed." Muti is almost fanatical about repeats in the score. When he recorded the Beethoven Seventh Symphony in 1978 with the Philadelphia Orchestra, he also recorded as a possible "filler" the *Leonore* Overture no. 3. However, the latter was not included, because with all of its repeats, the symphony left insufficient room for the overture if sound quality was to be retained. "You know that generally in the Beethoven Seventh conductors don't do all the repeats, and there are many important ones, especially in the Scherzo." The following season he played Mozart's *Jupiter* Symphony with all repeats, adding appreciably to the overall length of the work.

Because of his relative youth, Muti must rely on records for his knowledge of the great conductors of the past. Three of these—Toscanini, Bruno Walter, and Wilhelm Furtwängler—have impressed him most: "In Toscanini what I admire is not only the precision that he gets from the orchestra, but there is a *musical* idea, his conviction when he conducts a work. Furtwängler, this giant of music, makes mountains with his hands. For example, I like very much the Brahms Fourth Symphony conducted by Furtwängler. His conception is really like a monument. Very original and sometimes very personal. He doesn't follow all the indications of the score, and some rubato or rallentando when there is no rallentando, or morendo when it is not morendo. In Toscanini, the Brahms Fourth Symphony is much more controlled, more precise, no rubato like Furtwängler. But the line of Toscanini is so perfect that you can hear from the first note that he was so convinced about this line that after a few bars you love this way that Toscanini takes you with him until the last note. They are different, but so real, that you accept both."

However, when actually preparing a work, Muti seldom uses recordings. "Only when I want to know something special, as, for example, if I should do the Bruckner Seventh Symphony, I want to know the recordings of Furtwängler or Bruno Walter, just to have an idea of tradition of interpretation." Otherwise, he starts by studying the score itself before working with it at the piano. "I realize at the piano what I learn from the score, and then I go back to the score without piano."

Given his Italian heritage, Muti stresses the singing line in music. "Every part in the score should sing, not only the melody and then nothing. Toscanini always said that every note in the score is not a second actor, but is a first actor."

The sound he obtains from the Philadelphia Orchestra—varying as it must from Mozart or Beethoven to Prokofiev or Ravel—is generally lighter, more transparent than one associates with it under Ormandy. The orchestra is, of course, exceptionally flexible in its response to different guests, but it responds to Muti with truly unified adjustment to his individual style. His attacks and releases are less sharp than Toscanini's but more so than Ormandy's. Nevertheless, there is a muscularity and slight density of texture in Muti's conducting that are not quite Toscaninian. He falls, in these respects, between the lean intensity of his great compatriot and the lusher and more relaxed sound that has been for so long Ormandy's hallmark.

Muti's repertory extends, as he says, from Vivaldi to Penderecki. He plays more Mozart and Beethoven, for instance, than do some other conductors of his generation and plays them well. He is also a very sympathetic interpreter of such mid-romantics as Mendelssohn and Schumann; when he conducted the Philadelphia Orchestra in the latter's Fourth Symphony in New York, Harold C. Schonberg of the *New York Times* called it "one of the more impressive Schumann Fourths in recent memory." Muti has a great flair for Russian music: he plays and records a great deal of Tchaikovsky, being especially successful in the earlier symphonies. One of his greatest successes—in London, Philadelphia, Florence, and on records—has been Abram Stasevich's conflation of music from Prokofiev's score for Eisenstein's film *Ivan the Terrible,* a long and colorfully orchestrated piece for soloists, narrator, chorus, and orchestra.

If Muti's repertory is eclectic in these respects, he has yet to explore one composer whose music is very "in" with conductors and audiences today: "Mahler is a composer I don't conduct. I conduct only a few things, especially with voices—*Das Lied von der Erde, Lieder eines Fahrenden Gesellen,* but not the symphonies. I am more interested now in Bruckner than in Mahler. Maybe because now Bruckner is for me

(121)

more solid. I am sure that I will conduct Mahler in the future, but for the moment he is a composer who is out of my line."

Nor is he especially interested in the Second Viennese School. Among contemporary composers, Muti likes the work of Krzysztof Penderecki, Györgi Ligeti, Witold Lutoslawski, and Luciano Berio. He admits that he is woefully unacquainted with American music. Copland and Schuman are names he knows, but he has not played their music. Even the names of younger American composers are quite unfamiliar to him. He is frank about this, and he hopes to correct his lack of familiarity with American music in due course.

Although he conducts both symphony and opera in Florence and London, there are no plans for him to offer this combination in Philadelphia. Perhaps the memory of the orchestra's financially disastrous opera season in 1934–35 and the strife-ridden history of independent opera companies in the city offer grounds for caution. There are reports that Muti was offered and declined some sort of post with the Opera Company of Philadelphia, the most recent and soundly based of the city's succession of competing opera ventures. Nevertheless, he told Dan Webster, "It is my dream to do opera in some form with the Philadelphia Orchestra. That sound! I suppose it hasn't been done recently because of the cost, but I would like to find a way." Elsewhere, he has expressed the hope, rather wistfully, of one day hearing *Otello* and *Falstaff* played by the Philadelphia Orchestra.

Such is EMI's interest in Muti that, once his designation as Philadelphia's principal guest conductor was settled, it was important that he record with the Philadelphia Orchestra as well as the Philharmonia. Although Ormandy and the orchestra were already under long-term contract to RCA, this was modified to permit both Ormandy and Muti to record for EMI as well. The Beethoven Seventh Symphony is the first of a projected Beethoven series that Muti will record in Philadelphia; the Sixth is already on tape. He has also recorded Stravinsky's *Firebird* and *Sacre du Printemps* as well as the Mussorgsky-Ravel *Pictures at an Exhibition,* a repertory that he and EMI regard as especially appropriate to the Philadelphia's virtuosity; more Stravinsky is under consideration.

In Philadelphia, Muti has already become a familiar figure in music circles and with his audiences. However, although he enjoys being stopped on the street by a Ravenna opera lover denouncing a Ronconi production, he finds comparable encounters in Philadelphia less flattering. "Do you know," he asked Webster, "that people stopped me in the street in Philadelphia and said, 'Maestro, we enjoyed your program, but next time will you play Brahms's Fourth?' That, I think, is provincial."

With Ormandy approaching his eightieth birthday in November 1979, there were mounting indications that his retirement was imminent. Newspapers and wire services carried reports, of varying reliability, of lapses in the conductor's firm grip on the orchestra. Early in 1979 he announced that the 1979–80 season would be his last as music director of the Philàdelphia Orchestra. Amid an outpouring of tribute to Ormandy's unique forty-four years' tenure came official confirmation that negotiations were in progress with Muti. A month later came the expected official announcement: Riccardo Muti would succeed Ormandy at the beginning of the 1980–81 season. He will conduct for ten weeks in his first season of thirty-nine concerts, fifty-five appearances in fourteen weeks in 1981–82, and fifteen weeks for sixty concerts in the final year of the contract. (As principal guest conductor he had spent eight weeks each season in Philadelphia.)

The Philadelphia Orchestra has laid a firm foundation for this transition to new leadership. Muti is well known from increasingly important appearances since 1972. Muti, for his part, has had ample opportunity to discuss his long-range role in Philadelphia with everyone there, and elsewhere. There is, in fact, a precedent of sorts in this: although different designations were used then, Ormandy's accession to the music directorship of the Philadelphia Orchestra in 1936 was preceded by six years of ever closer association as guest conductor. Then, however, a crucial consideration was Ormandy's willingness to devote himself exclusively to Philadelphia; this is obviously not the case with Muti, who remains, for the time being at least, principal conductor in Florence and with the Philharmonia Orchestra in London.

The gradual increase in Muti's seasonal commitment to Philadelphia will give him ample opportunity to adjust his life to the requirements of directing one of the greatest orchestras anywhere. In his interview with Webster early in 1978, he anticipated the choices that both he and the Philadelphia Orchestra now face: "I know that I am entering a time for decision. I do know that I have no interest in simply taking an orchestra and maintaining its level. Anyone could do that. You step on the podium and conduct, one, two, three, four, and bow. For me there must be exploration, something more than maintenance—and I think the orchestra needs that, too. I have told [the trustees of the Philadelphia Orchestra Association] that I would not be able to settle in and do nothing but conduct the orchestra. I think they understand that it is necessary for me—and good for the orchestra—that I conduct opera and work in different settings."

ZUBIN MEHTA

ONE of the elder statesmen of concert music in this country once remarked almost defensively of Zubin Mehta, "You know, he's much
more serious than people give him credit for being. Actually, he is hard
to get to know, but when you do know him, he is a wonderful person
and fine musician."

In the fall of 1978, the New York musical community came,
much to its surprise, to agree with this appraisal of the new music director of its Philharmonic. Once the newspaper strike that had blanketed
the first few weeks of Mehta's tenure was lifted, critics who had for
years pigeon-holed him as a flashy conductor of late-romantic music
suddenly discovered that he could conduct surpassingly beautiful and
sensitive performances of early Schubert symphonies. At the same time,
players in the Philharmonic, whom he had disparaged just a decade
before, found him, as they had in his rare guest appearances, frank,
considerate, and as professionally musical as any artist who had
held that position for many years. If some of his interpretations were
questioned, most were admired, and all agreed that the Philharmonic
sounded exceptionally fine. The orchestra that Mehta had described as
one given to walking over conductors was responding to his leadership
with technical brilliance and enthusiasm seldom heard recently from the
stage of Avery Fisher Hall.

Moreover, Mehta was taking a deep interest in the Philharmonic
as an institution, working closely with the producers of two national

telecasts presented "live" from Lincoln Center when he had been conducting there in his new post barely a month. Early in his tenure at the helm of the New York orchestra, he conducted it in much of the George Gershwin music that accompanied Woody Allen's film *Manhattan*. His commitment to the Philharmonic was total, and his delight in being in New York, a city he had once scorned, extended from keen anticipation of sampling its extraordinary musical life to a sheepish admission that there were times when he almost found himself rooting for the New York Yankees against the Los Angeles Dodgers in the World Series. Mehta was not being disloyal to Los Angeles, where he and his wife adore the souvenir-cluttered Brentwood home which they plan to keep as their headquarters between his engagements in New York, Italy, Vienna, London, and Israel. It is just that, when Mehta commits himself, he commits himself fully—to wherever he is working, to his family, to his friends, and, above all, to the music he loves.

As conductor of the Israel Philharmonic Orchestra, he is if possible more Jewish than an Israeli. When his friends and symphony women's committee admirers throng to his dressing room after a concert, they are likely to find a place of honor occupied by Mehta's parents, Zubin often engaged with his father, Mehli, in intense discussion of the finer points or accidental bobbles of the performance just over. Visitors from India and Israel or old friends from Vienna receive a typical Mehta welcome before attention is given to others. He once berated some of the ladies considered indispensable to the survival of the Los Angeles Philharmonic for their treatment of the orchestra musicians as social inferiors, and on certain occasions, he has insisted that the musicians be included in after-concert parties which he would not otherwise attend.

As a conductor, he combines an extraordinary natural talent with a highly disciplined technique honed for more than two decades by training, experience, and ruthless self-examination of his strengths and faults. That talent was recognized as early as the late 1950s in Vienna by Josef Krips, who hailed the advent of "another Toscanini!" Mehta was at that time finishing intensive study with Hans Swarowsky at the Vienna Academy of Music. After a few years and many opportunities to fill in for a succession of indisposed elder colleagues, Mehta found himself musical director of two major orchestras in North America at the age of twenty-six. Though he left Montreal after six years, he stayed sixteen in Los Angeles, building its orchestra into one of the best in the country and, at the same time, refining, deepening, and expanding the training his talent had already received.

Although his career was to develop in opera and symphony in America and abroad, and although he soon assumed a leadership role with another orchestra in faraway Israel, the Los Angeles Philharmonic was where he grew into mature mastery and where he proved his mettle. His development was by no means in a straight line, clear as it may seem in retrospect. There were such diversions as a "Switched-on Bach" telecast and a joint appearance at UCLA with Frank Zappa. Moreover, there were, as he later described them, "marriage problems" with the Philharmonic.

His role at Los Angeles received the full glamorizing treatment that only southern California and Hollywood can bestow. While his face glowered down immobile from billboards on Wilshire Boulevard, its expressive original, with flashing eyes that cannot be captured in a picture, was communicating with an orchestra that he was teaching to respond to him. The Nehru-type jackets worn by ushers in the Dorothy Chandler Pavilion, the adulation of the symphony ladies who thronged to its top-floor dining room hoping to catch a glimpse of the intensely masculine conductor dousing bland American food with Tabasco sauce, the fluorescent portrait hung in the loge-level bar were part of the presence of Zubin Mehta in Los Angeles—his permeation of the Philharmonic, the Music Center, and the city's cultural life. To more purist minds, they were a vulgar phenomenon that Mehta could have banned if he had been more active in his asserted indifference, but they were also the basis of the material success that he brought to the orchestra and to the performance arts center perched on the hill overlooking downtown Los Angeles on one side and the serpentine strands of the freeways that converge on the other. The Music Center, the dream of civic leaders inspired by Mrs. Dorothy ("Buffie") Chandler, might well have been realized without Zubin Mehta, but he was certainly the force that made the job easier.

When Zubin Mehta came on the Los Angeles scene, he was making a career of filling in for cancelling colleagues in Vienna, Montreal, and Israel, as well as Los Angeles, on each occasion winning such success that he quickly established long-term relations. A spectacularly promising student at Tanglewood in 1958, he came in second to his friend Claudio Abbado for the Koussevitzky Prize and was introduced by Lukas Foss to his own manager, Siegfried Hearst. An elderly Central European, Hearst specialized in managing conductors; among his other clients were Otto Klemperer, Leopold Stokowski, and a promising Hungarian, Georg Solti. While Mehta returned to England to spend two miserable years as assistant conductor of the Royal Liverpool Philharmonic, Hearst went to work on his behalf. For one concert with the Canadian Broadcasting Orchestra in Toronto, the fee was so modest that the Indian government helped out by paying Mehta's travel expenses. More important were two concerts in the summer of 1960—one conducting the Philadelphia Orchestra in Robin Hood Dell and the other with the New York Philharmonic in Lewisohn Stadium. "Those were package deals of Siegfried's," says Mehta. "Both wanted Stokowski, and he had to have a rest. So Siegfried said, 'If you take this young Indian, you can have Stokowski.' " Pierre Beique, manager of the Montreal Symphony, heard one of these concerts, and when Igor Markevich, another Hearst client, canceled a concert a few months later, he remembered Mehta and booked him for a concert that was such a success that negotiations were shortly started for Mehta to succeed Markevich as music director of the Montreal orchestra. Although he left that post in 1967, he retains strong bonds with Montreal. After all, it was his first major symphonic job and the scene of his first operatic conducting. Moreover, it is the home of his two children and his first wife, Carmen, whom he met and married in Vienna and from whom he was divorced in 1964. She subsequently married Zubin's accountant-brother, Zarin. The conductor therefore visits his Montreal family regularly

(130)

and still makes guest appearances from time to time with the orchestra there.

Meanwhile, Solti, having enjoyed success both with the San Francisco Opera and the Los Angeles Philharmonic as guest conductor, had signed a contract with the latter to become its musical director in the fall of 1961. In view of his commitment to Covent Garden in London, Solti needed a full-time assistant in Los Angeles. At Hearst's suggestion he met and heard Mehta and was favorably impressed, but by the time he was ready to offer Mehta the assistant position in Los Angeles, the Montreal post was imminent. When Hearst reported this, Solti dropped the idea of Mehta assisting him in Los Angeles, as the whole purpose of this post was to have someone on the job when Solti was away. However, when the ailing Fritz Reiner canceled two weeks of concerts in January, as did Markevich for the following one, Hearst proposed Mehta to fill in, knowing that he was well regarded by Solti.

Mehta made his debut in the old Philharmonic Auditorium on the evening of January 19, 1961. William Severns, now manager of the Music Center but on the Philharmonic staff at that time, recalls that he did not attend the evening performance on the nineteenth and heard nothing extraordinary about it the next day. However, he was backstage during the repeat of the program on the next afternoon for a predominantly female audience. Even from backstage, he could sense the extraordinary enthusiasm of the audience. "I thought that Siegfried had hired a claque," he later recalled. ("He was quite capable of that," Mehta remarked long after.) But there was nothing artificial in the enthusiasm for Mehta that snowballed in the next two weeks, despite the fact that a week after his Los Angeles debut, his engagement as music director in Montreal was announced.

What happened next remains a matter of who is recalling events. At best it may be described as misunderstanding, breakdown of communications, and wrong assumptions by the key people involved. Mehta still asserts that although he was the center of the storm, he was also an innocent bystander. Except, of course, to the extent that his personality and conducting had a devastating effect on the decision-makers at the

(131)

Philharmonic, not least Mrs. Chandler, who decided that Mehta must fill the still-vacant post as Solti's assistant and conduct eight of the weeks that Solti would be away the following season. Here communications apparently broke down; Solti felt that he had not been properly consulted when, following Mehta's third week as substitute conductor, the Philharmonic announced that he had been engaged as associate conductor for the next three years. A month later, Solti, by cable from Germany, resigned the post that had never really begun to fill, citing "irreconcilable differences." "The last three months," he was quoted as saying in Frankfurt, "the board has made its decisions contrary to my rights." Hearst had to walk a tightrope. He was representing both conductors and, in a letter to the *New York Times,* tried to defend both without antagonizing the Los Angeles people with whom he now hoped to contract for Mehta's services as music director. Mrs. Chandler appointed an advisory committee, including Jascha Heifetz and Gregor Piatigorsky, who, according to their spokesman, eventually submitted but one name to Mrs. Chandler's board—Zubin Mehta. In November 1961 his appointment as music director, effective the following season, was announced.

The Philharmonic had been performing for years in an old church-owned auditorium in downtown Los Angeles, and one of the dreams of Mrs. Chandler and her supporters was a new home for the orchestra. Performance arts centers then being a fashion, plans were already well under way to erect a handsome music center near the city and county government buildings on a hill adjacent to the center of the city. In addition to a 3,198-seat pavilion for orchestra and opera, there were an intimate theater for drama and a larger, more conventional one, for ballet, plays, and musicals. By locating the center in an urban renewal project adjacent to the city and county government buildings, considerable public funds were obtained. Part of the center's long-range upkeep was assured by a massive underground garage that served the government offices by day and the center's patrons at night. Nevertheless, some $19 million dollars of private contributions by individuals, foundations, and corporations had to be raised. Combining her own by no means inconsiderable personal ability with the influence of her husband's newspaper, the *Los Angeles Times,* Mrs. Chandler led this campaign with singular energy and organizational ability. The business community of the far-flung Los Angeles metropolis was canvassed as it never had been for anything connected with art, frequently by determined ladies carrying shopping bags emblazoned with the Music Center's cause. Like their leader, they simply refused to take no for an answer. Although the center was already under construction when Mehta arrived in Los Angeles, the prospect of his taking over the orchestra, and the success of his first two seasons with it, provided a central theme for the final stages of the fund-raising. There is no question that his intensely masculine youth contributed to the enthusiasm of Mrs. Chandler's workers. This was the beginning of the glamorization of Mehta in Los Angeles, a process that, once it gained momentum, was to continue with different themes and variations until his highly emotional farewell concerts in the spring of 1978.

The orchestra that Mehta joined as music director in 1962 shared many elements of his Viennese orientation. For more than a generation, the cinema and broadcast studios of Hollywood had attracted to the Los Angeles area many first-rate orchestral musicians, including Jewish exiles from Central Europe. Some of them had gravitated from the studios to the Philharmonic; others had pupils who joined the orchestra. There was an important colony of Austro-German exile artists and intellectuals in the Los Angeles area—among them Alma Mahler, Thomas Mann, Bruno Walter, and Arnold Schoenberg. The latter not only attracted students in composition but also, in his university teaching, had a notable influence on the theoretical training of the younger generation of Los Angeles musicians. Moreover, although their tenure with the Philharmonic was neither consecutive nor very long, both Otto Klemperer and Edward van Beinum had left their stamp on the orchestra. When Bruno Walter made his last recordings with what was dubbed the Columbia Symphony Orchestra, its personnel was drawn largely from the Philharmonic. Immersed as he was in the Viennese tradition, young Mehta was much at home stylistically with what he found in Los Angeles. From the outset, he saw there an opportunity to shape an orchestra in the image of the Vienna Philharmonic, which was always his ideal.

In later years, Mehta referred to what he called "marriage problems" between himself and the Philharmonic. He had come to the orchestra with a well-filled reservoir of goodwill among the players; as soon as Solti resigned, the musicians petitioned the Philharmonic board to replace him with Mehta.

"I was badly advised by management and well-meaning players of whom to get rid of in order to improve the orchestra, and I signed a request to get rid of nine musicians. I couldn't have made a worse tactical mistake. There was a storm, of course, and the nine musicians were not fired. The first year went well, nobody was fired, but I started my work of building the orchestra almost immediately. There were a few vacancies to get good people into. In those days you couldn't get many good string players. We didn't audition nationally, like we do today; the union didn't allow that in those days. It was quite plain sailing; gradually one musician either retired, or was deceased; not many were fired. In my sixteen years, I have engaged sixty-three new musicians; I have fired less than ten."

During the next seven years the orchestra started touring and making records. Mehta himself was filling guest engagements with such prestigious organizations as the Philadelphia Orchestra, Vienna Philharmonic, Berlin Philharmonic, and Metropolitan Opera. But there was still room for improvement in the Los Angeles orchestra. There were a few weak principal players. Mehta and the orchestra manager, Jaye Rubanoff—"my absolute breath, my conscience, my right hand and left administrator"—were running the orchestra between them. "Between the two of us, we weren't strong enough to take certain decisions. So that's when Fleischmann came in." Ernest Fleischmann was born in Frankfurt, Germany, grew up in South Africa, where he started his career as a conductor and then became impresario of the Johannesburg Festival. He moved to London in 1959 as manager of the London Symphony Orchestra and later worked as a record producer there. In 1969,

Mehta told him, "Please come, because I need you. I need a strong person to stand behind some drastic decisions I have to take."

"The main people to be replaced were some woodwind soloists and there was a storm and unhappy mood in the orchestra. The master contract says that you must give a player a year-and-a-half notice, and that year and a half is, believe me, murder—murder for both. That's where these marriage problems came from.

"It was not nice. I was brought before an arbitration board. Ernest stood behind me and did not give in. I told the orchestra when they gave me a present before I left Los Angeles, 'Look, let's face it. I have made some mistakes. We did it the wrong way; we were sometimes crude and crass with the players.' I had to make music with them. When the head of General Motors has problems with his mechanic, let's say, he doesn't breathe and phrase with him all day long."

Thanks to Fleischmann's handling of personnel matters and to his close work with Mehta, the Los Angeles Philharmonic now enjoys exceptionally good labor relations. Frequently contracts are completely settled months in advance of their effective date. "Some orchestras negotiate until 11:59, but we hope to have a contract in May for next October," Mehta has observed.

"There has been a trust, confidence developed between management and orchestra, which I find unique in the United States. The orchestra knows, I am convinced, that the management is not out to get them in any way, that the management knows that if there is inflation they will have to give a raise. The management has convinced them to uphold the musical standards together. The orchestra is really conscious of that at the negotiations."

Because of the international contacts that Fleischmann enjoyed in centrally located London, he made another important contribution to the Los Angeles Philharmonic. Since Siegfried Hearst died early in Mehta's career, he has had no manager, no personal representative, no press agent. Had he been affiliated with an influential New York manager like Ronald Wilford, he might have had more success in getting top guest conductors and soloists to appear with the Los Angeles orchestra.

"In order to have a good season with guest conductors, you have to have a real personal contact with the musicians. In Montreal, a lot of great artists would come there because of their friendship with Pierre Beique. They wouldn't come to Los Angeles because no one knew them there. Fleischmann had that kind of connection. He took a lot of the load off my shoulders arranging and organizing tours, obtaining artists from abroad, convincing some of the big conductors to come here. It was not possible between Jaye and myself to entice a lot of good conductors, and I was rightly being accused of not having good guest conductors. The best thing for any music director is to get absolutely top-notch guests to take care of your orchestra. It is no fun to come back after two and one half months and find the orchestra full of bad habits, believe me."

Another area in which Fleischmann proved invaluable was in his direction of the summer season at the Hollywood Bowl, where the Los Angeles Philharmonic plays every summer. Although both the Philharmonic and the Bowl are part of the same overall organization, Fleischmann is executive director of the Philharmonic and general manager of the Bowl; at the Philharmonic, he shared responsibility with Mehta as music director, but at the Bowl he is, in effect, artistic director as well as manager. Here he finds full scope for his unique combination of artistic imagination and showmanship: in the summer of 1977, there were thirty-eight concerts by the Los Angeles Philharmonic, plus a few other events; nearly half a million attended, an average of just over twelve thousand per concert.

Nevertheless, what was probably Fleischmann's most brilliant managerial coup came after Mehta announced that he was going to the New York Philharmonic. Faced with a typical problem of succession—made much more difficult by Mehta's popularity in Los Angeles—Fleischmann succeeded in persuading one of the great conductors of our day, Carlo Maria Giulini, to accept the music directorship of the Los Angeles Philharmonic. One reason he could do so was that he himself could assume much of the artistic administration that Giulini was known to dislike. Another very important reason was the reputation that the orchestra had built under Mehta.

The working relationship between Fleischmann and Mehta was very close during the nine seasons they worked together in Los Angeles. Each had great respect and affection for the other. Neither tried to draw hard or fixed lines of authority: Fleischmann welcomed Mehta's suggestions for Bowl programming and for special Philharmonic promotion; Mehta valued Fleischmann's musical taste and artistic advice. Although both based their ideas of what the Philharmonic should be doing on solid musical integrity, they shared a "feel" for such special promotional events as the joint concert with rock star Frank Zappa, the composer "Marathons," and the television events, all of which brought Mehta and the Philharmonic more publicity than his solid day-to-day achievements with the orchestra.

Although he received much national publicity and more than a few critical brickbats, Mehta now sees such performances as the Zappa collaboration as experiments that didn't come off: "I didn't do that to only increase the audience. It was my insatiable curiosity as a musician. I meet a man like Frank Zappa. He talks about how, on tour with his rock group, he used to go to libraries and look at scores of Varèse, Stravinsky, and Bartók. He really taught himself composition, orchestration, etc. I was so impressed by this man's voracity and tenaciousness. It developed in one conversation with Zappa that we wanted to make music together. It didn't turn out to be a particularly rewarding experience. It was consciously done to entice young people. The concert with Zappa was part of Contempo. In the first part of the concert, I did parts of *The Rite of Spring,* the *Intégrales* of Varèse. It was not a rock concert really. I told the public, this is a concert of contemporary music, the second part of which will be devoted to a composition by Mr. Zappa."

Although Mehta conducted the Philharmonic in an award-winning television program devoted to Ravel's *Boléro,* he has considerable reservations about the medium's potential for serious music. But he would do more television work "if I met a writer and producer who could do it as artistically as possible.

"I think *Boléro* is an artistic film, on top of being educational. I

(137)

get tired of doing just straight concerts on television, where it becomes sort of a young people's guide to the orchestra, you know. The cameras zoom to clarinet to flute to bass to pizzicato. I think it distracts the audience. When I look at other people's concerts, especially if it is a piece I know, I find myself not listening and just looking at pictures."

Nevertheless, such highly publicized ventures were fundamentally peripheral to Mehta's basic ambition in Los Angeles—building the Philharmonic into an orchestra of first-rank international status. If there remains some doubt as to his success in this, there were occasions in performance, as well as on records, when the Philharmonic unquestionably ranked among the top American orchestras, as Fleischmann and Mehta would have us believe it did. The horns, trombones, and tuba under Mehta are surprisingly similar to the rich but never heavy brass of the Vienna Philharmonic, but the trumpets can have a raw edge and occasional inaccuracy that can spoil the stunning effect of Mahler's Third Symphony in an otherwise superb performance. If the woodwinds lack the virtuoso presence of some top orchestral soloists, they sound superbly blended and even in quality; of eight coprincipal woodwind players, three are young women, despite Mehta's occasional disparagement of women in symphony orchestras. Some of their lack of presence may be the fault of the acoustics of the pavilion and a stage shell that frequently emphasizes brass and percussion. The same acoustic vagaries hamper easy projection of the sound of the string basses and cellos. Mehta can correct this in balancing when he wishes to. The strings generally lack the richness that Mehta would like in his effort to realize a true Viennese sound. This is in part a matter of the instruments themselves and in part a matter of an American, as opposed to the Central European, technique, which is, on the other hand, the tradition behind the Israel Philharmonic, whose warmer string sound pleases Mehta greatly.

Inevitably, in the course of eighteen seasons together, Mehta and the players of the Los Angeles Philharmonic developed a highly economical means of communication. This made it possible for them to prepare a superb performance of Mahler's long and complex Third

Symphony with something less than five hours of rehearsal, half of it in an acoustically intolerable and physically cramped rehearsal studio; virtually everybody had played it a couple of years previously when they and Mehta had devoted much more time to its preparation. Sometimes Mehta would skip over a passage completely, merely reminding the orchestra how they had played it before. In other places that had not gone so well earlier, Mehta was extremely exacting, especially in matters of rhythm and balance. On the other hand, he would suggest shortcuts: "Begin that phrase just a bit early; there are so many notes to play. Just so you *end* with the rest of us," he would suggest to a wind player.

With a new piece, there are no shortcuts, although his command of the score in advance is much in evidence. For a new work, he likes to have the composer present from the beginning and generally finds that this leads to mutual satisfaction all around. However, he bitterly recalls an experience with a György Ligeti premiere in Los Angeles for which the composer was not only present at all the rehearsals but was most exacting in his demands. To make matters worse, the performance was criticized as underrehearsed.

In one of his guest appearances or when tackling a work new to his own orchestra, Mehta works through the music section by section at first, attempting to get all the details right before putting a whole piece or movement together. Although he is on first-name terms with the players in the orchestras he regularly conducts, there are limits to familiarity when the pressure is on. He can be quite irritable and demanding, especially if he senses any inattentiveness from any player or section. (He was somewhat more formal and less abrupt in his first rehearsals with the New York Philharmonic, although there was ample evidence of cordial camaraderie from the beginning). Most of the time, however, his rehearsals are very relaxed, with occasional humor from both sides of the conductor's music stand. But levity must be relevant, not distracting. Mehta's rehearsals move extremely fast and cover a great deal of territory in a short time.

Thanks to his long tenure with two orchestras, Mehta has been able, at a crucial stage in his development, to explore and learn a much bigger repertory than if he had been jumping from one guest engagement to another. His very earliest exposure to music in Bombay, where he was born in 1936, was in chamber and orchestral music from Bach through Brahms. He heard this both from his father's symphony orchestra in Bombay and from records of European classical music played constantly at home. Nevertheless, he recalls the staggering impression he received on arriving in Vienna and hearing the Philharmonic there play Brahms. Equally stirring were his first encounters with such later Austro-German composers as Mahler, Bruckner, and Richard Strauss, whose music remains to this day the virtual backbone of Mehta's repertory. When Mehta speaks of his musical roots being in Vienna, he has in mind these late-romantic composers, as well as the Second Viennese School. With the Viennese composers of a century earlier—Haydn, Mozart, Beethoven, and Schubert—Mehta's achievement is much more uneven than it is with the music of composers who were, at times, still vividly remembered by his older teachers and whose tradition was still a real force. Among earlier Viennese composers, Haydn generally fares well under Mehta's baton, being more straightforward and emotionally uncomplicated than Mozart, whose music still escapes Mehta. He has yet to conduct any opera by Mozart. On the other hand, as he demonstrated in the Schubert cycle during his first year with the New York Philharmonic, his early Schubert is delightful. With later Schubert, like the Ninth Symphony, he seems to have the same problem as he often has with Beethoven—possibly too much respect; here his performances are orchestrally and stylistically impeccable without conveying a more personal involvement in the melos of the music in the manner of Furt-wängler, a conductor whom he greatly admires.

The programs of his first New York season, like his Los Angeles repertory, included a good measure of contemporary music, some of it in first performance; in Los Angeles he premiered considerable music by composers of the region. His approach to twentieth-century music, old and new, seems to be colored by his affinity for such late-romantic composers as Richard Strauss and Mahler, but he has a keen understanding of music in the tradition of Schoenberg, Berg, and Webern, having been introduced to the Second Viennese School by his Vienna teacher, Hans

Swarowsky. Some of his earliest successes in Vienna and Tanglewood were with Schoenberg's music.

Despite the fact that Mehli Mehta had studied violin for several years at the Curtis Institute in Philadelphia with Ivan Galamian, when it came time to send his son Zubin to study abroad, it was Vienna. There Hans Swarowsky was regarded as the leading teacher of conducting in his time. Mehta found Swarowsky extremely strict and more than a little dry. However, the musical discipline that he instilled in Mehta was basic to his development as a conductor. Mehta won a conducting contest at the Royal Liverpool Philharmonic on his way to Tanglewood in 1958, of which he says, "If Swarowsky hadn't taught me how to hold the fermatas in the Beethoven Fifth, I wouldn't have won that contest." Musical analysis as taught then at the Vienna Academy of Music was very traditional, although Mehta did encounter some of the more unconventional approach of Heinrich Schenker in outside contacts. At the Academy, however, theory and analysis were taught by Erwin Ratz, also known as an editor of Mahler's scores and director of the International Mahler Society. When Mehta expressed an interest in seeing original materials in the Mahler archives, Ratz invited him to his modest flat, where he produced a pile of rare manuscripts from under his bed.

Unfortunately, Mehta never actually heard Furtwängler conduct. "I had a ticket for a concert when I first came to Vienna, but it was canceled and he died soon after. The influence of Furtwängler could be constructive only after the rigid schooling of Swarowsky. Without something like Swarowsky's absolute basis of sticking to the black and white of the notes and nothing else, the Furtwänglerian influence can be disastrous, as is sometimes the case with people who are his disciples. The conductor must ascertain the intentions of the composer, and Furtwängler was important for what he read between the lines. Since classical composers did not notate scores like Stravinsky and Bartók did in minutest detail, we can only ask ourselves, with knowledge of their style, what they really want. Knowledge of other works of the same composers is important: if you don't know Mozart's operas and piano concertos, you really cannot do his symphonies. If I did not have that strict classical basis, I could not even have admired Furtwängler. God! He really understood, because he had that same classical background. Yet he read between the notes; he read such things in the Adagio of the *Eroica.*"

Mehta is well acquainted with the Furtwängler style through recordings and tapes, many of them not published commercially or even surreptitiously. On a number of occasions he has shared discoveries of Furtwängler insights with his friend Daniel Barenboim over the long-distance telephone.

Recordings by composers of their own music are important to him, but with limitations: "I used to go to Stravinsky's recording sessions here in Los Angeles. I knew what he could get out of an orchestra and what he couldn't. There are a few Richard Strauss recordings available which are very objective. In music that so oozed love, care, sometimes unabashed declarations of beauty, he seemed as if he felt ashamed. Willy Boskowsky, a concertmaster at the Vienna State Opera, told me that at one performance of *Rosenkavalier,* Strauss leaned over to him and told him every hour what he had earned during that hour. That's a rather empty musical thing. *Till Eulenspiegel* doesn't suffer under Strauss's baton because it's that kind of piece. But when you hear Clemens Krauss conduct Strauss, you know that Krauss was his favorite conductor. So why shouldn't I give my own view of *The Rite of Spring* also?"

Mehta's study methods vary according to the music at hand: "If I am studying a classical score, I really first dissect and analyze it. I don't have to hear it. I hear it when I am looking at it. More complex scores I work out at the piano. I cannot tell you how I studied *Gurrelieder,* for instance. I didn't use any system. I just learned it by practice. It is a piece really without form, just a series of songs, each with a different structure—no classical structure at all. It becomes very complex to learn. I memorized it, and it took years before I could really do it. I say this because there are a lot of pieces which I do not learn from memory."

Mehta agrees with Barenboim's observation that two such quite different conductors as Szell and Furtwängler had an equally keen sense

of structure. "Those two approaches weren't too dissimilar. Maybe Furtwängler made a little bit more rallentando, but Szell's bridge passage
was also very carefully thought out. He didn't linger over it. In other
words, an actor saying the same line—Gielgud or Olivier—both have
the same structure but the expression will be different. I don't think that
makes those two so different in my eyes.

"I can always tell when a conductor has no sense of structure. First
of all, if he has no sense of tempo relationship. There are many conductors that have not even thought of a tempo relationship between the
adagio and the allegro of a classical work. I believe that all internal
tempo changes in classical music until early Beethoven were interrelated.
In the whole second-act finale of *The Marriage of Figaro* the tempos
are interrelated. In the Beethoven First Symphony, the Adagio is related to the Allegro. In a conductor's treatment of the *Schlussgruppe,*
I can always tell when he knows that he is at the end of the exposition
and beginning of the development. Invariably, Beethoven's codas are
either very intensely orchestrated or have a new surge of life, like the
first movement of the Fifth. I can always tell when a conductor doesn't
do anything with it, is not even conscious of it.

"These are things you never read from these experts in the newspapers. That is why I, none of us, can take them seriously; we don't
consider them colleagues, really. We work out so meticulously in the
Mozart G-minor Symphony the bridge to the recapitulation because it
is one of the jewels of all time, and then nobody notices it."

It is typical of Mehta that he will digress in the course of serious
discussion of music to express his views of critics who do not take his
work seriously. The antagonism that prevailed in Los Angeles between
him and Martin Bernheimer of the *Los Angeles Times* is legendary.
There may well have been, as some have speculated, personal grounds
for this that have nothing to do with music or writing about music.
Fleischmann, who arrived on the scene after Bernheimer's harsh criticism
of Mehta had become well established, quickly enlisted on Mehta's side
and has himself drawn Bernheimer's fire both for his part in the glamorization of Mehta and for his artistic policies at the Hollywood Bowl.
Nevertheless, Bernheimer had a very definite musical point of view

underlining his week-by-week comments on Mehta's artistic performance. He generally liked the conductor's work in Wagner, Richard
Strauss, Bruckner, and Mahler. Although he commended Mehta for
using a reduced orchestra for Mozart and Haydn, he criticized the conductor for failing to get below the surface of the music. Bernheimer
noted, following a 1972 performance of Handel's *Messiah,* that although Mehta was not necessarily a baroque specialist, he was hardly the
sort of musician who could turn his back on scholarship:

> Not all the way at least.
>
> His "Messiah" enjoys the distinct advantage of being small in scale
> and transparent in texture. It employs a chorus of 52, scaled down to
> 40 for the more intimate moments, and an orchestra of 40. No cast of
> thousands for Mehta.
>
> The maestro also sanctions the interpolation of a variety of embel-
> lishments, occasionally alters rhythms for the unwritten but imperative
> "notes inegales," and utilizes both a harpsichord and an organ for the
> continuo part. Bless him.
>
> Unfortunately, paying lip service to these authentic performance
> practices does not automatically produce an elegant performance. This
> year's celebration never convinced one that our maestro has totally liber-
> ated "Messiah," or his thoughts on the work, from the realm of inflated
> romanticism.
>
> Many of the scholarly devices applied were applied timidly, incon-
> sistently and/or arbitrarily. Some indulgences of the 19th century
> lingered on.

There is always a tendency of the local critic to become impatient
and sometimes bored with the local conductor, whose work can become
too familiar; the relationship between Bernheimer and Mehta has its
counterparts in many other cities, including New York. Yet some of
what bothered Bernheimer in Mehta is reflected in Thomas Willis's
Chicago Tribune review of a Los Angeles Philharmonic concert on tour
in 1972:

> It was without question the best conducting I have heard from Mehta
> and the best playing from an obviously improving orchestra. . . . Mehta
> can generate enormous energy from his players. He knows how to pace

the flow of a Mahler movement, even when he is going too fast for internal music conditions. The explosions in the outer movements had their desired incendiary effect. The waltz had its moments of charm and wit. The Adagietto found its balance points in place. But the interpretation was basically middle-of-the-road, substituting energy for spirituality, and external drama for precise and careful analysis. For all of the excitement, I still felt that I was floating on the surface instead of being submerged. With Mahler you should be able to drown and return to life.

At the same time, Martin Bernheimer has also been rather puritanical in his caustic comments on the glamorizing of Mehta in Los Angeles. Shortly after Mehta's appointment in New York was announced, *New York* magazine carried a feature article of which the title "Don't Call Him Zubi-Baby" was followed by a subheading quotation from text: ". . . Zubin Mehta insists that he despises the personality cult. But his resistance to it has been, at most, eminently passive. . . ." To such criticism, Mehta replies that he has never at any time in his career employed a press agent; he has not even had a personal manager since Siegfried Hearst's death, and if there is a personality cult, it is the creation of the media. That may be true as far as he is concerned, but the Los Angeles Philharmonic and Music Center have not hesitated to capitalize on his potential for glamorization—not necessarily as an end in itself but rather as an essential to the completion of the Music Center and an expansion of the Philharmonic into an orchestra of international stature. If it sometimes more than bordered on Hollywood vulgarity, that is the style of the city. Critics who complained of the ushers wearing Nehru-style coats and of the garish portrait of the conductor in the bar neglect to mention that in another bar located on a lower level there are several exhibition cases, some containing models of operatic decor, one the costume of Robert Merrill as Escamillo in *Carmen,* and still another the gown designed by Yves St. Laurent that Mrs. Chandler wore the opening night of the Pavilion.

The inclusion of the operatic memorabilia is significant, for the Pavilion was designed from the beginning to house opera, ballet, and music theater generally, in addition to the symphony orchestra. Just as

Mrs. Chandler originally hoped to include a major conservatory at the Music Center, like the Juilliard School at the Lincoln Center in New York, she once cherished hopes of establishing a regular season of opera in Los Angeles—something more than the two-week stand of the San Francisco Opera in the cavernous Shrine Auditorium. The inclusion of Los Angeles on the Metropolitan Opera's spring tours in 1948 and 1949 was strongly supported by Mrs. Chandler and her husband's newspaper. For a brief time, there was even talk of extended stays by the Met in Los Angeles once a proper theater might be built to house it; this may have been the germ of the Music Center idea. The San Francisco Opera gave its annual performances at the Pavilion in 1964, an engagement that involved a prohibitively high local guarantee, since the Pavilion has only slightly more than half the number of seats in the Shrine Auditorium. The San Francisco company returned to the Shrine in 1965 for its last appearances in Los Angeles.

With the abandonment of Los Angeles by the San Francisco company, the way was cleared for the establishment of a resident opera company at the center. At the time, there was speculation that Mehta himself was strongly inclined to head such an effort; he had, after all, been combining opera and symphony in Montreal. Looking back, Mehta believes that Mrs. Chandler herself was not particularly interested in opera at this time. This may have been the case, although the Music Center board later engaged George London to explore the feasibility of establishing a company in Los Angeles. Meanwhile, the Center started to bring the New York City Opera to Los Angeles, at first as a stopgap and eventually as a regular event in the Pavilion. Moreover, Mehta's operatic activities developed elsewhere—in Montreal, at the Metropolitan, and in Europe—and he may well have been happy to see the resources of the city concentrated on the Philharmonic. (The Philharmonic itself plans to bring staged opera to the Chandler Pavilion in 1982, a coproduction with Covent Garden of *Falstaff*, conducted by Giulini.)

In his memoirs, *5,000 Nights at the Opera,* Sir Rudolf Bing bemoaned the difficulty he encountered in engaging experienced conductors for the Metropolitan Opera. "Today talent is found too soon," he wrote, "and sent off to conduct difficult operas at international festivals." Just before making this comment, he recalled Zubin Mehta's career at the Metropolitan: "I went to Toronto to hear Zubin Mehta conduct *Tosca,* and he was *funny*—but he was clearly very talented, and the risk was worth taking. Except for *Tosca,* every opera he conducted at the Metropolitan was one he learned for the first time for that purpose."

Mehta is understandably annoyed with Sir Rudolf's summary treatment of his four seasons at the Met. In the first place, he points out, it was in Montreal, not Toronto, that Bing first heard Mehta conduct. Only in that city did he conduct both opera and the symphony orchestra in the then new Place des Arts. His operatic repertory in Montreal included, in addition to the *Tosca* that Bing heard, *La Traviata, Aida, Carmen, Otello, Tristan und Isolde,* and *Salome.* Whenever this work duplicated his work at the Metropolitan, he generally coordinated his own study to prepare for both productions.

"First of all, when Mr. Bing invited me, I told him I wasn't ready. Then I accepted doing *Aida* at the old Met, which was very well received. He then offered me everything—but no German opera. That is where his big mistake was. I had to learn Italian operas for him, whereas I had grown up with Mozart and Wagner in Vienna and he wouldn't let me do them. I would have been on much better footing at the Met had I done the operas that I grew up with. I made certain mistakes in agreeing to do operas like *Otello* for the first time at the Met. I did *Otello* at the Met with a minimal rehearsal because it was a revival. When I arrived in the theater, I was told that Mr. Krips wanted extra time for *The Magic Flute* that he was doing with Chagall, and they gave him two of my rehearsals. I should have at that time walked out and said, 'Find somebody else.' But I was too young. Maybe I needed a manager. I said, 'Oh, I'll do it,' and *Otello* wasn't good. *Trovatore* was the only opera where I really did something at the Met. It was a new production, a production that I didn't like too much, but I was happy with my work in it. Then I did *Carmen* with Jean-Louis Barrault; it was an unhappy birth. I could not influence that man out of the kind of symbolic staging he did. I suffered, he suffered, the company suffered, everybody suffered. I couldn't do my best, although I knew *Carmen* very well; I *wasn't* conducting it for the first time. Since I saw the entire house being so mean to that man, I took up his cause and tried to instill excitement into that production which just wasn't there."

Mehta recalled the failure of *Otello* in an interview with Alan Blyth of *Gramophone*:

"My first *Otello* was at the Met, and I didn't consider it a success, but I was tempted because of a near-ideal cast—Vickers, Gobbi, and Caballé—but I didn't have the orchestral preparation I needed, so I couldn't keep the line. I was doing it phrase by phrase. Line seems to me the most essential thing in any performance: you must conceive the end at the beginning. Too many climaxes won't work. That goes as much for a Bruckner symphony or the *Eroica* as for *Otello*."

In all, Mehta conducted seven operas at the Metropolitan Opera in four seasons, 1965–69, an average of thirty-six performances a season: *Aida* at his debut December 29, 1965; *Carmen*; the world premiere of Marvin David Levy's *Mourning Becomes Electra*; *Otello*; *Tosca*; *Il Trovatore*; and *Turandot*. "At the Met I used to drive Rudolf Bing crazy with contracts," he told Marcia Winn in a 1978 interview for the *New York Times*. "It really bugged him. 'Why don't you have a manager I can fight with?' he'd say, and I would say 'No, no, I don't want that.' So I would negotiate my own contract." Mehta's operatic conducting at the Metropolitan Opera received mixed response from the critics. Irving Kolodin in the *Saturday Review* found him interesting but inexperienced. Reviewing the conductor's Met debut in *Aida,* Kolodin expressed "admiration for what he achieved by innate talent and a cool command of the situation, wonder that he had not prepared himself better for the routine of this highly complicated calling." However, Winthrop Sargeant of the *New Yorker,* a very early admirer of Mehta, was more sympathetic:

It was a remarkable job of conducting—the finest I remember in any Italian opera during the Bing administration—and it is worth analyzing. In the first place, Mr. Mehta is young enough not to have been influenced by that great master of yesteryear, Arturo Toscanini, who was a supremely gifted artist, one whose effect on other conductors was to inspire widespread imitation. This was not a good thing, since it led the imitators to follow the most obvious and superficial aspect of the Toscanini style: namely, his adherence to rigid and speedy tempo. Now Mr. Mehta has a musical personality of his own, and the tradition it springs from is Central European, coming down from men like Furtwängler, Walter, and von Karajan. He is not a rigid tempo man, as is nearly every other younger conductor now before the public. He knows when to give a little, when to let the singer breathe, when to permit a slight deviation from the steady pulse of the music—things that are matters of taste and artistry rather than rules and regulations. Moreover, Mr. Mehta has a phenomenal sense of musical line, by which I mean an intuitive feeling for the form of musical phrases, their interconnections, and the relative stress to be placed on their component notes. In addition, he has a way of displaying the texture of a score as a jeweler displays the facets of a diamond. Elements one never particularly noticed before suddenly come to life in his interpretations as he lifts one or another into prominence. This habit, though it would result in mannerism if pushed to excess, helps to make each Mehta performance a fresh inspiration. And beyond everything I have mentioned, Mr. Mehta has a degree of authority—an ability to arouse eighty or one hundred men under him to special efforts—that is found only in born maestros. On Monday night of last week, I watched all these things carefully. The long melodic lines of the prelude were beautifully formed; the climactic moments were waited for and consummated at precisely the right moment; nowhere did one find a sense that Mr. Mehta was driving his singers—he allowed each of them such vocal license as is called for at cadential points, bringing down his baton firmly only when good taste or the exigencies of ensemble called for the gesture. Mr. Mehta is probably the most important find among conductors that Mr. Bing has made during his career here.

Actually, Mehta was happier with the opera he did in Montreal, "because they were my own productions," he says. "I must stress that I have no ambition to stage-direct, but I am very involved always. The Met just didn't let me be involved in anything. I was always guest conductor; I had to go in the pit and accompany the singers. I was never shown a sketch, never a design of a costume. I cannot do opera that way. I have to be totally involved or else I don't function as well. Except for *Salome,* which I completely left to Rudolf Heinrich because I admire him so much, I took everything else in Montreal personally. I sat down with the designer, I said I want this here, I want a door there. In other words it was a total concept, and that's where I flourish best.

"Recently Covent Garden let me do the same thing, and *The Girl of the Golden West* has been an absolute total success. It was my concept that the Girl of Golden West is not Minnie on a white horse. It is not Dorothy Kirsten looking like Calamity Jane, you know, like a rich Calamity Jane. It is not a John Wayne film with polished bars and naked-girl pictures. It is shabby old pre–Civil War; they haven't found much gold; they are poor, and this poor little virgin who hasn't been kissed has to give them some spiritual assistance, etc." *The Girl of the Golden West* was a great success in London and was later recorded under Mehta with most of the Covent Garden cast.

More controversial was a new production of *Die Fledermaus* that premiered on New Years Eve 1977: "I said, 'Look, I can't do this in English, but we have a cast who doesn't speak German, and 90 percent of the audience won't understand German, so what are we going to do?' I don't want *Fledermaus* like I see *Rosenkavalier* at the Met where people wait for one waltz to the other and don't really understand it at all. When you see *Rosenkavalier* in Vienna, the audience laughs all the time. At the Met, have you ever heard people laughing? No, they just sit, and they wait from one tune to another. I said I don't want *Fledermaus* to be like that. This in German is a kiss of death. It's a realistic opera. Kiri Te Kanawa is a beautiful singer, but she can't speak German and there is no way she can be Rosalinda, a Viennese housewife. So we made her the English wife of Hermann Prey, who is a Viennese bourgeois, and she had a Viennese maid. She spoke sometimes English to the maid, sometimes German. With her husband the same thing. I can't take Orlofsky as a woman. I said I will not have Orlofsky as a woman. I cannot see this woman dressed in tails, with a big cigarette holder. It looks like a lesbian to me. Maybe in the last century it didn't look like a lesbian. I cannot bring myself to believe that's a Russian prince who has seen the whole world and finds nothing to amuse him. Of course, I was criticized for that." At the premiere there were special performances inserted in the party scene, including a Daniel Barenboim playing the Chopin G-minor Ballade and Isaac Stern in the last movement of the Mendelssohn Violin Concerto. Mehta also interpolated a passage from "Wotan's Farewell" when Eisenstein takes his leave from Rosalinda.

One critic with whom this production did find favor was Harold C. Schonberg of the *New York Times,* who was in London: "Mehta conducted a lively, well-knit performance. He has been trained in Vienna, and he understands operetta better than most musicians around. The music never lost its lilt, and yet it never sounded oversentimental. The way Mehta led his soloists and chorus into the languorous 'Brüderlein und Schwesterlein' was a lesson in delicate rhythmic pacing and spacing."

Covent Garden, where Mehta has also done *Otello* and *Salome,* is but one of several major opera theaters abroad where Mehta has been active. In Vienna he has conducted *Lohengrin* and was paid for performances of *Salome* that he never conducted there. These had been scheduled between Karl Böhm's earlier preparation of the opera and a special performance at a gala honoring him. Böhm had nothing against Mehta, he said, but didn't want someone else making changes in what he considered "his" production of *Salome.* However, after the Böhm gala, Mehta did conduct the Vienna State Opera in *Salome* during its visit to the Maggio Musicale in Florence. Shortly before being offered the New York Philharmonic late in 1975, Mehta turned down an appointment at the Berlin Opera as its musical director, despite success there with several operas including *Tristan und Isolde.* He refused that post in large part because he felt that his wife, Nancy, might not be happy in Berlin.

For the immediate future, Mehta's operatic activity will concentrate on Wagner's *Der Ring des Nibelungen.* As he noted in his comments on his Met career, Wagner is close to his Viennese roots. He has done both *Lohengrin* and *Tristan und Isolde* on a number of occasions. With the *Ring* he will be working on two separate productions in Vienna and in Italy during the same period of time. The Italian production will be the realization of a long-cherished hope of Massimo Bo-gianckino, intendant at the Teatro Comunale in Florence. During his days in the La Scala triumvirate with Cláudio Abbado and Paoló Grassi, Bogianckino had initiated a *Ring* to be produced by Luchino Visconti, with Wolfgang Sawallisch conducting. However, Visconti fell ill be-fore even *Rheingold* could be mounted, and at Sawallisch's suggestion, La Scala began this *Ring* by borrowing Gunther Rennert's Munich pro-duction. Meanwhile Bogianckino engaged Luca Ronconi to continue the cycle at La Scala. During a highly controversial production of *Die Walküre,* there was a great deal of friction between Ronconi and Sawal-lisch, which Bogianckino managed to keep under some control. By the time *Siegfried* was under way, Bogianckino had left for Florence; the production took place, but the conductor and the producer vowed never to work together again. Thus, La Scala was left with half a *Ring,* and Bogianckino's hopes remained unfulfilled.

Subsequently Bogianckino approached Mehta to do a *Ring* in Flor-ence at the same time he was doing it with different singers and pro-duction people in Vienna. Moreover, he saw this as an opportunity to complete the Ronconi production of the tetralogy, by arranging for La Scala to collaborate with Florence in a joint venture. The decor and cos-tumes of the earlier *Die Walküre* and *Siegfried* would be used again in both cities, a new *Rheingold* and *Götterdämmerung* would be designed, and all four operas would be produced by Ronconi, with Mehta con-ducting in both Italian theaters. Bogianckino brought Mehta and Ronconi together and found them compatible. The cycle was to be in-augurated with *Rheingold* at the Teatro Comunale during the 1979 Maggio Musicale Fiorentino and will be continued during the following three years in Florence and Milan. Meanwhile, Mehta will also be conducting the same music dramas in Vienna. Appropriately, the farewell present from the players of the Los Angeles Philharmonic to their de-parting music director was a handsomely bound set of scores of Wagner's *Ring* signed by every member of the orchestra.

Mehta's most important activity abroad for many years has been his close association with the Israel Philharmonic Orchestra. As so often happened very early in his career, it was a cancellation that opened the way for Mehta. When Eugene Ormandy canceled an appearance with the Israeli Orchestra in 1961, Mehta was only twenty-five. His success was such that the players declared that they wanted him back for the next twenty-five years. In 1969, he was designated the orchestra's musical adviser. "I was always musical director," says Mehta, "but couldn't be called that because of my contract in L.A. that said I couldn't be music director anywhere else." Apparently the New York Philharmonic is less possessive, because Mehta's title with the Israel Philharmonic was changed in 1977 to musical director. That step may also have been aimed to reassure the Israelis that his new position in New York was not going to diminish the important place of their Philharmonic in Mehta's career.

Although he declares, "There is no orchestra in the world that's as difficult as the Israel Philharmonic," Mehta obviously has a unique affection for it. Part of his feeling may be because he himself regards his own people, the Parsees, who emigrated from Persia to western India in the twelfth century, as "the Jews of India." This affection is also typical of Mehta's intense loyalties to certain people, institutions, and ideals that he holds dear. This is not, he points out, necessarily a Parsee trait but rather "just Zubin Mehta." When he describes the difficulty of the Israel Philharmonic, he is taking on something of that typically Jewish propensity of being critical of other Jews, without in any way betraying loyalty or affection. In fact, such criticism of one Jew by another can actually be an expression of solidarity—telling the outside world, "See, we can recognize our faults better than you can"—a counterpart of their expertise in telling Jewish jokes that they might resent from gentiles. From his long association with the Philharmonic and his Israeli friends, Mehta has picked up Yiddish expressions with which he liberally sprinkles his fluently expressive English. This empathy between Mehta and the Israel Philharmonic also embraces the strong friendship he has with Daniel Barenboim, Pinchas Zukerman, Itzhak Perlman, Isaac Stern, and Vladimir Ashkenazy among musicians.

When the Six-Day War broke out in 1967, Mehta was making his first appearance at the Casals Festival in Puerto Rico. He asked Casals to excuse him and flew off immediately to Israel, catching the last plane from Rome to Tel Aviv. He joined the Philharmonic and the Barenboims in presenting special concerts for the soldiers and civilians, knowing how important it was to the morale of the Israelis to hear the music they loved. Once the hostilities were over, the Barenboims were married, and the three artist-friends joined the Philharmonic in a special concert in the Fredric R. Mann Auditorium in Tel Aviv.

The Philharmonic is a cultural institution unique to Israel. Founded in 1936 by the Polish violinist Bronislaw Huberman, it attracted exiled musicians from Central Europe who were driven from their jobs in major orchestras by the Nazis. Huberman invited his friend Arturo Toscanini to conduct its first concert, and, until his death in 1947, persuaded other colleagues among leading soloists and conductors to appear with the orchestra at drastically reduced fees.

From the beginning, the Israel Philharmonic was organized as a player-governed cooperative. Its membership jealously guards its artistic prerogatives and has an extraordinary morale and pride; the Israel Philharmonic is, after all, more than a decade older than the state of Israel itself. Musical policy and personnel matters are determined jointly by Mehta and committees representing the players. "I sit with my ministers," says Mehta. Although the orchestra has been strengthened in recent years by an influx of players from Russia and other Soviet-bloc countries, about half of its players are sabras, native-born Israelis. During a tour to Russia with the Montreal Symphony, Mehta indiscreetly thanked a government official for sending the Israel Philharmonic such good exiled musicians; consequently the Los Angeles Philharmonic, despite its intensive touring with Mehta, has never been invited to the Soviet Union.

Mehta has observed that one aspect of the Israel Philharmonic's being difficult is that they often need to be inspired, rather than merely led, by their conductor. This places a special burden on him, but sometimes the flame will be ignited by a spark from an exceptionally fine solo phrase from one of the players. Under Mehta's leadership, the Israel Philharmonic has traveled widely—as far afield as Australia and New Zealand and frequently to the United States. An especially emotional occasion was in 1971 when the Israelis opened the Berlin Festival, preceeding their announced program with a performance of their national anthem. They have toured in the United States frequently, usually to help raise funds or sell bonds for Israel. Particularly since the Palestine Liberation Organization killings of Israeli athletes at the Munich Olympic games, the orchestra has traveled under tight security precautions.

When the Israel Philharmonic played in Carnegie Hall in 1972, with Mehta conducting and Barenboim as soloist, Harold C. Schonberg reviewed the concert in the *New York Times*:

It was a fine concert. The Israel Philharmonic is a topnotch orchestra, up to the highest international standards. Strings sing sensuously, first-chair men are uniformly proficient, everything fuses into a gorgeous mesh of sound. Zubin Mehta, who conducted the concert, has had a long-time association with the orchestra, and he is no shrinking violet when it comes to voluptuous sonorities and virtuoso effects. The orchestra gave him everything he asked for, with plenty in reserve. But if Mr. Mehta is a virtuoso, glamour-boy conductor, he is also a musician of sensibility. If he favors dynamic extremes, he also has the technique and control to use them in a tasteful manner. The last piece on the program was the Mahler First Symphony, and he made a very exciting thing of it. Exciting—and, happily, anything but superficial.

Mr. Mehta has developed into a conductor who reins his natural ebullience into the creation of musical structures. In the Mahler he organized everything with unusual skill, bending tempos just enough to lend variety without losing the line. His treatment of the dancelike episodes of the second movement was a lesson in stick control and dynamic plasticity, and the result was enchanting. This is *wienerisch* in the best sense of the word—suave, subtle, full of sentiment without ever becoming cloying. I have not heard it done better.

With Daniel Barenboim at the keyboard, Mr. Mehta conducted the Beethoven *Emperor* Concerto in an unusually lively performance. This was not the most precise within memory, not with the impetuous Mr. Barenboim tending to rush phrase endings, often finishing up a shade ahead of the orchestra, or sometimes blurring passages with a heavy pedal.

(155)

Nevertheless, the performance had character, and it was preferable to the letter-perfect but stale performances so frequently encountered. Pianist and conductor took a free view toward the score, employing tempo changes, taking the music at a spanking pace, using pronounced accents to emphasize the contours. There was a great deal of fervor to the interpretation, the work of two hot-blooded young men who also have exceedingly original music minds.

If Mehta has any complaint about the Israel Philharmonic, it is over the government's—not the orchestra's—refusal to permit the music of Wagner and Richard Strauss to be played. Several years ago, when the orchestra itself changed its policy on these composers, Mehta actually took some scores of their music to Tel Aviv, but the officials continued their ban. Nowadays, with a more conservative national government, the chance of a change is even more remote. However, Mehta is good-natured about this ban on music in which he is regarded as a specialist, pointing out that the Volkswagen is now the most popular car in Israel. Mehta is enough of a *Mensch* in Israel to be able to get away with comments that might otherwise be indiscreet; when he met Prime Minister Menachem Begin in New York just after the Camp David meeting in 1978, he impishly suggested that the Israel Philharmonic should play a concert in Cairo, a suggestion that Begin obviously regarded as premature.

Despite his activities elsewhere, Mehta is firmly committed to the Israel Philharmonic Orchestra. During a year when he is increasing his time with the New York Philharmonic and will be starting his *Ring* cycles in Florence, Milan, and Vienna, he is spending two months in Israel and will tour Europe with the orchestra for six weeks.

Zubin Mehta's move to the New York Philharmonic—announced in 1976 and consummated in the fall of 1978—had a certain inevitable logic to it. He had the international stature, a record of orchestra building and of commitment to a city and its orchestra, a substantial exposure through recordings, and, by no means least, the requisite charismatic glamour. All of these must have seemed desirable to New Yorkers in their search for a successor to the relatively colorless Pierre Boulez, who had followed not too successfully in terms of charisma the popular Leonard Bernstein. In any short list of prospects in the councils on the top floor of Avery Fisher Hall in 1975, Zubin Mehta's name must have loomed very large. He may or may not have been the first choice of the Philharmonic—Sir Georg Solti is reported to have stated otherwise—but there was a strong pull of logic in his direction.

Not that Mehta had made his path to New York easy. When the New Yorkers were seeking a successor to Leonard Bernstein in 1967, Mehta was included, by the media at least, among the prospects. However, when invited to schedule a guest appearance in the 1968–69 season, Mehta privately told Carlos Moseley, the New York managing director, that he would not accept it if he were being considered a candidate. Publicly, however, speculation continued, most notably in a Sunday feature article in the *New York Times*. Whether by premeditation or on an impulse, Mehta effectively doused any further speculation regarding New York with some very outspoken remarks at a reception in Los Angeles where he was overheard by wire service and weekly magazine correspondents. He expressed a low opinion of New York as a city in which to live and most emphatically described the players in the Philharmonic as little short of saboteurs and destroyers of conductors.

At the time, this incident was regarded simply as another instance of Zubin Mehta's constitutional inability to keep his foot out of his mouth when the media were around. But, in retrospect, he may have had other, much deeper, motives in effectively squelching New York speculation. This was the time of what he referred to as his "marriage problems" with the Los Angeles orchestra. Even if a New York offer were to have been made, it is not characteristic of Mehta to run away from problems. Nor is it in his nature to allow his name to be bandied about on a list of candidates. Moreover, though much had been accomplished in seven years as musical director, much remained to be done with the Los Angeles Philharmonic. Finally, Los Angeles had shown its faith in a twenty-six-year-old conductor by turning its Philharmonic over to him in 1962 and giving him a base on which to build a youthful international career. Loyalty to Los Angeles and pride may well have motivated Mehta to remove himself from consideration by New York so firmly. The very indiscretion of his remarks, although he later admitted that he had been rude, may have been intended to leave no possibility of his being seriously considered.

Mehta's schedule called for him to conduct at the Metropolitan Opera shortly after his Los Angeles outburst. Although he was an alien and therefore working in this country with union permission, Mehta was not a member of the musicians' union. However, he was called to account by Local 802 of New York. After claiming that he had been misquoted out of context and protesting that he had only the highest respect for the players in the New York Philharmonic, he was treated to a fatherly lecture on public relations by the local's president, Max Arons. Although the 1968–69 season guest engagement with the New York Philharmonic was canceled, he finally appeared with the orchestra for two weeks in 1974. He began his first rehearsal with a dignified yet frank apology for his earlier indiscretion. That engagement was a great success in every respect.

A year and a half later he was in New York on tour with the Los Angeles Philharmonic and was interviewed by John Rockwell of the *Times*. It may have been only an accident that he sounded less committed to Los Angeles and less hostile toward New York. Or he may have been sending signals toward Lincoln Center, although he later denied that he had any interest at that time. However, the well-informed Moseley must have known in December 1975 that Mehta had just turned down the offer from the Berlin Opera and was thus free of a commitment that could limit his time elsewhere. At the very end of December, Moseley flew out to Los Angeles, ostensibly to visit friends at Malibu. There he phoned Mehta's home, asking if he might drop by while he was in the area. Mehta still maintains that he had no inkling then that Moseley's call was anything but the friendly courtesy of a colleague.

"I have always maintained that I will not be on anybody's list, because I was just not available for any job. Carlos Moseley came to me in Los Angeles one day, described the situation, and outright offered me the job. I said I will think about it, and in three days I told him,

'Yes, I am seriously considering it.' I took two secret trips to New York and met at [Philharmonic Board Chairman] Amyas Ames's house, and they outlined the job for me, what my authority would be. I came back but discussed it only with my wife, who was overjoyed because she loves New York. Then I had all my internal tribulations to go through about this orchestra that I had come to love.

"Carlos, of course, had a lot to do with convincing me that now it's time after these sixteen years to move toward the center of things. I had not canvassed for the position, not at all. I had just refused the Berlin Opera a month before that, and I said to myself, there must be a reason that Berlin fell through. It is true that I called Danny, because he really knows the orchestra. I asked Carlos; I said he's the only person that I would like to call. I didn't call him until after those meetings in New York, until I myself was sure, then I called him. And he recommended it very highly because every time Danny guest-conducted in New York, he came and said, 'You know, what is all this talk? They are such nice people. Why does everybody say these things?' He was the only one who talked so positively about the New York Philharmonic. Then when I went to guest-conduct, I must say, I found that too. I found it no more difficult or easy to work with them than with anybody else."

Since Mehta had no manager, all negotiations were directly between him and the Philharmonic, and from all accounts, they proceeded very smoothly. One of his first concerns was the union contract under which the Philharmonic players worked; he studied it carefully and discussed it with the management to learn precisely how it would affect his work. He saw no difficulty in having to listen to players' advice in hiring new musicians as long as he had the final say. Given the lead-time with which orchestras and conductors both schedule their work, a host of logistics for the season after next—to say nothing to longer-range planning—had to be settled. These included finding time in Mehta's plans for sufficient time in New York—five to six months each year. In addition to the subscription season schedule, plans had to be set in motion for tours; a "get-acquainted" jaunt to Buenos Aires and Jamaica was set up to precede Mehta's first concerts as music director in

(159)

September 1978. Recording contracts presented some problem because the Philharmonic was a long-time CBS orchestra and Mehta an exclusive Decca-London artist; it was agreed that Mehta would record for CBS in New York, but for Decca-London with orchestras abroad, including the Israel Philharmonic.

Zubin and Nancy Mehta will keep their home on a hilltop in Brentwood. For one thing, Mehta's parents remain in the Los Angeles area, since his father, Mehli, is now established there as a conductor and violin teacher. Moreover, he has promised to return regularly to conduct the Los Angeles Philharmonic as guest. Despite these loyalties, Mehta has been increasingly excited about the prospect of working and living in New York. He looks forward to attending concerts by his colleagues and friends, something that the more limited music activity in Los Angeles did not offer to the degree that New York does. In fact, the possibility of being located in a major art center like New York played its part in Mehta's decision to make the move. From the beginning, Mehta took a keen interest in the overall institutional affairs of the Philharmonic to a degree that many other music directors nowadays do not concern themselves. Mehta wants to be involved with everything the Philharmonic does—not just his own concerts—if not directly, at least in discussing them and offering his suggestions. Nor is his concern meddlesome; he is genuinely concerned with the institution and offers constructive and often imaginative advice that is highly valued.

Following the announcement of his New York appointment, Mehta was able to squeeze two separate weeks at the Philharmonic into his crowded schedule before formally assuming his post. This first encounter with the orchestra—not as guest but as prospective music director—was awaited with some tension and trepidation, but both weeks came off well and were received warmly by the audiences and the media. Once he and the orchestra really started to work together in August 1978, there was instant rapport. For all the glamour surrounding the conductor and for all the fearsome reputation of the Philharmonic players, it was a coming together of experienced professionals. In one sense, Mehta had a fortunate break in his first weeks on the Philharmonic podium; the New York newspapers were on strike, and though there was television, magazine, and temporary daily coverage of the arts, Mehta and the orchestra were able to start working together without the intense glare of publicity. The members of the audience, too, had a chance to make up their own minds about Mehta without being told what to think in the press. Once the papers were printing again, working relations at Avery Fisher Hall had settled into routine. In mid-November, as Mehta completed his first series of concerts with the Philharmonic, Harold Schonberg summarized his impressions of the conductor so far in the *New York Times*:

Mr. Mehta is a romantic through and through, and he has been getting the orchestra to play with an unusually rich sound. His beat is an orchestra player's delight. It is almost textbook in its motions, moving in fairly large arcs in an unfussy manner. He works largely from the waist up; there are few of the leg motions and crouchings of other conductors. Indeed, there is something Toscaninian in Mr. Mehta's beat. . . . His actual behavior while working belies his reputation for flamboyance. He gives the impression of a serious musician doing his very best to get the very best from his orchestra. . . . Up to now he has conducted Schubert's Fourth and Fifth Symphonies, and the results have been impressive. He uses a reduced orchestra but does not have any doctrinaire ideas about style. The conducting is stylish nevertheless. He does not slavishly follow repeats or second endings; sometimes he uses them, sometimes not. Whatever he does in the matter of repeats is apparently governed by his ideas about form. . . .

In his Schubert, Mr. Mehta uses rather rapid tempos, adheres to a steady rhythm, but is not afraid to use expressive devices: a ritard here and there not written in the score, an unusual accentuation, an inner-voice emphasis. All of this was done without hitting the audience over the head; it sounded natural and unaffected. The performance of the Schubert Fourth Symphony was the finest that this listener has ever heard: it was lithe, sensitive, beautifully controlled, full of song, and yet never romanticized.

Curiously, Mr. Mehta's Beethoven has been less convincing. In the *Leonore* Overture no. 3 and in the Eighth Symphony there has been a rather pedantic approach. Everything has been correct, but the music has failed to come to life. It is almost as if Mr. Mehta is so determined to let New York see his respect for Beethoven that he refuses to let himself go. Where he is a wonderful colorist in Mahler, where his Schubert has such grace and style, his Beethoven sounds inhibited. All of a sudden the dashing Mr. Mehta is a kapellmeister.

He has accompanied several soloists, including such big guns as Vladimir Horowitz and Rudolf Serkin. . . . In the Rachmaninoff Third Concerto with Mr. Horowitz, Mr. Mehta showed that he could work with the most wilful artist. . . . A soloist like this is calculated to give a conductor nightmares, but Mr. Mehta was with the pianist wherever he went. At the big moments Mr. Mehta was much more than a mere accompanist; he saw to it that the orchestra had its say.

On the basis of what we have been hearing, then, the new conductor of the New York Philharmonic has a strong musical profile and has been making the orchestra play more alertly and with more color than it ever seemed able to do under Mr. Mehta's predecessor. Whether the love affair will continue remains to be seen. The Philharmonic has been known to turn around and bite, and conductors have walked away bleeding. But right now all is harmony.

Mehta's success in his first season in New York was such that, in May 1979, his contract was extended through 1986; he will conduct eighteen weeks of subscription concerts plus two to four or more weeks of touring and special events.

Still in his early forties, Zubin Mehta is already one of the most seasoned conductors before the public today. But he is young enough to have a capacity for artistic growth. The inhibition that Schonberg perceived in Mehta's Beethoven is not necessarily confined to New York concerts. One could hear it also in Los Angeles Philharmonic performances and on records. That restraint is also evident in much of his Mozart. For the moment, while he continues his work with the Israel Philharmonic, he faces two new challenges—Wagner's *Ring* abroad and making the Philharmonic his own orchestra in New York. Someday, however, Mehta may also feel the need to follow those of his Vienna roots that will lead him to Mozart opera.

Zubin Mehta is a paradoxical person and artist. He can turn maddeningly flippant in a serious musical discussion. He can mar an otherwise beautiful performance with flashes of the garish or vulgar. The same artist who can make such lyric music as Dvořák's G-major Symphony sound coarse and driven can be completely at one with the romantic sentiment of Schumann's *Spring* Symphony. However, the time is past when one can excuse as youthful indiscretion, however nobly motivated, the kind of comment he made about the New York Philharmonic in 1967 or his undertaking his first *Otello* under less than favorable circumstances in the harsh glare of the Metropolitan Opera. Ambition, southern California glamorization, protean talent, and sheer *chutzpah* may be forgiven in a young man, and the new, more serious environment of New York may temper some of Mehta's exuberance. There is no question that Mehta is a serious musician, extraordinarily talented, well trained, and thoroughly experienced. Nor is there any question of the unique greatness of his best work. Yet one can rightly wish for greater consistency in this paradoxical artist.

SEIJI OZAWA

THE tour of the Boston Symphony Orchestra to Japan in the spring of 1978, its first since it was there with Charles Munch many years earlier, was a profoundly emotional experience for its music director, Seiji Ozawa. Although he had conducted Japanese orchestras and visited Japan with three others from North America in the previous two decades, many Japanese did not regard him as highly as those abroad did. In their parlance he was not *nakami doshi* ("one of us"). His compatriots could not forget that when he returned to Japan in 1962 to conduct the orchestra of the Nihon Hoso Kyokai (NHK, or Japanese Broadcasting Corporation), after three years of study abroad, he treated Japan's most respected orchestra in a manner to which they were not accustomed. He had, in short, acquired Western ways of making music that offended older musicians. Although he continued to return to Japan to conduct other, less prestigious orchestras, the focus of his career centered in the West—Berlin, Salzburg, London, Paris, New York, Toronto, San Francisco, Chicago, and Boston.

When he went to Japan with the Boston Symphony, some questioned his holding so exalted a post as music director of the great Boston Symphony. Recalling what they regarded as the "golden age" of that orchestra under Charles Munch—Serge Koussevitzky had never conducted in Japan—the Japanese could not conceive that they would hear it under Ozawa as anything but an orchestra that had seen better days. One critic is reported to have explained attending the orchestra's first concert in 1978 solely out of curiosity to hear what was left of the once great orchestra of Munch.

In his concerts with the Boston Symphony, Ozawa established once and for all that he was a native son worthy of acceptance as truly *nakami doshi*. Even the most skeptical critics were bowled over by his Brahms and Berlioz, and Ozawa was deeply moved by his reception. In press interviews, he spoke with intense sentiment of his first teacher, Hideo Saito, who had died three years earlier. At the orchestra's farewell concert in Tokyo, Saito's widow sat in a place of honor, a picture of her late husband on a chair beside her. The concert over, Ozawa received the usual floral tributes from pretty girls in native costume, then stepped down from the stage, walked over and laid a spray of flowers before his teacher's portrait. The prodigal son had returned to triumph and was received again into the bosom of his people.

It was twenty years since Ozawa had boarded a Japanese freighter, the *Amaji-san Maru,* bound for Messina, Sicily, with a motor scooter, a guitar, and an ambition to pursue a career as an orchestra conductor. He left with the blessing, or more precisely at the urging, of his teacher, who recognized in young Seiji a talent such as had never before appeared in Japan.

Nowadays Seiji Ozawa speaks with great emotion of "my three old men," a term of deep respect to a Japanese. They were his father; his teacher, Hideo Saito; and the Alsatian-born conductor Charles Munch.

Ozawa's father was a dentist working in Hoten in Japanese-occupied Manchuria when his third son, Seiji, was born on September 1, 1935. Although his father was a Buddhist, his mother was a Presbyterian and brought the four boys up in her faith. All three of Seiji's brothers followed artistic or cultural pursuits. The eldest, who turned to his father's faith, is a sculptor who earns his living as an innkeeper. Another brother is a professor of German literature, and a third is an actor. As boys, the four Ozawa's sang in a Japanese version of the Golden Gate Quartet, learning gospel hymns from recordings. The family also lived for a time in Peking but eventually returned to Tokyo.

Close-harmony gospel singing aside, young Seiji's serious musical interest was the piano, which he first studied when he was eight. At six-teen he enrolled at the Toho Music School in Tokyo, and there en-countered the second of "my old men," Hideo Saito, who was head of the school.

Saito was typical of those Japanese who had embraced Western mu-sic during the years between the two world wars, when this completely foreign culture had a phenomenal vogue in certain limited circles in Japan. In the 1930s, the famous HMV "Society" recordings by pianist Artur Schnabel and singer Elena Gerhardt enjoyed surprising commercial success in Japan. Prince Hidemaro Konoye, after study abroad, founded the Imperial Music Academy and was the first Japanese conductor of Western classical music in Japan. Like Konoye, Saito studied in Ger-many, with the great cellist Emanuel Feuermann. However, the intro-duction of Western music did not come exclusively from Western Europe: a host of White Russian exiles passed from Siberia, through China, to Japan, and in many cases to the United States. Those who settled in Tokyo included a number of professional musicians who con-tributed greatly to establishing Western orchestral music in Japan be-fore and after World War II.

Ozawa has described Saito as the man to whom he owes the most: "The musical idea, his attitude toward music. He was absolutely great —in spirit, in inspiration, in his soul. He also had a very clear method about conducting technique. He taught that the conductor's hand must be like a language to the orchestra. The conductor must not use his mouth too much to the orchestra. That helped me a lot when I left Japan and went to Europe, because I did not speak any European lan-guage or English. I had to conduct and go through all those compe-titions, but he taught me how to handle an orchestra without words, just by my hands. Otherwise I couldn't make it."

Although young Seiji entered the Toho School to continue his piano studies, he suffered a serious injury to a finger while playing football. After he recovered, he could still play the piano, but the injury was such that it made a virtuoso career unlikely. Ozawa then concentrated on composition and conducting. At some point in his youth, Ozawa had encountered the sound of the symphony orchestra, both live and on records, an experience that was almost shattering for him. At the Toho School, most of the students studied stringed instruments, so the orchestra there was primarily a string ensemble. But it gave Ozawa his first opportunity to develop his natural talent for conducting, a talent enthusiastically encouraged by Saito. "I started with Haydn symphonies, Mozart serenades, the Tchaikovsky *Serenade,* the *Italian Serenade* of Wolf, and the Bartók *Divertimento."* The latter was one of the few contemporary works that Ozawa encountered in his early training. "The bad thing," he says, "was that I couldn't learn Mahler, Bruckner, or Wagner and all the big operas, which are difficult to learn. They are still difficult now."

However, there were several semiprofessional opera companies in Tokyo for whom Ozawa worked as piano accompanist in coaching and rehearsal of the singers. "Then, when they were secure, and everything was going very nice, the conductor would take over and the performance belonged to him." Years later, looking forward to his own first opera, Mozart's *Così fan Tutte* at Salzburg in 1969, he expressed a keen anticipation, "knowing that this time I get to conduct the performance too."

Nor did young Ozawa become well acquainted with traditional Japanese music and instruments, despite his family's early efforts to arouse that interest. Only after he was established as a conductor abroad and first encountered the concert music of such compatriots as Takemitsu which called for Japanese instruments did he seek out the native idiom during visits to Japan.

By the time he was twenty-four, Ozawa was recognized as an exceptional young musician. He had conducted both the Japan Philharmonic and the NHK Orchestras in concert and had been designated officially as the "outstanding talent" in Japanese music of 1958 by the NHK and the *Friends of Music Magazine.* But he was not content to remain a "local talent." Saito agreed and urged that he go to Europe for further study.

In the spring of 1959, Ozawa pursuaded a manufacturer to give him a motor scooter and pay part of his passage to help promote the vehicle in Europe; Ozawa washed dishes in the galley to pay the rest of his fare. He took along a guitar because he thought a musician should carry some sort of instrument. The *Amaji-san Maru* took nine weeks to reach Messina, where Ozawa disembarked. Traveling by scooter around Europe, earning money doing odd jobs, he eventually reached Paris, where he gravitated toward the Conservatoire. A student there, who later became his first wife, called to his attention a poster announcing a contest for young conductors to be held at Besançon. Ozawa entered the contest and won it, at the same time arousing the enthusiastic interest of the third of his "old men," Charles Munch. Another judge, Eugène Bigot, was a long-time fixture in Paris music circles; he gave Ozawa some lessons and helped secure for him some conducting engagements in France. More important, Munch, then conductor of the Boston Symphony, urged Ozawa to come to the Berkshire Music Center at Tanglewood the following summer.

There Ozawa worked with the student orchestra, often receiving comments on his work from Munch and Pierre Monteux. He attended rehearsals and concerts of the Boston Symphony conducted by Munch, Monteux, and others and had a chance to discuss these with the conductor and other teachers. He joined the Berkshire Festival Chorus and sang in a performance of the Beethoven Ninth Symphony. An old-timer in the Boston Symphony later recalled Ozawa as he was then: "He used to run around on his motor scooter, always busy, always on time." At the end of summer he was awarded the annual Koussevitzky prize as the best conducting student. Madame Olga Koussevitzky, the conductor's widow and long a familiar figure at Tanglewood, took an interest in Ozawa and promised to recommend him to Leonard Bernstein.

Meanwhile, in another competitive audition, Ozawa was awarded a year's scholarship to study with Herbert von Karajan in Berlin. This included monthly sessions with Karajan himself, access to all rehearsals of the Berlin Philharmonic, and a chance, every three weeks, to conduct the orchestra in semipublic performances. Although Ozawa's conducting was influenced by Karajan, he finds it difficult to define that verbally. "In Japan, I had been taught in a rather strict way," he has remarked. "Karajan taught me flexibility—particularly how to phrase in a long line, especially in Strauss, Mahler, Sibelius."

Late in 1960, Leonard Bernstein, filling an engagement in Berlin, caught up with Ozawa at Madame Koussevitzky's prompting. The immediate result of an amiable meeting was an exploration of Ozawa's becoming Bernstein's assistant with the Philharmonic for a tour of Japan in the spring of 1961. He made his first appearance with the Philharmonic in April 1961, in a concert that he shared with Bernstein. Although he conducted several of the Philharmonic's Young People's concerts during the next two seasons and joined Bernstein and another of his assistants, Maurice Peress, in a performance of Charles Ives's *Central Park in the Dark,* which requires three conductors, he did not actually conduct the Philharmonic in a concert of his own until the summer of 1963 at Lewissohn Stadium. The *New York Times* reported of that concert: "He controlled the ensemble with skill and flair that he has shown before, his hands seemingly everywhere at once giving precise cues. . . . [He is] at home in music that is bright and sparkling [and] likes to stress the excitement he finds in the score." Another *Times* reviewer described a later performance in the same series as "a very fine concert. . . . [Ozawa's] conducting was anything but arduous. There is a great deal more in him than flash. [But he is] still trying to sort out proper tempos for certain sections of the Tchaikovsky Fourth." Ozawa returned to conduct the New York Philharmonic regularly through 1971.

Shortly after Ozawa's arrival in New York, Bernstein introduced him to Ronald Wilford, the leading manager of conductors at Columbia Artists Management, who showed an immediate interest in him. Ozawa recalls being in Wilford's office on Fifty-seventh Street in 1961 when Harold Zellerbach, president of the San Francisco Symphony Association, arrived in a last-minute search for a conductor to replace Dmitri Shostakovich, who had suffered what might be called a "political cancellation." As Ozawa recalls, "Ronald said 'How about this guy?' I had an interview, and so he said, 'Ok, let's try one week.' So I flew out and conducted. That was the first time that I conducted a whole evening program of my own in the United States."

Wilford was to continue to play a very important role in Ozawa's career. More than merely a booking manager, Wilford serves, with certain key conductors on his list, as a close friend and adviser in personal and business matters, devising their most advantageous financial arrangements for tax purposes. With vigor, sometimes ruthlessness, and total commitment to the artistic and business interests of his clients, he may be said to conduct the career of his conductors as brilliantly as they conduct the orchestras with whom he negotiates contracts on their behalf. Ozawa relies upon him with total faith; their only differences arise in occasional fiercely contested tennis matches at Tanglewood.

During his earliest years with the New York Philharmonic, Ozawa also regularly guest-conducted the Montreal Symphony, in the years when Zubin Mehta was first its musical director. He was also beginning to conduct in Europe and was engaged by the Minneapolis Symphony. From 1964 on, he conducted regularly at Tanglewood, and he began to appear with the Boston Symphony during its winter season in Symphony Hall in 1969.

Ozawa also returned regularly to Japan, to visit his family and Saito and to do some conducting. When the West Berlin Opera Orchestra visited Tokyo on tour, he was invited to lead one of its concerts there. He also resumed his earlier contact with the NHK Symphony Orchestra but with rather unfortunate results. The NHK orchestra was the most prestigious in Japan; its players, many of them trained in Germany or in the German tradition, were well paid and considered themselves the elite of Japanese instrumental music. At first they welcomed Ozawa, a native son who had made good abroad and had studied with Karajan, who was fervently admired in Japan. But Ozawa soon antagonized these players in various ways unacceptable to them: his interpretations of the classics were not "correct" in their view; he asked them to play music unfamiliar to them, both old and new; and he insisted that they play in time and in tune. In short, he lacked the respect that a twenty-seven-year-old Japanese youth should have for his elders by insisting that they play music his way, not theirs.

(171)

Protesting what they regarded as the youth's arrogance and complaining that he was too prone to French and American methods, the players boycotted Ozawa's rehearsal. Tension was briefly relieved by official intervention, but according to the NHK account, Ozawa then demanded an apology in writing. The concerts were canceled, but Ozawa himself created wide publicity when he turned up on schedule on the empty concert hall stage, with a full panoply of newsmen and photographers. He claimed that he was honoring his side of the contract, regardless of the action of the NHK and players: "I want to conduct an orchestra the way I think music should be," he told a *Time* correspondent. The NHK concertmaster dismissed Ozawa as "simply a poor conductor." Soon after, Ozawa sued the NHK, which has yet to invite him to conduct again. Nevertheless, when Ozawa visited Japan in 1975 with the San Francisco Symphony Orchestra, the NHK telecast one of their concerts.

However, Ozawa has continued to conduct in Japan, mostly with the Japan Philharmonic Orchestra, a player-governed cooperative in Tokyo. With that group he has played a repertory that the critic of an English-language periodical regarded as the most stimulating to be heard in Japan. On the number of occasions, Ozawa's programs included selections, such as Berlioz's *Lélio,* the Mahler Eighth, and Mozart's *Così fan Tutte* in concert form, that he was to program later in Boston or San Francisco. The Toho School and Saito remained major interests for Ozawa in Tokyo, and in 1964 he conducted the Toho String Orchestra during a tour of the United States. Nor did he confine his activities to Tokyo: he has at various times conducted orchestras in Osaka and Sapporo. More recently he has been working with a Japanese opera company that performs in Japanese. Its repertory has included *Boris Godunov,* given its premiere in Japan, and a concert performance of Bach's *St. Matthew Passion.* Ozawa feels that certain operas in the standard repertory might not go well with Japanese singers: he doubts if *Rigoletto* would be convincing and is not quite sure of *Carmen;* on the other hand, *Madama Butterfly* has always been popular in Japan. The company with which he works has perpetual financial problems, and Ozawa hopes to see it more firmly established.

Meanwhile, Ozawa's American career moved ahead securely in the mid-1960s because of a combination of Wilford's skillful guidance and Ozawa's talent for capitalizing on the "breaks" that came his way. One of these came in the same summer of 1963 that he first conducted the New York Philharmonic in Lewissohn Stadium. Georges Prêtre canceled a week of concerts with the Chicago Symphony Orchestra during the summertime Ravinia Festival.

To a large extent at that time, the artistic policy of this festival was dominated by a board of laymen, then headed by advertising executive Earle Ludgin. When Prêtre canceled on forty-eight hours' notice, it fell to Ludgin to secure a replacement for a symphony week at Ravinia, and he pressed Wilford, who was Prêtre's manager, to find a replacement of "international stature." Ludgin recalls suggesting one such conductor after the other, only to have Wilford explain why that particular musician was tied up elsewhere; and each time Wilford would end his explanation by singing the praises of an unknown Japanese conductor who, Wilford assured Ludgin, would be a sensation. Time being short and failing any more attractive prospect, Ludgin agreed to engage Ozawa, despite his typically Chicagoan misgivings about engaging an assistant conductor of the New York Philharmonic. The result was as Wilford predicted. Moreover, before the summer was out, Ludgin proudly announced that beginning in the summer of 1964, Seiji Ozawa would be artistic director of the Ravinia Festival.

Ozawa's five seasons at Ravinia were highly successful in a number of respects. He and the Chicago Symphony got on very well. The orchestra's recording activity had declined considerably after the death of Fritz Reiner, and both parties welcomed the opportunity for the orchestra to record with Ozawa, first for RCA and later for EMI-Angel. Moreover, the young conductor now had an American post where he could control the repertory, soloists, and guests and not have to take what was left over after a musical director had made his choices. For the Ravinia sponsors, Ozawa was the drawing card that they needed. Although he did not conduct all of the concerts, he appeared more than any of the guests. Moreover, working with Ludgin and the board of directors, he made some progress in planning a festival-type summer

(173)

season, rather than a succession of events. "I want to move in the direction of Tanglewood," he told an interviewer from the *New York Times* as he was beginning his tenure at Ravinia. "I want music to speak out at Ravinia. I want to show its versatility and its many faces." In retrospect, the reference to Tanglewood was ominous for Ravinia; that same summer of 1964, Ozawa returned as guest conductor of the Boston Symphony Orchestra at Tanglewood, where four years earlier he had been a student.

While the suburbanites who supported Ravinia with contributions and fervent attendance found him charismatic or at least "cute," the usually cantankerous Chicago music press welcomed him with open arms. They were delighted with his enterprising repertory and the quality of his performances despite cramped rehearsals. When Ozawa finally departed from Ravinia the critic of the *Sun-Times* glowed retrospectively, "So much of his work at Ravinia was brilliant improvisation, a high-wire act based on his own confidence and in his baton technique and the ability of the [Chicago Symphony Orchestra] to follow wherever he led them."

Although close to thirty when he arrived at Ravinia, Ozawa seemed much younger—fragile, delicately slender, willowy on the podium and, away from it, resembling a teenager in his moods and pleasures. He drove a white Mustang convertible with obvious élan, often to join friends in downtown Chicago for an Italian dinner or to enjoy an early-morning session of jazz on the Near North Side.

Originally calling for three seasons through 1966, Ozawa's contract was extended for another three, through 1969. In 1968, however, when another renewal should have been discussed, Ozawa asked to be released from part of the 1969 season in order to accept an invitation to conduct a new Jean-Pierre Ponnelle production of Mozart's *Così fan Tutte* at the Salzburg Festival. The release was granted on condition that he return as guest conductor in 1970. Already—as Ozawa, Wilford, and the Ravinia trustees knew—the conductor was considering a move to Tanglewood, where in 1970 he would become codirector with Gunther Schuller of the Berkshire Music Center. In 1969, however, he spent a busy fortnight with the Chicago Symphony—two weeks of concerts at

Ravinia and six recording sessions for EMI-Angel. There he was off to Salzburg for his first opera production.

By this time Ozawa's commitments were beginning to overlap. In the fall of 1964, after his first summer as director at Ravinia, he was a guest conductor with the Toronto Symphony Orchestra, which was looking for a successor to Walter Susskind. Again he had instant success; again negotiations followed, this time for Ozawa to become musical director of the Toronto Symphony beginning in the fall of 1965, a post that meshed nicely with Ravinia. Aside from convenient winter-summer scheduling, he could spread the same repertory over two different posts. Even before Ozawa assumed his duties as music director at Toronto, he joined that orchestra on a two-week overseas tour to the Commonwealth Arts Festival in Great Britain. There the critic of the *Sunday Times* reported, "Under Seiji Ozawa the Toronto Symphony gave one of the most stunning concerts I have yet heard on the South Bank. . . . [They] brought an unexpected element to a homely festival—orchestral virtuosity of the international class."

In four seasons with the Toronto Symphony, Ozawa won the hearts of his audience. The subscription season of the orchestra expanded both in number of concerts and in the size of its audience. The orchestra toured within Canada and to the eastern United States, winning praise for both the orchestra and the conductor in Carnegie Hall. As the wife of one player put it, "There is the most beautiful love affair going on between Mr. Ozawa and the members of the orchestra. They are giving 150 percent of themselves to each other." In 1968 he conducted the Toronto Symphony Orchestra on a tour of Japan.

But the demand for Ozawa's services was also growing elsewhere. He first conducted the Philadelphia Orchestra in 1965 and continued to appear with it as guest at the Academy of Music through 1972; at one point, reports of Eugene Ormandy's admiration for him fired rumors that he was heir apparent in Philadelphia. He was returning to Japan regularly for concerts with the Japan Philharmonic or its successor, the New Japan Philharmonic, which on one occasion he conducted in five performances in as many days of the Beethoven Ninth Symphony. Moreover, he was active with the New York Philharmonic.

(175)

But, possibly most important at that time, was the growing interest in Ozawa on the part of the San Francisco Symphony. To no one's surprise, Ozawa informed the Toronto Symphony in 1968 that he would not renew his contract when it expired in the summer of 1969.

Ozawa's first appearance with the San Francisco Symphony Orchestra, when Wilford persuaded Zellerbach to book Ozawa as a substitute for Shostakovich in 1961, was the beginning of a mutually happy but sometimes stormy relation between the young Japanese and the city of San Francisco. At times it took on many of the characteristics of a love affair—a courtship the outcome of which was sometimes in doubt; competition from other suitors; and a strained alliance that ended in a separation that saddened both parties.

Philip S. Boone, Zellerbach's successor as president of the San Francisco Symphony Association, recalls the extraordinary impression Ozawa made on his first appearance, an impression reinforced on each occasion that he returned as guest conductor. The city, facing as it does toward the Orient and accustomed as is no other American city to everyday dealing with resident and visiting Orientals, extended a warm welcome to Ozawa. Moreover, San Francisco has always looked askance culturally at Los Angeles, where, just as Ozawa was making his first San Francisco appearance, the Philharmonic was acquiring in Zubin Mehta a young resident conductor from the exotic East. Moreover, since Pierre Monteux's departure in 1952, the orchestra had failed to find leadership that would cement solid community support and respect: though able conductors, each in his own way, neither Enrique Jorda nor Josef Krips earned the kind of success that the orchestra and community wanted.

By 1966, Boone and many others were convinced that Ozawa would be an ideal conductor for San Francisco, especially because he had acquired valuable artistic and administrative experience at Ravinia and Toronto. Once he had reached this conclusion, Boone recalls, he had considerable difficulty in pinning Ronald Wilford to a definite commitment or timetable. Finally, at Boone's request, Wilford came to

San Francisco in 1967 for what was mutually understood to be a decisive discussion of Ozawa's future with the San Francisco Symphony Orchestra. At this point, Ozawa's commitments at Ravinia and Toronto were drawing to a close. Although Boone may have had an inkling of possible Boston interest in Ozawa, Wilford must have been clearly aware of it. (Boston was at that time going through its post-Leinsdorf sharing of William Steinberg with the Pittsburgh Symphony). Moreover, Leonard Bernstein was leaving the New York Philharmonic and Ozawa's name was on speculative short lists as his successor. However, Ozawa quite firmly disclaimed any interest in the New York post: "I don't think I would want the job at this point. I have a lot of conducting to do, and I enjoy moving around. Besides, where do you go from the New York Philharmonic?"

The result of Wilford's visit was that negotiations for Ozawa and a gentlemanly termination of Krips's services proceeded in due course toward a successful conclusion. By the time the association was ready to announce Ozawa's engagement, it was embroiled in a work stoppage at the beginning of the 1968–69 season. When the negotiations with the union and players became acrimonious, Joseph L. Alioto, then mayor of San Francisco, stepped in. During one all-night session at his home, he asked the members of the negotiating committee, "If you had your choice of any conductor you know anywhere, whom would you choose?" The answer was clear—Seiji Ozawa. Once the stoppage was over and concerts were resumed, the association announced Ozawa's appointment as music director, effective in the fall of 1970.

Much to the delight of San Franciscans, Ozawa did everything possible to become one of them. He and his second wife, Vera, bought a home high up in the Twin Peaks section of the city, with a view of the Golden Gate Bridge, the city, San Francisco Bay, and the region beyond it, all spread out in a dramatic panorama. It was a view that Ozawa, normally a reluctant interviewee, delighted in describing, with gestures, to the press. There, in due time, two children—a boy and a girl, Yukiyoshi and Seira—were born to him and Vera. There was no doubt that San Francisco held a very special place in his affections because of its Oriental and cosmopolitan flavor, the beauty of its physical setting, its sophistication, and the warmth with which he was received everywhere.

And Now Ozawa! announced the posters, brochures, and billboards that flooded the city when he took over the orchestra. Attendance at symphony concerts in the War Memorial Opera House broke all records, each year higher than the last; in his second season, attendance reached an unprecedented 93 percent of capacity. The media fondly reported his doings, his idiosyncrasies, and his colorful personality. The orchestra, long overshadowed in glamour by the San Francisco Opera with which it shared the Opera House and competed for philanthropic support, shook off the staid reputation it had had under Ozawa's predecessors. Ozawa, whose physical appearance had been "square" and conservative in his early Ravinia and Toronto days, now presented the image of a high-culture hippie—a shaggy mop of hair, dhakshi shirts, cowboy boots, beads. For evening concerts he wore not the customary starched wing-collar shirt but a glossy white knit turtleneck. He arrived at rehearsals wearing Levi's, Italian leather boots, and a loose shirt with Japanese lettering.

In Toronto, Ravinia, and San Francisco, Ozawa's repertory was decidedly individual. During his six seasons as music director in San Francisco, for instance, he conducted no Schubert symphonies, only three by Beethoven, but six of Mozart and fourteen of Haydn. He scheduled virtually no major music by Mendelssohn or Schumann, but played all four symphonies and the *German Requiem* of Brahms. Always a colorful interpreter of Berlioz, a composer much favored by his mentor Charles Munch, Ozawa offered a broad representation of the French master's concert music, plus *Béatrice et Bénédict*. There were two symphonies of Ives and three by Mahler, including the Eighth. To honor the hundredth anniversary of Schoenberg's birth, he programmed virtually all of that composer's orchestral music, including a splendid performance of *Gurrelieder*; no other American orchestra matched Ozawa's San Francisco in so lavishly paying tribute to one of the towering figures of twentieth-century music. He also played a great deal of Richard Strauss, Bartók, Debussy, and Ravel. In this six-year span, he also surveyed the full range of Stravinsky's evolving styles. He was obviously building his repertory: except for concertos, usually chosen by soloists, Ozawa repeated only four works during this period—Beethoven's *Eroica*, the *Daphnis et Chloé* of Ravel, *Le Sacre du Printemps*, and the *Symphonic Dances* from Bernstein's *West Side Story*.

Under Ozawa, the San Francisco Symphony began to regain the international repute it had not enjoyed since the departure of Pierre Monteux in 1952. During his service there, the orchestra made a few recordings for Philips and Deutsche Grammophon, both companies with which Ozawa was making records with other orchestras. In 1973, he and the orchestra toured Europe, including the Soviet Union, and, in the following year, Japan, which the orchestra had previously visited with Krips and where Ozawa had already toured with the Toronto Symphony and the New York Philharmonic. These recordings and tours greatly enhanced the pride that the city took in the revival of its orchestra under Ozawa.

In San Francisco, Ozawa had a better chance than in his previous posts to demonstrate his ability to develop a truly polished virtuoso orchestra sound. Whereas he was recalled in Toronto as having produced a rather raw tone from the orchestra, the San Francisco critics commented on how successfully he improved the string sound of the orchestra. Ozawa attributes his sensitivity to strings to his early training at the Toho School, where the orchestra with which he worked consisted mainly of strings. Moreover, says Ozawa, he has been very lucky in both San Francisco and Boston with the concertmasters who were already there when he arrived. "Two really great string players—first Stuart Canin in San Francisco, then Joseph Silverstein in Boston. Canin and I worked very closely to make the strings sound great. After all, you can have great wind soloists, great percussionists, but the conductor's basic work is the strings of the orchestra—bowing, vibrato, intonation."

From his first appearance in San Francisco, Ozawa was warmly welcomed by the media. Columnists such as Herb Caen mentioned him frequently, and the newspaper music critics—the *Chronicle* and *Examiner* had at least two each—were generally delighted with his work,

(179)

although they modified their praise when Ozawa carried the orchestra beyond its depth or what was felt to be the bounds of good taste. When Ozawa began his last stint of guest-conducting, before actually becoming music director, Robert Commanday wrote in the *Chronicle*:

> Ozawa is where the excitement is, and vice versa, even when he miscalculates. . . . Haydn's melodies, too, acquire a special kind of lilt as Ozawa finds in them their exact points of weightlessness. . . . The orchestra changes its style for him, playing so that they carry through the tone more (in the von Karajan manner), tapering off or lingering past the ends of phrases, thus implying musical continuance through the text. . . . [In the Mussorgsky-Ravel *Pictures at an Exhibition*] his conducting was the performance, captivating for its characterization, of all that was happening, peeping chicks, minstrel song, quarreling, gossiping, etc. The orchestra, which followed him happily down the primrose path in fullness of spirit, was not used to balancing and controlling tone and intonation at this level. Its weaknesses glared. . . . The performance was both vivid and rough.

In his first season as music director, Ozawa programmed the Scriabin *Prometheus—Poem of Fire* with a light show that followed the composer's own notation in the score. Except for lights on the music stands borrowed from the opera pit, the stage and auditorium were in darkness to heighten the effect of the play of colored lights. Hewell Tircuit reviewed the performance for the *Chronicle*:

> Brilliant! Absolutely faithful to the composer in style, and awesome to behold. Those lights, that 120-piece orchestra representing the cosmos around man (the solo piano), as he searched for intelligence (or fire) was an astounding accomplishment.

Reviewing the performance of the Brahms Third Symphony early in 1974 Arthur Bloomfield declared in the *Examiner*:

> As far as the orchestra is concerned, well, Ozawa had nursed it through a necessary period of loosening up following the Krips regime and, on

top of that, created a bigger, rounder, warmer sound than subscribers had previously heard. . . . I could not help feeling that the San Francisco Symphony is moving toward the style of the Philadelphia Orchestra of Stokowski's time. Not all the way, of course, because our band doesn't sound that lush—which is probably a blessing—but the local emphasis on mellowness is more "old Philly" than the steely modern Cleveland, which is okay with me.

But, in this Garden of Eden, there was the inevitable serpent— two of them in fact, the Boston Symphony Orchestra and the stubborn power of the musicians of the San Francisco Symphony Orchestra.

Thomas D. Perry, the long-time manager of the Boston Symphony, has said that the union of Seiji Ozawa and the Boston Symphony was preordained when the young conductor arrived at Tanglewood in 1960. A protégé of Charles Munch, well liked by the orchestra, adored by the audience, and admired by management, Ozawa soon established himself, first at Tanglewood and, after 1969, at Symphony Hall, with the trustees of the orchestra as a young man with a future in Boston. Although he had been through the Philadelphia rumor mill in the late 1960s, along with Zubin Mehta, his direction Boston-ward was clearly indicated in 1969 when it was announced that he would be codirector of the Berkshire Music Center beginning in 1970, the summer before actually becoming music director in San Francisco. If that did not arouse worries in San Francisco, certainly the announcement from Boston two years later, that Ozawa would become music director of the orchestra there in 1973, did. When the story of the Boston appointment was prematurely leaked in the media, indicating that he was leaving San Francisco, Ozawa flew westward between rehearsals and concerts in Philadelphia, to promise the orchestra players personally that he had no intention of deserting them.

To be sure, there were reassurances that the young conductor would be a "two-castle man," as described in a *Time* article, directing both orchestras. However, Ozawa had to cancel a few concerts in San Francisco because of a strained neck suffered from having to bend his head backward while rehearsing the chorus and orchestra of La Scala in the Mahler Eighth Symphony. For some time he had to wear a stiff neckbrace. With his dual duties in Boston and San Francisco, plus increasing guest engagements abroad, it is said that Ozawa was traveling fifty thousand miles a year. There were reports, and not only in jest, that he was studying the scores for his next engagement in midair.

Nevertheless, San Francisco tried to put a good face on sharing Ozawa with Boston. In a March 1974 article entitled "Why Isn't Ozawa Here More Often?" Tircuit wrote:

> First of all, . . . he can be shared. Secondly, the concept of a music director sitting on his orchestra like a faithful hen hatching is thoroughly dead in our time. The only way that that can be managed is if the conductor is so poor that he has no guest offers, or if a maestro is so apprehensive that guest conductors might show him up.
>
> Ozawa conducts more San Francisco Symphony concerts per season than the vast majority of American music directors. He leads fourteen of twenty-four weeks of subscription concerts. . . . Ozawa may not be here as much as we would like, but he gives the Symphony better measure for the money than most. . . . His other posts have nothing to do with the situation. We can have him for fourteen weeks a season or not at all. . . . There are those who enjoy panic, and have convinced themselves that Ozawa will pull up stakes and decamp for Boston. I don't.

Two months later, the announcement of plans for the 1974–75 season called for Ozawa to conduct thirteen weeks—"a shade more than he will be giving his other orchestra, the Boston Symphony, during the winter of 1974–75," reported the *Examiner*. Ozawa's schedule in San Francisco was further reduced the following season to eleven weeks, less than he was spending that winter in Symphony Hall.

Meanwhile, in an effort to bolster the musical leadership of the orchestra, its management and board announced in May 1974 the engagement of Edo de Waart as principal guest conductor, beginning with six weeks in 1975–76. De Waart had enjoyed success as guest conductor in San Francisco, and his choice for a position paralleling that of Colin Davis in Boston and Carlo Maria Giulini in Chicago was widely hailed. By the summer of 1975 the conducting staff of the San Francisco, on hand or in prospect, included Ozawa as music director, de Waart as principal guest conductor beginning that fall, Niklaus Wyss as resident conductor, and David Ramadanoff as assistant conductor.

The final blow, by now generally expected, came in July 1975 with Ozawa's announcement that the following season would be his last as music director of the San Francisco Symphony. He stopped off on his way to Japan to disclose this personally to some forty players of the orchestra hastily assembled for the purpose. In 1976–77, he would conduct ten weeks, serving as musical adviser but without administrative duties. After 1977, he would be available for as much as six weeks a season as guest conductor, but actually has not conducted there since early 1978. "I love San Francisco," Ozawa declared in announcing his decision. "I'll keep my house here. What a city for an Oriental! For anybody, but especially for an Oriental. And the orchestra is now playing fantastically too. But a music director should stay longer with his musicians." Many San Franciscans agreed with this last statement, wished that he had chosen their city, but recognized, in spite of their own feelings, that no conductor in his right mind would choose San Francisco over Boston.

The question of administrative duties had developed between Ozawa and the San Francisco Symphony Association rather early in his tenure as music director. They became a serious problem in the personnel crisis of 1974, which some felt might have been avoided or at least alleviated had Ozawa been on hand at every step of the rather complicated procedures stipulated in the contract between the association and the musicians' union. On the other hand, others feel that Ozawa was expected to deal with administrative matters—admittedly having artistic implications—that could or should have been handled by the orchestra's management. On this question, as on all other aspects of what has come to be known as the Jones-Nakagawa affair, Ozawa is extremely reticent.

The nationally publicized confrontation between the San Francisco Symphony Association and the players of the orchestra had its roots in the very powerful, and in some respects unique, position that the players and their union had established in successive working agreements with the association. If this reflected to some degree a willingness of the association to make concessions, it also reflected the fact that the musicians' union was a strong one in a city well known as a "union town." Members of the union and orchestra players like to recall that in the mid-1930s, when the San Francisco Symphony was virtually bankrupt, it was the musicians' union that spearheaded a political campaign to secure tax support for the orchestra, one of the first such steps taken in the United States.

Like local unions the world over, the musicians of San Francisco had long limited the ability of the symphony orchestra to import players from other cities in and out of the United States in competition with local talent. Once that restriction was relaxed in 1968, the musicians sought further implementation of their concession in 1972. In an effort to promote harmony between the players, management, association, and conductor, the association ceded virtual veto power over granting permanent tenure to new players after a probationary period; in effect, both the conductor and the players had to agree to retain such players. This players' veto was unique among American orchestras.

Since Ozawa refuses to discuss the matter, it is impossible to determine how aware he was of these restrictions on his authority when he agreed to come to San Francisco. In his first years as music director, he succeeded in making some important personnel changes, and when the orchestra's tympanist was hired away by the New York Philharmonic, he engaged Elayne Jones, a New York musician who had played in Stokowski's American Symphony Orchestra and was free-lancing in New York. He also engaged as first bassoonist Ryohel Nakagawa, who held that post at the New York City Opera. Early in 1974, when the time came for the orchestra to confirm these players for permanent tenure, they were turned down overwhelmingly by the committee and later by the full orchestra, although several other players were approved. In the orchestra committee vote, it was obvious that a majority of the seven members had assigned extremely low scores to both Jones and Nakagawa. Ozawa himself felt that they deserved higher rating and was amazed at the committee's opinion. At that time, he made it clear publicly that he firmly believed that both players deserved permanent status in the orchestra.

There is no question that this rejection reflected two factors. In the first place, Nakagawa was the first Japanese to join the orchestra and Jones was both a woman and a black, minorities long underrepresented in American orchestras, especially in principal positions. A second factor was that many players in the orchestra saw in Jones and Nakagawa an opportunity to undermine Ozawa, who was rumored to have a list of players in the orchestra whom he wanted to replace or demote. Such reports, whether true or not, unquestionably created insecurity.

Even before the Jones-Nakagawa affair, Ozawa had made important personnel changes. Some players thought he had gone far enough. Said one, quoted in the *New York Times* in June 1974, "Ozawa sure ain't happy. These two were his favorites, and it's a slap in his face. . . . Today we get the transient conductor. They fly all over the country; they play here only ten or twelve weeks a year. They bring in all the stars they can, kick out anyone they want, and then, whoops, they are gone. A couple of years later they move on to bigger things and you are left with whatever is left, if you are left."

However, both the press and the public were strongly on the side of the two players and, by inference, of Ozawa. At each concert, as the musicians took their places on the Opera House stage, a round of applause from the audience greeted the appearance of Jones and Nakagawa. Alexander Fried, dean of the city's music critics, writing in the *Examiner,* quoted George Szell: "A conductor can't be a good guy and make a great orchestra." In March 1975, while both players were in a second probationary period, Commanday wrote in the *Chronicle,* "Meanwhile Ryohei Nakagawa and Ms. Jones continued to play beautifully on a par with the best of their 'peers' and under emotional strain and pressure which must be horrendous. At the same time, their colleagues continued to defend the principle of home rule, the sanctity of the contract, and the committee's rights in the face of a higher principle of what is musically just."

Although Nakagawa was not inclined to file legal charges, Elayne Jones did not hesitate to accuse her colleagues in the orchestra, the union, and the association of discrimination on grounds of race and sex and brought suit to regain her post in the orchestra. For a year, while the case was pending in the courts, both Jones and Nakagawa were "rehired" on probation. In the fall of 1975, the court ordered another vote on Jones by the players' committee—one that would settle the matter. The vote went heavily against Jones, who sued again and lost again, this time with Ozawa stating that he agreed with the vote of the orchestra committee. He has never explained his change of mind on Jones's qualifications.

In an interview for the *New York Times* on the occasion of his fortieth birthday, a month after he announced his departure from San Francisco, Ozawa made one of his rare public references to this affair: "The Elayne Jones case really did not force me to leave San Francisco. What wears you down is all the administration work that music directors have to do now—auditions, meeting with the union, talking with the Symphony Association, all that. San Francisco wants a music director who can spend more time there, and they are right. I think a music director should stay longer with one orchestra for long periods instead of flying back and forth. Maybe age has something to do with it, but I like it better this way. Besides, you get more work, more recordings."

His duties at Ravinia and in Toronto and San Francisco did not keep Ozawa from filling important engagements in the United States and abroad. He conducted the New York Philharmonic frequently, both in New York and on tours of the United States and to Japan. For ten years following his Philadelphia debut he conducted that orchestra regularly in the Academy of Music, Robin Hood Dell, and Saratoga. During and after his Ravinia tenure, he also appeared with the Chicago Symphony in its winter season in Orchestra Hall. Although his San Francisco contract apparently permitted him to guest-conduct extensively, this activity has virtually ceased in the United States since he settled in Boston.

In Europe, his early connection with Karajan led to regular appearances with the Berlin Philharmonic, both in Berlin and Salzburg. He has also been a frequent guest conductor of the Orchestre de Paris and, at the time of Solti's resignation in 1974, was rumored to have been offered the directorship of that orchestra before Barenboim was engaged. He has, in any event, made a number of recordings with it in recent years as a part of his Deutsche Grammophon contract.

Ozawa has given relatively little attention to opera. He has conducted staged performances of *Così fan Tutte* at Salzburg in 1969 and Tchaikovsky's *Eugene Onegin* at Covent Garden in 1974. The former, which caused him to curtail his Ravinia work, is one of the skeletons in Ozawa's artistic closet; it was, from all accounts, a dismal failure. More successful was the Covent Garden performance, related no doubt to the fact that the music director of the Royal Opera, Colin Davis, is Ozawa's principal guest conductor in Boston. His return to Covent Garden in the spring of 1978 for a new production of *Rigoletto* was canceled when it became impossible to assemble a satisfactory cast; Ozawa hopes that this will be reinstated in the near future. Ozawa conducted partly staged concert versions of both *Così* and *Onegin* at Tanglewood and elsewhere; the Mozart opera, in particular, was very successful at Tanglewood. In addition, he has presented similar performances of Ravel's *L'Enfant et les Sortilèges* and Berlioz's *Béatrice et Bénédict* and the first act of Wagner's *Die Walküre*. There is no question that opera appeals to Ozawa, but he has yet to find a sustained milieu for his interest. That may develop in Paris, where he is doing a double bill of *L'Enfant et les Sortilèges* and Stravinsky's *Oedipus Rex* in 1979 and has been booked for a 1980 premiere of a new and as yet untitled opera by Olivier Messiaen.

Ozawa generally conducts the Boston Symphony Orchestra in ten out of twenty-two subscription weeks at Boston, plus several weeks on tour to New York and other cities during the season. Colin Davis, as principal guest conductor for at least four subscription weeks, also tours with the orchestra. In addition, Ozawa is director of the Berkshire Music Center at Tanglewood, a combined summer music festival and summer school for the training of advanced music students. Traditionally, since Koussevitzky founded the center, the music director of the Boston Symphony has been its director. This scheme was interrupted when William Steinberg, dividing his time between the Boston and

Pittsburgh orchestras while in failing health, was unable to accept the Berkshire summer responsibility. From 1970 until he became music director of the Boston Symphony, Ozawa was codirector with Gunther Schuller of the Berkshire Music Center. Leonard Bernstein, whose association with the center goes back to its earliest days, was adviser to Ozawa and Schuller. However, once Ozawa began his Boston Symphony tenure, he also became sole director of the center. Although Schuller remains in charge of its educational aspect, Ozawa takes an interest in it and, on occasion, conducts the student orchestra.

Of all American orchestras, the Boston Symphony has the greatest diversity of activity—the Boston Pops and Esplanade Concerts under Arthur Fiedler; the summer program at Tanglewood; the Boston Symphony Chamber Players; and extensive radio and television productions. As music director of the Boston Symphony, Ozawa has overall direction of all these undertakings, although demands on him vary greatly since some, such as Fiedler's Pops, have become virtually self-contained. Nevertheless, the administrative demands on Ozawa in Boston seem to be less onerous than they were in San Francisco. The Boston management recognizes where Ozawa needs help in artistic administration; with its substantially larger staff, it can relieve him of many details he found trying in San Francisco. Moreover, the orchestra personnel situation in Boston is, to say the least, less of an adversary one between players and management. Boston feels secure in having Ozawa, and Ozawa feels secure there—conditions that seldom prevailed in San Francisco.

A special warmth seems to surround Ozawa at Symphony Hall. When Ozawa's father fell ill in Tokyo, Perry insisted that he leave for Japan immediately despite the fact that a concert was scheduled that night. When Ozawa worried about the program, the soloist, and other details, Perry and his staff took over all the problems, and Ozawa was confident that they would be handled as well as if he had been on the scene. When he describes his pleasure in the family home in Newton, he expresses his gratitude to the Perrys for having helped find it. He is chauffeured to and from it in a limousine bearing the seal of the

Boston Symphony Orchestra on its front doors. Unquestionably the "care and feeding" of conductors is a fine art in Boston.

Although Ozawa is relatively young and the product of a culture alien to that in which the players of the Boston Symphony Orchestra were brought up, there is an extraordinary understanding between him and them. This is akin to Perry's feeling that Ozawa became a prospect for the Boston Symphony Orchestra from the day he first arrived at Tanglewood in 1960. The players have seen and heard him grow up as a conductor, and it is hard for them not to assume an almost parental feeling toward the still frail-looking young man. Such familiarity might breed contempt were it not that Ozawa's talent is so extraordinary, his command of the orchestra so deep and firm.

Ozawa's first hero is his teacher Saito, whose influence, one gathers, was as much idealistic as it was technical. After Saito, another "old man" is Charles Munch, not only in gratitude for helping him very early in his career but also for the sincerity for the feeling that he conveyed in his conducting; Munch's influence is also reflected in Ozawa's fondness for the music of Berlioz. Karajan is another conductor to whom Ozawa is indebted artistically; the special polish that he obtains from the Boston Symphony Orchestra nowadays is definitely analogous to Karajan's work with the Berlin Philharmonic. However, he does not subscribe to Karajan's way of conducting with his eyes closed: "That takes a lot of time to master," he says. "I do it with my gestures, my eyes, my body, and some feeling. You can't control a hundred musicians with one baton."

Even if English came more easily to him, Ozawa would probably nunicate with his orchestra physically rather than ver players and audience alike have observed that Ozawa is a completely natural-born conductor, bodily and by temperament. Harry Ellis Dickson, in his delightful book on the orchestra and its conductors, *Gentlemen, More Dolce Please,* says that of all conductors whom he has played under in his many years with the Boston Symphony Orchestra, Ozawa has the greatest natural gift. But no man can conduct by instinct alone, and Ozawa has developed an impressive conducting technique. Despite what seems to be the spontaneity of many of his performances, he rehearses in close detail. He has a keen ear for intonation, timbre, and balance and will work over a passage with separate sections of the orchestra before blending them. He obviously has a clear idea of the components of the sound he wants, because the final combination seldom needs additional polishing.

Ozawa is at his best in romantic and early twentieth-century music, although his Haydn series at San Francisco was widely praised. He has a special flair for the orchestral virtuosity of Berlioz, Mahler, Ravel, and Stravinsky but can be surprisingly effective in Brahms as well. His performances of Schoenberg, especially *Gurrelieder,* have had great audience impact. Similarly he has had great success with the music of Messiaen, especially the *Turangalîla* Symphony, which he recorded with the Toronto Symphony. He feels no special obligation to explore contemporary music in general, preferring to play the few scores that appeal to him. However, as part of a six-orchestra commissioning project supported by the National Endowment for the Arts, he was committed to performing five new compositions commissioned by other orchestras.

Ozawa's performances have received a mixed press, especially in New York. Although his Berlioz has been frequently praised, Irving Kolodin of the *Saturday Review* felt that his 1969 reading of the Requiem "fluctuated between the flamboyant and the frustrating." On the other hand, Donal Henahan of the *Times* was very favorably impressed by a New York concert by the Boston Symphony under Ozawa in 1974:

Any good conductor knows what a major orchestra can do and how to get it to perform up to the top level of its ability. A few superior conductors are somehow able to seduce an orchestra into playing better than it knows it can, and knows what to do when such transcendental accidents take place. Ozawa as the Boston Symphony's musical director had his musicians operating beyond even their own lofty levels at Avery Fisher Hall on Wednesday night.

Boston critics have been more measured in their assessment of Ozawa; after all, they hear him more frequently, on his good days and on his bad days, not just when he is "on show" with the Boston Symphony in New York. Early in Ozawa's tenure as music director in Boston, Michael Steinberg wrote for the *Boston Globe* a comprehensive comment on his work:

Ozawa himself is a huge success with the players and with the public. He has a good ear, a clear and ready technique, abundant vitality and charm. Orchestras enjoy working with him and they really play for him. . . . The orchestra, in a high state of morale and strong condition technically, played beautifully this past season—it should have been still more beautiful if Ozawa had insisted on a real pianissimo—with only rare lapses from a standard that has not been obtained here for twenty years.

As an interpreter, Ozawa defies generalization. It is tempting to say that he excels in flashy repertory—Ravel, Tchaikovsky, Rachmaninoff, *Firebird*, and such things—but that would be selling short one of the great Brahms conductors of these years. It also fails to take into account his failure, by the most demanding standards, with Berlioz, Debussy, and Mahler, where he delivers the brilliant surface but not often much else. He is less pressured than he was a few years ago into performing pieces he is not quite finished learning, but even now he occasionally gives the impression that he has not thought deeply and not enough. Pieces whose coherence hinges on getting the relationships of tempi to one another right—Verdi's Requiem and Schoenberg's *Transfigured Night*, for example—suffer from the shallowness of his consideration and misunderstanding of questions of tempo and musical character.

Steinberg's successor at the *Boston Globe,* Richard Dyer, recently expressed the opinion that Ozawa has become a less interesting conductor than he was earlier, although he continues to polish the ensemble playing of the orchestra. In the summer of 1978, Dyer wrote a long article summing up his view of Ozawa, in which he said in part:

It is, of course, impossible to go along with those who say that Ozawa is a bad conductor, because there is no sense in which that is true. . . . Ozawa knows how to create an instant rapport with the orchestra, music and audience. His body is a superb instrument of communication. . . . Ozawa has a vital sense of instrumental color and he knows how to build an orchestra and how to keep it trim. . . . I have never heard a BSO musician express personal dislike for the musical director, and the work they do for him, when roused, invalidates Goddard Lieberson's famous remark, "Show me an orchestra who likes its conductor, and I will show you a bad orchestra."

Dyer goes on to recall that the best performances that he had heard from the Boston Symphony Orchestra the previous season had been, with one exception, under guest conductors:

The one Ozawa performance this season truly comparable to what the guest conductors achieved was the Berlioz *Symphonie Fantastique*, which got better through the Boston series and across Japan until that most astonishing performance in Tokyo, after which the orchestra joined in the audience's ovation.

Ozawa's worst performances are not incompetent. They are not un-musical. They are not self-serving—his reputation in some quarters as a flashy conductor is wholly undeserved. But his work is subject to dam-aging lapses of taste. . . . Worse than such lapses, for they are only oc-casional, is Ozawa's fairly consistent inability to get far beyond that instant rapport with music, orchestra and audience, beyond the general sense of things. Too much of his work is superficial and the very worst of it is ignorant (in the sense of "unaware").

Just as Dyer points out that it is wrong to dismiss Ozawa as flashy, one should not be misled by Ozawa's hippie hair style and dress. He is fundamentally very conventional in his musical ideas and orchestral technique. He is equally conservative in his private life. At last count, the Ozawas owned four houses—in Newton, the Berkshires, San Fran-cisco, and Tokyo—and each means a lot to Seiji Ozawa. He cannot bring himself to part with any of them, even the one in San Francisco, which is now probably superfluous to his career. Speaking of it, he repeats his by now familiar description of its dramatic view and admits that his attitude is one of compromise—renting it out rather than selling it. Although he has taken out his first citizenship papers, he is uncertain whether he wants to complete his naturalization. Especially after the emotion-packed tour of Japan in 1978, he is less certain. He wants his children—Yukiyoshi and Seira (a combination of her parents' given names)—to grow up as Japanese.

The 1978 tour to Japan, may, in fact, be a turning point in Ozawa's career. In establishing himself as firmly in Japan as in Europe and America as one of the great conductors of his generation, he may have opened the door to his becoming a major force in modern Japanese culture. The home in Tokyo was purchased after that tour. His "old man" Saito is said to have expressed the hope that one day his protégé would carry on his educational work at the Toho School. On the other hand, when pressed on his future, Ozawa eagerly discusses his plans with the Boston Symphony—a round of the major European festivals in 1979, a triumphal tour of the United States in honor of the orchestra's one-hundredth birthday in 1981, and the celebration of Bartók's hundredth birthday that same year.

Nevertheless, there is increasing evidence that Ozawa's success in the 1978 tour of Japan may be turning him toward the Orient. After that tour, his wife and children remained in Tokyo when he and the orchestra returned to finish the Symphony Hall season. During the unexpected free time opened by the cancellation of the Covent Garden *Rigoletto*, Ozawa returned to Japan and then visited Peking, where he had not been for sometime. Whereas his previous visit had not been a completely happy one, he was warmly received in 1978: for example, he was given a full tour of his childhood home this time, although he had been allowed to see only its exterior on his previous visit. He also had extensive contacts with musicians and initiated arrangements for Chinese students to come to Tanglewood. The most important result of this visit came after President Carter's December announcement of diplomatic recognition of the People's Republic of China: Ozawa and

(193)

the Boston Symphony Orchestra were invited to visit China in March 1979.

In Shanghai and Peking, Ozawa and the orchestra gave five concerts, the last combining the Boston and Peking orchestras. The tour had obvious diplomatic overtones and was something of a media event: a CBS production crew traveled with the orchestra, and the *New York Times,* in rare deference to an out-of-town orchestra, sent its senior music critic, Harold Schonberg, to send back copious and glowing reports of the tour. In addition to performing, the players of the Boston Symphony Orchestra had ample opportunity to work with Chinese musicians and to mingle with them informally. Most important, the entire tour was a personal triumph for Seiji Ozawa—an Oriental returning in 1979 to the land of his birth to enjoy a triumph equaling that of his visit a year earlier to Japan.

Ozawa ordinarily dislikes giving interviews: it is said at Symphony Hall that he views the role of the press department as keeping the media *away* from him. Yet in Tokyo he gave two very revealing interviews—one to the Japanese press and the other to the English-speaking. At the latter, he said, "It was unbelievable that the Boston Symphony Orchestra should ask me to be its musical director. It is a traditional orchestra, and I am not a traditional musician. I come from Japan, which has no history or tradition of Western music, and this is a tremendous disadvantage to me; I have so much music to learn. This disadvantage may also be an advantage to me, because, as my great teacher Professor Saito said to me, I do not have bad traditions; I can choose the feelings of Latin, German, French, and Russian music."

Of the many paradoxes in Seiji Ozawa, he may have come closer than anyone else in defining the crucial one. If his lack of "bad traditions" is an asset, his lack of any tradition may be at the root of what Dyer terms his superficiality. And the very natural-born-ness of his great talent may make it difficult for him to get to the meat of a musical work until, as in the *Symphonie Fantastique* (a speciality of another of his "old men"), successive performances carry him closer and closer to its heart.

EDO DE WAART

THE actuality of succession—becoming a successor rather than waiting in the wings as an heir apparent—became a reality for the young Dutch conductor Edo de Waart when he succeeded Seiji Ozawa in 1977 as music director of the San Francisco Symphony Orchestra. The transition was rather faster than anticipated, unquestionably accelerated by Ozawa's growing commitments in Boston and very possibly by his desire to disentangle himself from the special "administrative duties" that the Jones-Nakagawa affair involved.

A year after Ozawa officially began his duties in Boston, the San Francisco orchestra announced the appointment of Edo de Waart as its principal guest conductor, a post widely assumed to indicate an orderly succession, although de Waart himself denies that he saw it that way. In any event, all agreed that Ozawa's absences from San Francisco would be compensated by extended visits from an outstanding young conductor whose style sharply contrasted in many ways with Ozawa's. However, even before he officially became principal guest conductor, de Waart immediately became the leading candidate for succession once Ozawa announced his intention to leave the San Francisco orchestra.

The process thrust de Waart into the limelight in San Francisco under rather trying circumstances, once he was officially designated to succeed a popular conductor toward whom the city might be said to have intense though ambivalent feelings—strong affection, sense of loss, and angry resentment at being abandoned by Ozawa. Into that rather precarious situation, then, came a hearty, businesslike young Dutchman who lacked the exotic charisma that had so endeared Ozawa to San Francisco. Comparisons may be odious, but they were present throughout de Waart's first years in San Francisco, even before he became musical director.

With his blond curly hair, beaming blue eyes, and cherubic face, de Waart might, with proper costuming, have easily stepped out of a painting by Rembrandt or Frans Hals. In reality, he has a certain trimness, a lean muscularity that are decidedly modern and thoroughly masculine. It is not surprising to learn that by the time he was thirty-four, he had been married four times. To a reporter who asked him why he bothered to get married, he once replied that it was probably his Dutch Calvinist background.

But there is little of the Calvinist in Edo de Waart's obvious enjoyment of his musical talent or in the energy with which he puts it to use. He is just as articulate in talking about music and his career as he is in commanding or persuading an orchestra to play well for him. He combines idealism in his approach to art with a hardheaded sense of responsibility to it and to himself. He seeks no overnight miracles in San Francisco, recognizes that Ozawa is a hard act to follow, but is confident that he has the talent and tools to achieve his goals in San Francisco.

Edo de Waart was born in Amsterdam in 1941. His father was a professional chorister with the Netherlands Opera, his mother a member of an amateur chorus. He heard a lot of singing at home: his father especially liked the art songs of such composers as Schubert, Schumann, Duparc, and Fauré. As a child, he occasionally attended performances of orchestras or opera with his parents. He remembers attending concerts in the Concertgebouw, where he sat with his father in the seats behind the orchestra (when they were not occupied by a chorus) so that he could watch the conductor. He has vivid early memories of Edward van Beinum and Otto Klemperer: "I remember going to a youth concert one day and then van Beinum talking to one of the members of the orchestra in the galleries. He was standing there with his foot leaning on something, I still see exactly. I must have been nine, ten years old. I just stared at him. I also remember that at one of the youth concerts, Otto Klemperer conducted, and it is too bad that I had not yet reached the age of understanding by that time. I am sorry that I never heard him more, because that, of course, was his great time, the fifties."

Although his first music lessons were at the piano, he turned to the oboe at thirteen, and three years later entered the Musieklyceum, one of two professional conservatories then in Amsterdam. Among the older teachers there the memory of Willem Mengelberg was still vivid: de Waart's instructors in oboe and woodwind ensemble had both played under the long-time director of the Concertgebouw Orchestra and gave the young oboist a strong sense of the tradition of orchestral music in the city. Although the oboe was de Waart's major area of study at the conservatory, he was also interested in conducting, especially after spending six weeks in the summer of 1960 at Salzburg as an auditor, not student, of the conducting class of Dean Dixon, the black American conductor who had a much more important career in Europe than in the United States: "Dean Dixon took conducting very much from the psychological point of view. He was always talking about the psychological side of it and how a conductor himself should not be excited but should get his players excited and things like that, and it was a very worthwhile experience. We were also allowed into rehearsals, for the festival to watch Böhm, Karajan, and Fricsay."

Although he was only an auditor of this class, de Waart realized that he was as qualified as most of the students there, and on his return to the conservatory in that fall, he began to study conducting. "I never really decided to become a conductor. I always wanted it very badly, but never decided 'I am going to be a conductor.' I was always thinking, if I have the talent, I would like to be a conductor. I was very —well—sober about it. When I went to New York for the Mitropoulos Competition in 1964, I thought to myself, you know, if I am thrown out in the first round, I might as well stay a good oboist and not become a bad conductor. . . . Looking back, I think now that I was always going to be a conductor, but I didn't know it then." To enhance his knowledge of string instruments, so indispensable to conducting, he also studied the cello.

When he first graduated from the conservatory, de Waart played oboe in the Amsterdam Philharmonic, but a year later, in 1963, joined the Concertgebouw. Meanwhile, at a seminar sponsored by the Netherlands State Radio Corporation, he spent six weeks of intensive conducting study with Franco Ferrara. Thanks to the facilities of the Radio Corporation, there was ample opportunity for the students to work with various staff orchestras.

For de Waart, study with Ferrara was an extraordinary experience: "He didn't actually teach, strangely enough. I cannot say that there were definite things that he told you to do or not to do. If someone would do something terrible, he would shake his head and put his head in his hand, like, 'My God, how can he do that?' And if someone was good, he would give a short nod, and that would be as good as we ever would get. More than anything he was a great personality, a man of incredible sincerity as a musician, with a magnetic power about him.

"He let me conduct and encouraged me a lot. The main thing that he did for me was making me see that music was quite a lot else than I thought it to be till that time. I had become very preoccupied with the organization of music—the structures and all that. He would never step up on the podium, because he would be afraid that he would collapse. That was the reason why he stopped conducting himself, but he would stand next to you and say, 'Ho, ho, ho, wait,' and then he would conduct a little. Just looking at him and listening to what he was saying, you could learn more from that man in those six weeks than from anybody else in four years. I learned in those six weeks the basic traits of the profession, much deeper than I had in three years preceding as a conducting student.

"I still remember one time, when we were in one of the radio studios during the lunch break. He said, 'Come on,' and he played on the piano *Till Eulenspiegel,* and it was fantastic. No orchestra could play it like that. He had been for seventeen years concert master of the Santa Cecilia in Rome, but he played the piano incredibly. He could play orchestra scores and everything was there, and it was a total command, not just technically, but very musical, very sensitive.

"I remember one day he had me do the Beethoven Fifth, the opening, and I just couldn't get it right. That is very much a matter of self-confidence. If you know what you do is clear, it is not difficult at all, but when you start doubting yourself, it becomes very difficult and the musicians do not know what you mean. And so, I couldn't do it. My whole day was spoiled. At the end of the second session in the afternoon—he always called me Waart-eh—he said, 'Waart-eh, again, do you like to do Beethoven Five again?' The whole day I had been busy in my head getting it ready, and I stood before the orchestra, I raised my hand and there it went right. I got a big hand from the orchestra, and he was smiling. In that way, he got me to find the answer myself and to cope with the problem."

In June 1964, de Waart made his public conducting debut in Amsterdam with the Netherlands Radio Philharmonic Orchestra. He was still playing oboe in the Concertgebouw that fall when he saw on the orchestra manager's desk a leaflet announcing the Dimitri Mitropoulos Competition for young conductors to take place a few weeks later in New York. With a leave of absence from the Concertgebouw, de Waart entered the contest and was one of six winners that year. He was one of the three who were to be Leonard Bernstein's assistants at the Philharmonic the following season, the other three to serve as assistants with other orchestras. The competition was for de Waart "a thoroughly unpleasant experience. Competition brings out something that has nothing to do with music: it is survival of the fittest."

In the months following his victory in that contest, the twenty-three-year-old de Waart had a number of conducting engagements in Holland. He also conducted a performance of Stravinsky's *L'Histoire du Soldat* at Spoleto. These performances, appearances in chamber music, and his competition achievement led him to embark with keen anticipation on his season as assistant conductor at the Philharmonic. "It was the most useless year of my life. I think I conducted altogether two hours, maybe twenty minutes before an audience. I was completely lost, lonely, depressed, bored out of my senses." His conducting before a public was at two childrens' concerts, when he conducted a part of the Ravel orchestration of Mussorgsky's *Pictures at an Exhibition,* a pianist played part of the original piano version, and Bernstein finished off with the big orchestral climax. On the other hand, Bernstein did pass specific advice on to his assistants. "Bernstein has a fabulous analytical gift. He once explained to me in three sentences the structure and problems of the Violin Concerto by Chavez. That gift is his great strength in explaining the music at his youth concerts."

Returning to Amsterdam, however, he found much more satisfactory work awaiting him. The Concertgebouw Orchestra appointed him assistant conductor under Bernard Haitink; in all he revisited the United States on two of that orchestra's tours. More important, his colleagues in the Netherlands Wind Ensemble invited him to become their conductor. This group of young musicians, all de Waart's contemporaries, had originally been organized by an older man, an instructor in chamber music whose health declined, leaving the group virtually leaderless. In 1966, de Waart began to lead them. With the ensemble he made tours of Asia as well as Great Britain, Spain, and other European countries. In 1969, he conducted the ensemble in the first of series of well-received recordings on the Philips label, his first recordings and the ones that gave him his initial international exposure.

Soon after becoming assistant conductor of the Concertgebouw, he was engaged by the Rotterdam Philharmonic Orchestra as its codirector with the older French conductor Jean Fournet. A few years later, in 1973, he became sole principal conductor of this orchestra, a post he was to hold until 1979.

The Rotterdam Philharmonic is one of seventeen full-time professional orchestras in the Netherlands, all of them receiving support from the national government as well as from their respective municipalities. In Rotterdam, the city provides about two-thirds of the Philharmonic's expense, the national government about one-third. Box office income is negligible because ticket prices are kept low and there are fewer concerts than is usual in the United States. Of an orchestra numbering ninety, forty string players are foreigners. There are not enough

Dutch players to staff the orchestras, all of which have a distinctly international atmosphere.

Despite the size of the government subsidy, there is relatively little interference in the running of the orchestra. It is governed by a board of five—two designated by the city; one by Friends of the Orchestra, a community fund-raising group; and two by the players. Although the mayor must formally approve the committee's action, this is usually automatic except in such special situations as the choice of a permanent conductor, budgets, or public protest over too much modern music on the Philharmonic's programs. Another committee works with the conductor to determine what players shall fill vacancies and, in unusual cases, how to deal with incompetent players. New musicians are on probation for one or two years, permanent tenure being decided by the audition committee and the conductor.

"Initially I did [a lot of youth concerts], but I feel that the phenomenon of youth concerts where you pack two and one half thousand yelling and screaming kids without help from anybody into a hall is not good. For them it becomes a terrific adventure and they run all over the place, and you have to start behaving like a schoolmaster. It has nothing to do with music and I feel that unless you get help from the schools, this is a thing of the past. . . . I think you should try to go to much smaller groups that can almost surround the orchestra and sit very close and can see and be really drawn in."

De Waart's success in Rotterdam was undoubtedly helped by the opening in 1968 of the new Doelen Concert Hall. "It turned out to be a very good modern hall," says de Waart who has unhappy memories of the early days of Philharmonic Hall in New York's Lincoln Center. "It has the characteristics of every modern hall and is bright and brilliant but lacks warmth and—to a certain extent—sensitivity that maybe comes with age."

Under de Waart's direction, the Rotterdam orchestra has traveled a great deal, such touring being financed partly by the government and partly by the organization of Friends of the Orchestra. In addition to travel on the Continent and to Great Britain, the Rotterdam Philharmonic has been to the United States three times under de Waart's direction, and as his last official duty as conductor, de Waart will take the orchestra to Asia in 1979.

When the orchestra visited New York late in 1977, Alan Rich reported in *New York* magazine:

> The Rotterdam Orchestra is not quite of first-class quality; its winds, in particular, have a fuzzy, rather nasal sound. It plays with good clarity, and its strings, while without much resonance, form a responsive unit, agreeable if not remarkable. De Waart is, however, quite remarkable. For a man of his tender years, he behaves himself with great reserve on the podium. His beat is graceful and clear, and his every movement seems to draw some kind of orchestral response. He uses a baton, he uses a score; he does not, in other words, show off. . . . The Beethoven he performed [the Seventh Symphony and the *Leonore* Overture no. 3] was set off with a fine sense of drama and with control over structure that made the climaxes occur where they belong. Dashing young conductors are all over the place nowadays; conductors with de Waart's brand of intelligence are not.

Edo de Waart has been fortunate in having received virtually all of his musical training and launched a career—conducting a chamber ensemble, symphony orchestra, and opera—entirely in his native land. With a father who is a full-time professional chorister with the Netherlands Opera, young Edo grew up hearing operatic chitchat at the dinner table. When that company went through a serious crisis early in the 1960s, the young conductor heard a great deal about its problems. A new music director at the opera was dissatisfied with the quality of the orchestra, and when he insisted on reauditioning half the players, the entire orchestra went on strike. The company ceased to operate. Later a new Netherlands Opera Company was formed, more of an administrative structure than a full performing company. It offered eight to ten productions a year, in *stagione* scheduling, and gave as many as ten performances in each of perhaps five Dutch cities.

Since the country was already well supplied with orchestras, the company engaged one or another of these for each production. In this

the American premiere of the three-act version of Berg's *Lulu,* the offer from Bayreuth took precedence.

When first in Santa Fe, de Waart had an American manager who had done nothing for him; the Santa Fe engagement was handled by his London manager, whom he asked for help in securing a more active representative in New York. This was Ronald Wilford at Columbia Artists Management, who, in the next few years, succeeded in booking de Waart as guest conductor with most of the major orchestras in the United States, both in their summer festival seasons and during the winter on their home base.

When he conducted a Ravinia Festival performance with the Chicago Symphony Orchestra in 1978, John von Rhein of the *Tribune* found his performance of the Franck Symphony in D-minor worthy of comparison with Pierre Monteux's legendary performance and recording with the same orchestra in the 1960s: "Both conductors had a way of sustaining linear tension and drive without ever pulling or pushing the tempos; of scaling each climax with a larger architecture always in clear view; of building intensity without lapsing into hysteria. . . . De Waart paced it beautifully. . . . He knew precisely how to draw together the thematic parts into a cohesive and dramatic whole."

During the same summer, he conducted the Boston Symphony at Tanglewood, where one critic commented, "He treats Beethoven as a composer who, for all his later storm and stress, came out of the classical tradition. The result was a Fifth Symphony that shouted triumph at the world, yet retained an early-nineteenth-century shape and feeling."

For his part, de Waart admires the professionalism of the orchestras he has conducted in the United States: "They are there to do a job. And they are prepared to do that; they are usually prepared to go as far as you want them to go. In other words, they are not terribly stuffy, they do not live on their great tradition; they do not say, 'Well, we played under Brahms himself, you know. What are you saying to us?' I find a general lack of haughtiness in the American orchestras, a really down-to-earth professionalism very congenial. And then if I want to inspire them, that is fine with them. The responsibilities lie very much where they should lie—on both sides—and it is not very often in

America that you have to whip an orchestra into action. They may battle over their contract, but once they do their work, they do their work, and that is an attitude that I admire greatly.

"Many of the big cities in Europe have had an extremely rich tradition, with the composer coming to do his own work, or a protégé of the composer like Bruno Walter coming to Amsterdam, or the relationship of Mahler and Mengelberg. In the United States, compared to Europe, what strikes you . . . is the lack of tradition. . . . It is all new, brand new. Americans have a great knack of tearing down their beautiful landmarks and putting up parking garages instead, and that's very sad. Only for people like Isaac Stern do you still have Carnegie Hall. That's one of your best concert halls, and God knows what an ugly office building would have stood there now."

From his playing oboe in the Concertgebouw Orchestra, de Waart recalls that he could easily tell whether a conductor was himself primarily a pianist or player of an orchestral instrument: "Maybe not when he has conducted for twenty years, but in his first five or ten years, you can pick him out. You know those who have only played the piano and really never played a lot of chamber music. They ask for different things. It's very often more studied, less really bread and butter things, the real things that have to be done. When I played in the orchestra, I could always tell, and I know that many of my colleagues could. Sound production very often, technical things like bowings, tonguing, breath, where to take the breath for wind. Pianists can go along for hours, and if a conductor does not ask for phrasing, you know that he was a pianist."

String bowing is a very important element in phrasing; that is the main reason de Waart studied cello at the conservatory while preparing to be a conductor. He relies a great deal on his concertmasters for their expertise in bowing. He has a sense of differing tension and relaxation between an up-bow and a down-bow that is very important in his way of conveying the music. When working with one section of the orchestra in rehearsal (the strings, let us say) he expects the rest of the orchestra to pay attention and observe how he wants other players (winds or brass) to play the same phrase. Though normally very patient in his work, he cannot stand lack of attention. "We should take our work seriously. If we don't, then we should go somewhere else—play for the Rockettes, or something."

Just as he admires businesslike professionalism in American orchestras, de Waart himself is very businesslike on the podium. He does not emulate his great fellow Hollander, Willem Mengelberg, whose garrulity was the source of orchestral legends that de Waart must have heard many times from his teachers. Unlike some of his contemporaries, de Waart is seldom addressed by his first name, though there may be closer familiarity in Rotterdam or in San Francisco after he has become better acquainted there. His verbal instructions are precise, technical rather than metaphorical. His gestures are mainly from his arms and hands; he seldom throws his whole body into his conducting. During rehearsals, he often sits on a high stool as opera conductors do. He will, when necessary, move his hands independently—rhythm in the right, expression or cues in the left. His baton seems an extension of his whole body and thus of the musical intelligence and feeling of the conductor himself.

De Waart admits that he has difficulty in developing a systematic method of study: "The one most frustrating thing in my first ten years as a conductor was how to learn a score. I still remember that I would go totally crazy up to Szell and ask him, 'How do I learn it? How do you learn a score?' And I really have never gotten an answer from anybody, because nobody really ever knows. I have found out for myself that the only way that I can get a work in my system is by having a good working knowledge of the piece at first rehearsal, and the rest is done there. In other words, I am not the kind of conductor who could do it all at the table."

Nevertheless, de Waart does not come unprepared to rehearsals: "If it is a Mozart or Beethoven symphony, which I either played or I can read dry, if I can really read and hear it, I would not use anything—a recording nor piano—but sit and mark the score up where I thought the important lines were. For phrasing, I have a system in which I periodize the phrases into four, eight, six, three, two, one bar. That is very important, because that gives me a very good structural foundation. Then I try to get a good feeling about what the composer is trying to say, by either knowing the score or listening to a record. Listening to a record is done for one purpose only, not to get the interpretations, but to judge what the piece is like, what are its possibilities. If you do Mahler's Sixth and you listen to Bernstein and Haitink, you hear two totally different versions. When I did my first *Falstaff*, I listened to Toscanini a lot, which I thought was the absolute great *Falstaff* and I still think so. There is no other recording that comes even close to what that does. Then later when I listened to a tape of myself or listened again to Toscanini, I still had my own tempi in my head.

"I am extremely picky to whom I would listen, because there are conductors and I listen to their records, and I get physically unwell. If I would do Schumann, for instance—I've never done anything else than the Third Symphony—I would go to George Szell's records and listen to them, because he seems to be the only one who can bring clarity to the dense texture. I would listen, how does he do that, what does he do, how far does he carry his retouchés. With the Italian repertoire, invariably I turn to Toscanini. With Wagner, I would listen to Furtwängler very much. The romantic symphonies, Klemperer a lot. I never met him but I have learned a great deal about music-making from his style of work."

As for the Toscanini-Furtwängler polarity that still pervades much conducting today, de Waart sees his own position as one of developing maturity: "I think when my days are over that I would be more toward Furtwängler's side than Toscanini's side, but I think I can only come to that point by departing from an absolute fidelity to the score. One has to start out with the score and then maybe over the years, when one gets more confident and enriches his life and nature, one will add to those scores."

De Waart's inclination to allow his own experience to ripen artistically has its parallel in his attitude toward his career, as is vividly illustrated by the fact that he did not share the general view in San Francisco that his appointment as the orchestra's principal guest conductor was a prelude to his stepping up to the music director's post. Even after

Ozawa announced plans to leave San Francisco, de Waart told an interviewer from *Musical America* that only a "fantastic offer" could get him out of Rotterdam. When Robert Commanday of the *San Francisco Chronicle* talked with him in Santa Fe during the *Falstaff* production in the summer of 1975, de Waart was most convincing in his disavowal of candidacy for the post being vacated by Ozawa. Yet, in the following spring, it was announced that de Waart would indeed succeed Ozawa in 1977. What had happened in the meantime? Or was de Waart misleading the press the preceding summer? From the announcement in December 1974 that he would become principal guest conductor, it was generally assumed in San Francisco—by the association leaders themselves, by the orchestra, by the public, and by the media—that de Waart was in fact being groomed to succeed Ozawa, whose inevitable departure was only a matter of time. Strangely, de Waart did not see it that way. "I thought it would be very nice to have a steady job in America, six weeks a year in a certain place, and I never went any further because my heart was completely and totally with Rotterdam at that point."

De Waart's public statements in the summer of 1975 had two motives—discretion and an assumption on his part that he was not the automatic heir apparent. "I think basically what happened is that in everything I do, there are very much two sides. I don't say I do this and then absolutely do it. I always think, Is it really right? I was being careful not to make myself a candidate for that job, which by that time was open. Seiji had just said he would leave, and of course I was besieged by people who said, 'Now you are going to be. . . .' I never had more despicable thoughts about people than when I read an interview where someone says, 'Yes, you know, I really would like that job because I think I could. . . .' When you get into that, that is terrible. If I expressed an interest, that makes it very hard for the board to pass me up and not have very hard feelings after that. Secondly of all, I was generally not that interested.

"The strange thing is that when I got the offer, I could have never known what a difference it would make to have a solid offer. And when I got the offer, and I thought, I could really be the music director of one of the really great American orchestras, in what is one of the great cities of this country. It's not New York. It's not a rat race. You are not always in the spotlight. It's a good situation, and I need a change. Initially I thought I would do it together with Rotterdam, but my first year already proved that that would be impossible. One can only have loyalties to one side. And they are too far away from each other. If it was Rotterdam and London, that's fine. That's an hour. But ten hours difference is impossible. So that's what happened that summer."

Unquestionably de Waart knew he was taking on a difficult task, especially in the aftermath of the Jones-Nakagawa affair. As had been done before Ozawa was engaged, the members of the orchestra were consulted about their preference, and their response was strongly in favor of de Waart, whom they knew well. Given the tensions still prevailing even after the Jones lawsuit had been resolved, it would have been disastrous for the association to have designated a new musical director whom the players did not like, for de Waart's attitude toward the musicians was well known—implicitly by how he treated them and explicitly when he said that he had no intention, in San Francisco, Rotterdam, or anywhere else, of "fighting the orchestra." When he discussed the matter with his manager, Wilford made it clear that the decision was up to him but pointed out that he must know what he was getting into and that the job involved a lot more than merely conducting.

In de Waart's first season as music director, he conducted twelve of twenty-four weeks in the season but will increase his work in San Francisco to sixteen weeks in the last year of his present three-year contract. After that, the season itself may be longer, and de Waart hopes to handle about two-thirds of it himself. The association hopes that he will spend extra time in San Francisco on artistic administration if necessary. One problem in the personnel procedures involved in the Jones-Nakagawa crisis was that Ozawa was not on hand when crucial deadlines in the process occurred. However, should such problems recur under de Waart, he counts on the considerably more aggressive new manager, Peter Pastreich, to work with him while in residence or by phone in carrying out these administrative duties. In many respects, the

administration of the San Francisco Symphony Orchestra had fallen behind the pace of professionalism of other orchestras in the United
States. Board leaders, such as Boone, were involved in administrative
matters that had grown beyond the old-fashioned personal concern that
was characteristic of a time when orchestras had much shorter seasons
and less need for tight professional administration. Significantly, de
Waart's taking over as musical director was followed in less than a
year by a change in the orchestra's management.

De Waart is fully aware that relations between management and
personnel are quite different in Rotterdam and San Francisco. In Holland, orchestral players are under contract to the government as state
employees. Working with orchestras in the United States, de Waart has
learned that players can be very literal in holding a conductor to work
rules—length of rehearsals, scheduling of breaks, overtime, and other
provisions that force a conductor to plan his work more precisely. That
is something he did not encounter in Rotterdam, but he is quite prepared to plan in San Francisco.

On the less specific issues of orchestra morale and players' attitude toward the conductor, he says, "If there is a problem, there are two
sides to blame. I do not think that the management and board were always in the past terrifically efficient or humane. I do not think that the
union and the musicians were that wise or that mature in everything. It
boils down to a partial breakdown in communication on many issues—
assuming that the other side will think this or that, instead of asking
someone, 'How do you feel about it?' I prefer a very open approach
where you are not playing games and not trying to look someone down
in the eyes. Our musicians are as positive or negative as in any other
orchestra. Bad handling has blown the situation out of proportion and
then it comes to the point where one cannot back off anymore because
pride becomes involved on both sides."

In San Francisco, de Waart continues to build much the same orchestral repertory as he had offered in Rotterdam, which was just as eclectic
as his operatic bill of fare. Admirers of Josef Krips enjoy his readings
of the earlier Vienna composers. In his first season, he introduced to
San Francisco one of the delightfully long-winded Mozart serenades that

he had previously recorded with great success in Dresden. He also introduced a symphony from Haydn's middle period. He has great expertise in the Second Viennese School: he himself conducted the *Three Orchestral Pieces* of Berg and the Schoenberg *Variations for Orchestra* in their San Francisco premieres, and one of the guest conductors programmed music of Webern. "In Holland I have the name of being a radical," he says with a laugh. "But here in San Francisco I have a name of being a conservative." He likes contemporary music—especially Lutoslawski, Berio, and Dallapiccola—and prefers it "when you can detect it is written by a human being and not by a computer. I get very edgy with a score that asks only for numbers, figures, counts and has nothing to do with professionalism and is written so badly that I have to explain it for forty-five minutes to the orchestra. I like Berg and Schoenberg very much. That kind of music I am particularly fond of. The Berg Chamber Concerto and Violin Concerto are masterpieces. Webern I have somewhat more problems with. It gets a little too cerebral now and then. I very seldom program anything without a purpose. If I will be here six or seven years, we will have done everything of Mahler, and there may be a possible recording project in seven or eight years."

A major challenge facing de Waart during his tenure in San Francisco will be the opening of a new performing arts center, designed primarily to house the San Francisco Symphony Orchestra. Ever since it was opened in 1932 the War Memorial Opera House has served both the San Francisco Opera and the city's symphony orchestra: since the major opera season in the fall extends to the end of November, the symphony orchestra season runs from then until early June. This arrangement also makes it possible for the opera company to recruit its orchestra from symphony personnel. (For the San Francisco Ballet and for the spring season of opera in a downtown theater, an entirely different orchestra is employed.) However, when the San Francisco Symphony Orchestra has its own home away from the Opera House, there will be several radical changes.

The War Memorial Opera House has never been suited to the orchestra. Acoustically, it is too dry, lacking in resonant tone, despite efforts to design a succession of shells for the stage. Even during the symphony season, the orchestra must adjust its concert and rehearsal schedules to accommodate other tenants—the San Francisco Ballet, traveling companies, and concert attractions. The new hall, located across the street from the Opera House in San Francisco's spacious Civic Center, has been designed with the orchestra as a prime consideration. De Waart arrived too late on the scene to play a role in planning this new building, although he offered some advice on some matters such as dressing rooms and practice facilities. The opening of the new performing arts center in the fall of 1980 will have a major impact on the scheduling of music performance in San Francisco. The opera season will no longer have to be cramped into three fall months, and the orchestra will be able to begin its season earlier. Despite fears that there will be competition for audiences, it is generally agreed that the city is now large enough to have both an orchestra and an opera company running at the same time: surveys have shown that there is an approximate 15 percent overlap of audiences. If the experience of other cities is any guide, there will probably be a net increase in both audiences, thanks to better scheduling.

Of equal importance will be the impact of this new scheduling on the orchestra players. Once the symphony and opera seasons are running simultaneously, there will be no more chance for the two to share personnel than would be possible with the New York Philharmonic and the Metropolitan Opera. In effect, two distinct orchestras will be needed, offering overall more employment for San Francisco musicians and very possibly drawing on the present second orchestra that plays for the ballet and the spring opera season. The result may well be to relieve some of the tension in the orchestra now shared by opera and symphony. These changes will have an effect on de Waart's activities in San Francisco, and he, in turn, will have an opportunity to play a part in shaping the outcome of this revolution in San Francisco's musical life.

One of de Waart's hopes is that the new facility will open the way to a major summertime festival in San Francisco that will utilize the musicians' services more economically (they already have a year-round contract) and provide a focus for the city's already strong attraction as a tourist center. A "room tax" levied on hotel and motel guests' bills is partly spent on tourist promotion, with a major portion going to support San Francisco's art activities, which are viewed as a major tourist attraction. The San Francisco Symphony received about $315,000 of the total raised by this tax toward its 1978–79 budget of over $6 million. De Waart shares the hope of many that the addition of the performing arts center to the city's varied aggregation of art facilities—major museums, theaters, private galleries, parks, and recreational centers—will give the orchestra a chance to develop a major music festival in the city. He argues that San Francisco is the most cosmopolitan city in the United States enjoying a comfortable summer climate and a physical setting second to none.

At the same time, de Waart detects a certain provincialism amidst San Francisco's highly vaunted cosmopolitanism. For decades, the city's music critics have been pressing the San Francisco Symphony to engage more local musicians as soloists. They see an ominous connection in the fact that the orchestra's conductor is managed by a New York agent who also books soloists with the orchestra. Nor are the music directors the only ones suspected of knuckling under to New York managerial pressure. When Alfred Frankenstein, long-time art and music critic on the *Chronicle,* was asked who would succeed Ozawa at the Symphony, his reply was, "Ron Wilford hasn't decided yet."

"Everytime you think there is a major talent," de Waart has replied, "I will listen to it, as long as you understand that if I do not think that person is good enough to appear with the San Francisco Symphony, I will not use that person. At least someone is listening now. But we have to be careful not to become too provincial here—a great danger in a city like this so isolated from the rest of the world."

When de Waart first guest-conducted the San Francisco Symphony in 1974, the critical reception was warm but tinged with a "wait and see" attitude. On that occasion, Robert Commanday wrote in the *Chronicle,* "He is a big talent, conducts large, gets large sonorities, sharp attacks, and has the explicit physical equipment that audiences like. De Waart has control, authority, quick reflexes, but how interesting a musician he is still remains to be heard."

De Waart's accession to the music directorship was not given the almost hysterical promotion that Ozawa's was a few years earlier. Once established in his first season as music director, de Waart's reception in the critical press was considerably more reserved than it had been while he was a guest conductor. Although this puzzled and at times annoyed de Waart, it is actually rather a common phenomenon for local critics in any city to be more exacting in their appraisal of the man who is to be in charge of an orchestra for several years. At least one critic, not in the daily San Francisco press, viewed de Waart as an unmitigated disaster, especially in comparison to Ozawa, but this was regarded as an extreme view. The orchestra management has been reluctant to release authoritative attendance figures, but informed and regular patrons noted vacant seats in areas usually occupied by season subscribers and what seemed to be a slight decline in single-concert attendance. With the professional music community outside the orchestra itself, de Waart established some early cordial contacts: he has visited the San Francisco Conservatory, talked with its faculty and staff, and heard some students—not by way of formal audition but rather to orient himself in prevailing music standards.

As his first season as music director drew to a close, de Waart himself was concerned with some of the adverse criticism he was reading in the press. He tried to distinguish between what he felt was unfounded or irrelevant comment and truly informed criticism. When one critic, possibly even younger than de Waart, wrote, "The depths of Mahler's Sixth remain unplumbed," the conductor exploded: "He has heard me do six programs, and he has made up his mind already. I am coming into a new situation, feeling my way with a totally strange orchestra in a hall that doesn't sound very good. I am not here to be exciting. I am here first to get the orchestra to play well. This was my first Mahler Sixth; if, at thirty-six, I would have given a fantastic performance, where can I go from there? How can I be compared with records by Bruno Walter when he was sixty, Toscanini when he was eighty, Furtwängler when he was in his absolute prime, Karajan when he was sixty? I am sorry, that is impossible."

However, when he returned to San Francisco for the beginning of his second season, de Waart candidly acknowledged that his first year's work as music director did not show him at his best. In retrospect, his effort to discharge his administrative duties as music director conscientiously may have impaired his work as a conductor. He was no longer merely a guest conductor. "I am the one to be blamed if the winds play out of tune, the brass are sour, or the strings weak," he told Commanday in a preseason interview late in November 1978. "Here there is so much more that concerns me. . . . The time has come for me to stop being a teacher all the time. That was one weakness in Szell. At night he couldn't let go. He was still checking the things he told them to do." This interview took place after a long summer in which de Waart interrupted intensive study in a houseboat on Lake Powell on the Colorado River in Arizona with only a few guest engagements at such summer festivals as Ravinia, Robin Hood Dell, and Tanglewood. Returning to Europe in August, he conducted *Tannhäuser* at the Holland Festival, conducted both the Rotterdam Philharmonic and the Amsterdam Concertgebouw in concerts and recordings, and then, just before returning to San Francisco, filled in for the ailing Solti at the Chicago Symphony Orchestra so successfully that he was engaged to return the following season. During the weeks following his return to San Francisco for his initial stay there of five weeks, there was much evidence that he was carrying out his resolve to put his concern for artistic administration out of his mind when he was actually performing. As early as his second subscription concert, Commanday concluded a glowing review of an all-Beethoven concert with this general comment: "De Waart conducted Wednesday in a new, outgoing, and more committed way, yet without undue tension. It was gratifying to experience the growth in him, the change and positive effect that sounded in the orchestra's playing."

Six months earlier, de Waart tried to place his reaction to the critics' reception of the Mahler Sixth in a larger perspective: "One cannot expect to grasp the tremendousness of that piece in five rehearsals and one performance at age thirty-six. Then one can say, 'Why do you do it?' Well, once has to be a first time. I see my life not as doing two years here, two years there. I have, maybe if I am lucky, another thirty-five years measured out to me where I can be active. I see maybe ten to fifteen devoted to growth, to build a base. When you build a pyramid it takes very long to lay the foundation. The higher you go, the less time it takes as it gets narrower and narrower. I think if one is building a really solid foundation, not one five feet long but one that is a hundred feet long, it takes a long time. Yesterday we played it for the second time. It was another Mahler Sixth. I am the first to acknowledge that it was still not the greatest, but it was much looser. I didn't care so much anymore about the structure, because I knew it. When I touch one of the truly great masterworks like that, it is difficult, hard, desperate music, and I cannot go wild the first time."

JAMES LEVINE

NATIONAL telecasts from the Metropolitan Opera House in New York have made him a familiar figure to millions—the roly-poly figure, the rotund face with its double chin, the lively blue eyes behind prominent spectacles, and the halo of Afro-cut brown hair. On a night when he is conducting, the black-tie dinner jacket that he sometimes wears in the pit or for a live intermission interview is almost as much of a hallmark of his informality as the bright sportshirts and cardigan sweaters he wears when interviews are taped in advance of the telecast. But most impressive is his fluency of speech: he talks the way he conducts—smoothly, clearly, intelligently, and with obvious pleasure in what he is communicating. His colleagues across this nation and in Europe all know him as Jimmy. His audiences and the public at large are learning that his last name rhymes with *divine.*

James Levine was thirty-three when he became music director of the Metropolitan Opera, not the first to hold that position in name or in fact but certainly the first to have authority and responsibility that even Arturo Toscanini did not wield between 1908 and 1915 in that company. Levine is one member of a triumvirate that also includes patrician Wall Street lawyer Anthony A. Bliss as executive director and the British theatrical producer John Dexter as director of production. In 1976 these three faced the awesome task of restoring artistic respect and financial stability to the most elephantine performance arts organization anywhere in the world. With more than half its 750 employees under a year-round contract with fourteen unions, committed to presenting twenty-four different productions in a season of thirty subscription weeks, plus touring and park performances, and faced with an annual operating deficit in excess of $12 million, the Met had come to be regarded by many as a virtual impossibility, a dinosaur wobbling toward inevitable extinction. Nevertheless, the Metropolitan Opera did survive and in fact moved rapidly toward regaining its waning artistic stature. It is generally agreed that James Levine played a crucial role in this process of rehabilitation. To be sure, the work of Bliss in administration and fiscal management and of the board of directors in raising millions of dollars to keep the company solvent has also been crucial, but Levine gave them a musical product that they could be proud to sell, that the foundations, corporations, private contributors, and government art agencies were equally proud to support out of enthusiastic respect rather than grudging obligation.

James Levine made his debut at the Metropolitan Opera on a Saturday afternoon, June 5, 1971, conducting *Tosca,* sung by Grace Bumbry, Franco Corelli, and Peter Glossop. It was an out-of-season June Festival performance offered during one of those weeks in which the Met found it more economical to use the services of its year-round staff in performance than to pay them for doing nothing. Robert Herman, one of Rudolf Bing's assistants, had heard Levine conduct the same opera in San Francisco, liked his work, and kept him in mind for the future. When a conductor was needed for the June Festival *Tosca,* the Metropolitan called Levine's manager, Ronald Wilford, at Columbia Artist Management. Levine had serious misgivings about getting mixed up with the Met at all. As a teenager commuting every other week from Cincinnati to New York to take piano lessons from Rosina Lhevinne at Juilliard, he haunted the old Metropolitan on Thirty-ninth Street every Saturday it was performing when he was in the city. Later, as a full-time conducting student at Juilliard, he attended Metropolitan performances and rehearsals several times a week and knew many of the singers there or from his summers at Aspen. He also heard all about the Met from his teacher, Jean Morel, who was on the company's conducting staff at the time. During six years as George Szell's assistant at the Cleveland Orchestra, Levine heard chapter and verse about the artistically impossible working conditions in this company. To Levine's misgivings, Wilford replied that all the Metropolitan needed was conductors willing to fight its handicaps tenaciously: "I said, 'But Ron, you can't function if there aren't decent artistic conditions.' 'It's a myth,' he said. 'Conductors have to create those artistic conditions in conjunction with the administration.' When I asked, 'Are you telling me that I could have any kind of influence on that at this stage of the game?' he replied, 'All I'm telling you is that if you go into the Met and do within their system better work than they are doing now, that will be forthcoming.' I thought that was a most idealistic point of view, but sure enough, the day after my debut, Goeren Gentele called Ronald and asked if I would become principal conductor on the strength of that *Tosca* performance."

Following that performance, Allen Hughes was cautiously complimentary in the *New York Times*: "If it is impossible to jump to valid conclusions on the basis of a single performance from a conductor, it can be suggested that Mr. Levine, who is twenty-eight, may be one of the Metropolitan's best acquisitions in some time. He conducted a performance that was vital, precise, and splendidly paced. The balances between voices and orchestra were excellent, and those within the orchestra were adjusted to achieve a nice interplay of textures and colors."

However, Levine's initial success was no surprise to those who knew him. It was no surprise to Morel, ill and still somewhat bitter at his pupil's refusal to stay at Juilliard as his assistant. Had he lived to see the day, it would have been no surprise to George Szell, who, despite their differences, had great respect for a young assistant who had a phenomenal grasp of the repertory. It was no surprise to Victor Babin and his wife, Vitya Vronsky, at the Cleveland Institute of Music, where Levine had virtually created a student orchestra of imposing quality. Nor to Jennie Tourel, whose classes Levine had accompanied at Aspen. Nor to Rosina Lhevinne, who regarded "Jeemey" as one of the most talented young pianists she had ever taught. Nor to Walter Levin of the LaSalle String Quartet in residence at the University of Cincinnati, who had not only coached Levine in chamber music and music theory but also instilled in him important basics of professional idealism. Nor to former fellow-students at Juilliard on whom he used his impressive powers of persuasion to play voluntarily in orchestras he organized for school concerts. Nor to Wilford, who had been in touch with Levine for several years, much of the time with no commissions, advising him, "bringing him along," and eventually booking a few performances for him, all the time knowing that he was cementing a strong bond with an extraordinary young musician.

That debut in 1971 was a beginning of a relationship between Levine and the Metropolitan that ripened and strengthened rapidly. During the next season, Rudolf Bing's last, he not only conducted *Tosca* but took over *Luisa Miller* when Fausto Cleva died and, in another June Festival, stepped in at the last minute to conduct *Falstaff,* one of the most difficult of all operas for the conductor. Donal Henahan reviewed that performance for the *New York Times*:

> Mr. Levine, who had not previously conducted the work at the Metropolitan, settled in like a veteran and led a lovely, lively performance. . . . Mr. Levine put a welcome bounce and energy into the performance, and the orchestra sounded in tune with him and with itself throughout a score that presents some of opera's most tricky problems. The pace was quick but never breathless in the ramshackle way that is too often offered to unsuspecting audiences as "Falstaffian" fun. Mr. Levine made Verdi's quick changing contrasts work in scene after scene, giving the music of the "Merry Wives" and Fenton a nimbleness that threw the buffoonery of Sir John and his cronies into witty relief. Several scenes . . . were managed with the kind of carefully judged theatrical timing that draws gasps of delight from the audience.

A few weeks earlier, he had conducted "The Star-Spangled Banner" that opened the farewell gala to Rudolf Bing. By this time he had agreed to become principal conductor of the Metropolitan Opera, a post new to the company in which he would be on hand much of the season, conduct a significant number of operas, and be general deputy to the new music director, Rafael Kubelik, especially during the latter's absences in Europe. Although Gentele's death in a motor accident in

Sardinia that summer did not technically affect Levine's place in the Metropolitan structure, it created some uncertainty as to just where he, or anybody else, stood when the Met board of directors asked Schuyler G. Chapin, Gentele's assistant, to take charge but only as acting general manager. Levine's role became even more difficult as Kubelik's weaknesses as an administrator and his absences from the house created further uncertainty in the lines of authority, although Chapin was, in May 1973, relieved of the onus of the "acting" in his title. Meanwhile, despite a growing number of commitments that had been made elsewhere before his role at the Metropolitan had been determined, Levine was carrying a growing load there—three operas in 1972–73, four in 1973–74, and five in 1974–75.

Upon Kubelik's resignation in February 1974, Chapin recognized that Levine was his logical successor as music director of the company and started exploratory discussions with him and Wilford. In the fall of 1974, the Metropolitan board appointed Anthony A. Bliss as executive director over Chapin, who shortly learned that Bliss was exploring the possibility of engaging a European conductor as music director. After Bliss was persuaded that Levine was a preferable choice, he took over the negotiations with Wilford and Levine. Chapin had all along taken the position that although a music director of Kubelik's or Levine's stature was absolutely necessary at the Metropolitan, he should still be subordinate to the general manager, who should have final authority over all matters, including the artistic. In earlier negotiations on Kubelik's contract, Wilford had sought that full authority for the music director, but Gentele successfully retained the power of the general manager intact. In the end, Levine's contract specifically gave him the authority that Kubelik had unsuccessfully sought and that Chapin as general manager had resisted.

That unprecedented power was indispensable to Levine: "My relationship with Gentele, short as it was, was fine, beautiful. My relationship with Kubelik as principal conductor was clear-cut. I was to be in residence five months a year and, as the contract stated, to assist the music director in the musical supervision of the company. By the time that contract took effect, Gentele had died; Kubelik resigned a while later. The people I had signed the contract with were no longer there. The board was treating Schuyler like an interim thing. I found myself in a very difficult no-man's-land. Here was Schuyler trying to execute Gentele's plans, Kubelik's wishes. In other respects plans were only half made. People knew that the musical authority closest to him was me. Sometimes he consulted me, sometimes he didn't. Other times he consulted me and did not follow my musical advice. So, when he asked me, on behalf of the board, to be music director, I didn't want to accept a position that wouldn't function. I was tired of having responsibility without authority. I wanted very clearly to have direct contact with the board because the last time the other principals of the contract were no longer operative shortly after the contract began.

"After six months deliberation, my ultimate acceptance was based on several factors. First of all, my conviction that the greatest artistic contributions historically have always been made by people who were willing to do building, who were willing to stay in one place and work with people and develop a rapport in subtle areas. Second of all, I wanted to live in one place, and New York is a wonderful place to live. Third, I had a wonderful relationship with the company from the moment I walked in the door, which has only grown more wonderful. Fourth, most of my intelligent, sensitive, friend-adviser colleagues said, 'Look, you're the one for the job; you know opera; you know the American situation; you know the house from the inside; you've been there and understand what all the problems are; you have the energy; and you love the company.' "

Levine's engagement as music director, on his and Wilford's terms, was announced in the spring of 1975. After the Metropolitan returned from a tour to Japan in June 1975, Schuyler Chapin and the Metropolitan board came to the parting of the ways. The present triumvirate—with Levine responsible for music, Dexter for production, and Bliss in overall charge of both, plus responsibility for the financial stability of the company—was instituted.

It is interesting to compare this distribution of authority with the administration of other major opera theaters. At such major U.S. companies as the San Francisco Opera, Chicago Lyric Opera, or the Opera Company of Boston, authority flows from one general director—Kurt Herbert Adler, Carol Fox, and Sarah Caldwell, respectively. In many European opera houses, which are in effect autonomous quasi-government agencies, much depends on the personalities involved. Herbert von Karajan left the Vienna State Opera years ago because his artistic authority was being limited by government functionaries. Although the Paris Opéra is controlled by the government, Rolf Liebermann has very strong authority because he was brought to Paris to restore that theater to international glory and he demanded power as a condition of his moving from Hamburg to Paris. The power of Claudio Abbado at La Scala grew steadily as he demonstrated his artistic achievement, but he is still much circumscribed by political and practical considerations. Until 1975, the Metropolitan has always centered power in the general manager—Gatti-Casazza, Johnson, Bing, Gentele, and Chapin. The success or failure of the new triumvirate at the Metropolitan will depend less on the system than on the people involved.

For its 1977–78 season, the Metropolitan Opera published a handsome full-color booklet, which included an article by Robert Jacobson entitled "The Right Balance." In it he quotes Levine as saying, "The way we presently work is that Bliss does everything having to do with liaison with the government, the board and money, and he stays in touch with us [Dexter and Levine] insofar as every artistic decision will affect financial policy."

Levine elaborated on this: "For instance, we wanted to do a revival of *Die Frau ohne Schatten* and the costs per performance were enormous. We said, 'Look, it's available to us, and we can do it in this period. We feel it's artistically important—there's a big clamor for that production. It has not been possible to have it back at a high enough quality until now.' Although Bliss is the functional head of the administration, his input to us and output from us are basically from the standpoint of economic balance. He never says, 'I think you should do this artistically, or I don't think that you should do that.' "

It is important to note that despite Anthony Bliss's preeminent position, both Levine and Dexter have access to the board of directors and, more important, to the executive committee and the leading officers on the board.

Where the actual production of opera is concerned, Dexter and Levine work together, keeping Bliss informed and working within the policy and financial parameters he and the board set. Although there are theoretical areas of responsibility—the visual and audible, as it were —opera is basically lyric theater, and lines cannot be drawn too rigidly if any kind of total affect is to be achieved.

Dexter describes how this works from his point of view in the same article: "I think this collaboration is unique in that you almost never get two strong people who have so much aesthetic agreement. It's peculiar— our conversations are short but intense. We accept preconceived things that we both think about. Beginning with *I Vespri Siciliani,* we knew that we shared an approach to the theatre, a relationship. It's not a maestro on stage and one in the pit. We share an aesthetic, yes, but we share more a sense of time and pacing. I work intensely in blocks of three or four months and then go away. I jam it in, and we share this sense of pace. When we did *Lulu,* he had his orchestra rehearsals and I my stage rehearsals. At the first piano technical rehearsal we realized that the way the sets had been designed and made, plus the efficiency of the stage crew, there was no need for a tech. Jimmy said we would put the orchestra in the pit the next day, so we had everything one day earlier than scheduled, an extra day to tidy things up."

However, the collaboration between Levine and Dexter is by no means limited to working together on specific productions. Levine conducts some productions staged by other directors, Dexter stages operas that Levine does not conduct, and there are some productions in which neither is directly involved. Nevertheless, each is responsible, in his own area, for everything that is performed in the house—Levine for how it sounds, Dexter for how it looks. Ultimately this goes back to planning, a process on which the two directors and their respective staffs must spend a great deal of time.

Jacobson has Levine describe the process in his own words: "How it works is that we have a long list of things we would like to see done

(228)

in this house as new productions—operas we have no productions of, operas we have productions of and that are no longer playable, everything from eighteenth century to contemporary that we feel would be a valid extension of the repertory. In other words, a working list so we can balance doing rarities with standard works, nineteenth century with twentieth, German and Italian, to achieve some kind of balance over one, two, three years. . . . Many of the decisions, like doing *Lohengrin* before *Tannhäuser,* are practical—to get them when you can best cast them.

"We work in three-year increments, because booking has to be done so far in advance that it gives you a little more perspective. What we tend to do then is pick out of our existing repertory all the pieces that we would like to see revived and then lay them out on a chart, which instantly shows that you have too many chorus pieces, too many non-chorus pieces, too many heavy pieces, too many this or that, speaking strictly pragmatically for rehearsals or setting the stage. You try to balance, and then somebody notices that there aren't any comedies—or too many comedies. Then you start casting, and it turns out that you get halfway down the cast of one opera and two crucial people aren't available. Immediately you see that with the people you have under contract you could do a good revival of so and so, so you call them up and see if they can. As this takes form, the next thing you know somebody who was slotted in this opera is now in that opera. . . ."

On another occasion Levine quite unabashedly expressed his pride in what he and Dexter had accomplished. "Here was this challenge beckoning," he recalled. "In any generation there are a few people who are cut out to this kind of work. We have seen an incredible artistic turn-around, more quickly than I thought was possible. In fact, in certain respects, I would have given at least three years to get to the point where it has gotten in one or two. I mean the way the orchestra is playing, the way the chorus is singing, the consistency of the casting, the expanding of the repertory, the upgrading of what was a real artistic instability. This has been substantially accomplished even in the first two years, and what I hope to accomplish over the next few is to achieve a consistently better standard, more exciting than anywhere else.

"I am not only speaking, by the way, of my end of it. John Dexter has done a miraculous job with respect to improving the way everything looks, the costuming, the refurbishing, the style of new productions, the reduction of heaviness in the productions which gives us a longer rehearsal day, the careful perception of what the practical artistic balances have to be in a period in which you are trying to turn something around financially."

Although Levine, like most artists, claims that he hates administration, there is no question in his tone of voice that he relishes such details, if not for themselves, at least as a means to an end. Levine unabashedly likes working with people. Although he may prefer collaborating musically, he also enjoys the inevitable human relations involved in administration. He has a clear perception of how he wants the Metropolitan to operate. One goal is what he calls quasi-*stagione* scheduling. Traditionally, the Metropolitan has been a repertory theater, in theory maintaining a company of performers who are available to perform a given group of operas throughout the season. Their rotation is determined in part by the work load on the singers and in part by the requirements of a subscription season so devised that each "series" will include a certain variety of operas without repetition. This has required, at the Metropolitan at least, giving seven performances a week—six evenings and a Saturday matinee every week for thirty weeks. The system worked reasonably well as long as major singers were willing to spend a full season or most of it exclusively at the Metropolitan. If this was not possible, frequent cast changes became necessary, and the quality of ensemble suffered. At its worst, the repertory system could degenerate into a succession of star-studded concerts in costume with scenery.

At the opposite extreme is *stagione,* in which each opera is prepared with a fixed cast and appropriate covers and then presented as many times as practical in a short as possible span of time. Producing each opera with its own cast in this manner results in much better quality of performance. Although practical considerations at the Met—seven performances a week and the requirements of the subscription system—make a full *stagione* presentation impossible there, Levine seeks to schedule many of his operas in this way: "We are finding that, out of twenty-four operas, for instance, we may be able to do twenty in *stagione,* which is fantastic. This gives us much better casting stability and a much better performance level from the company, who don't have to dredge an opera up every two weeks or so. There have always to be a certain number of repertory items that can fill in while you give the two or three days break that this or that opera needs. We've had some very exciting runs with barely any cast changes of new productions or major revivals where we gave all of that season's performances in four or five weeks."

Stagione scheduling is especially suited to the modern-day careers of international star singers, very few of whom are willing to settle down in one theater for a long time. Under any system of scheduling, "covers," or standbys, are a major problem, given the physical frailty of the human voice, to say nothing of the temperamental vagaries of star sopranos and tenors. In Europe, covers are not so great a problem: if a Tosca falls ill in Hamburg, there are probably three or four satisfactory substitutes within a few hours' flying time. For the Metropolitan, it is not nearly as easy to fly a substitute singer in and out in a day or so. Therefore, some singers are paid not to sing but simply to be within hailing distance of the Met for certain performances. Sometimes this is accomplished by double casting, but in many cases the cover seldom gets a chance to sing until toward the end of a run of an opera when he or she is scheduled to sing as a part of a bargain made to assure that all substitutes are of a quality to step in otherwise when needed. Throughout the history of the Met there have been legendary events involving ailing singers and a shortage of covers: the night in 1959 when a different tenor sang in each act of *Tristan und Isolde* or, more recently, the performance in 1978 of *Il Trovatore* when the Leonora, not a regular cover but a former member of the company, went on "cold" with a substitute conductor in the pit. Covers are one of the more nagging problems of casting at the Met, and casting is but a part of the overall artistic administration. Levine's staff now includes Joan Ingpen, a British opera administrator who is one of those rare people with an encyclopedic knowledge of where any singer is working at any given moment, his strengths and weaknesses, the current condition of his voice, and the state of his love life.

In any discussion about American and foreign singers at the Met, Levine finds himself walking a risky tightrope. If he emphasizes his desire to include the finest European singers in his productions, he is accused of discriminating against American singers who must go abroad to prove themselves before the Met will consider them, a charge less justified today than it was in the Bing regime. On the other hand, when he speaks of building a home for the best young American singers, he arouses fears that the Metropolitan will become a provincial house whose fans will be deprived of the stars whom they know from records and must also hear in person. Levine attempts to maintain some perspective on this issue by pointing out that some 50 to 60 percent of the "name" singers on the Met's current roster are Americans and that where singers are concerned, he wants, first, the very best from anywhere in the world and, second, Americans of all ages, especially young American singers to develop in appropriate roles. He wants what he calls an "international American opera company," but he has no intention of cutting off the international celebrities who are the lifeblood of big-time opera any more than he has of forcing outstanding young Americans to establish themselves abroad before he will consider placing them on the Met roster. At the same time that the Met has successfully wooed the once feuding Renata Scotto back with a succession of choice roles, it has offered the debuts of Ileana Cotrubas, René Kollo, Elena Obrastzova, Kurt Moll, Julia Varady, and Yuri Mazarok, to name but a few Met debutants during the Levine years.

Another very significant effort on Levine's part is to bring back to the Metropolitan some celebrated European singers, now past their prime, and to use them in ways that pass their vast experience on to younger singers; Fedora Barbieri, Renato Capecchi, and Italo Tajo have returned in this way to the Met, and Tito Gobbi was engaged to stage a new *Tosca*.

The handling of star singers is always a difficult task in a major international opera house. They have their friends in the press, their fans among the standees, and frequent social contacts with board members or financial supporters. They can bring a deluge of wrath down onto an opera executive for real or imagined slights. The withdrawal of a major singer like James McCracken literally days before he was to open the 1978 season, because he felt slighted in casting that season and the next, can send Levine and his staff literally "to covers" in lining up suitable replacements in over twenty performances. As Levine told a *Time* interviewer, "We try to reconcile the house's interest with that of the individual. One problem we face is that there are fewer great singers of the big-voice type than there were. And the lighter-voice singers have paid a great price for things they were really not up to, and so didn't have time to grow." Another problem, of course, is the intense competition between international opera houses in Europe and America: the number of great singers simply has not increased at the same rate as the number of major theaters, which compete not only with financial reward but also with incredible ingenuity in stroking the egos of celebrated singers.

In his attitude toward all these challenges Levine has dominated by an extraordinary enthusiasm for working with other musicians. He dates this from spending a summer at Rudolf Serkin's Marlboro School of Music when he was thirteen: "I really got bitten for good with the bug of making music with other people. It was very clear to me from that moment on that what I formerly thought I was going to do really wasn't right for me at all. I had always imagined myself turning into a pianist, but somehow that exposure in those six weeks of playing a lot of chamber music and working in that opera workshop finished that for me. I just had to work on operas and symphonies and oratorios and chamber works and lieder and not on solo piano sonatas and travel around all by myself and play. I remember coming home from there on the train with my father. He had to convince me not to give up the piano, so smitten was I with the idea of conducting and working on those large-scale works. And to this day I have no regret about that decision whatever. In fact, there's a very small solo repertoire that I enjoy playing. But, to spend my life immersed as I do in operas, oratorios, symphonies, lieder, piano chamber music is beyond any description, sheer ecstasy from beginning to end. I am just as happy that I am not traveling around playing the Liszt Concerto and the Rachmaninoff *Second* and the Prokofiev piano sonatas.

"I did keep on with the piano because my father and Walter Levin persuaded me that I would need the piano as a tool to coach singers, to play chamber music. My father actually said the thing that was ultimately persuasive: 'Even though you now think that it will be wonderful working with other people, there may come times when you will be awfully glad to be able to sit down in front of your own instrument and not have to worry about cajoling, persuading, rehearsing other people to do what you want them to do.' I still play a lot of chamber music and Mozart concertos and that sort of thing."

For all his involvement in administration, Levine is first and foremost a performer. He loves to perform—on a few occasions in the Met pit as many as five times a week—and he loves the process of preparing a performance, whether it be a cello sonata recital with his old friend Lynn Harrell, the Mahler Eighth Symphony, or a new production of *Lulu*. Fascinated as he is by logistics, it is the human relationship in making music that arouses his greatest enthusiasm. Everybody in the house calls him "Jimmy"; at first that familiarity aroused some concern among traditionalists, but it represents a collaborative spirit that he has brought to his work and with which he has imbued the work of others by his example and openness. He is everywhere in the house, day and night. If he must work late in his office on a night he is not conducting, he will slip in among the standees to catch a portion of the performance, dressed in loose slacks and a sport shirt.

However, when he is in charge he throws everything he has into rehearsal. Some conductors save their more energetic calisthenics for the concert; Levine is more active—amazingly so for a stout person—in rehearsal than in concert. He seldom gives orders or instructs his singers or players but seems to cajole and inspire them into working with him rather than for him. His command of the score is obviously impressive: he knows every detail and, what is more important, knows how each detail can be best performed by his colleagues. The result can be something like the chamber-music transparency and fluency of the Metropolitan Opera Orchestra's role in Berg's *Lulu* or the supple phrasing and interplay of inner voices and color in its performance of *Pelléas et Mélisande*. It can also be heard in the totality of Levine's performances of *Otello*, the opera he has performed most, in which there is unanimity not only of ensemble at any given moment but of all concerned—on stage and in the pit—in the moment-to-moment and act-to-act progress of the music from the opening thunder of its first chord to the tragic resolution of its dying harmonies. Through the best of Levine's work there runs a sense of exuberance, of joy in music, that lends a special quality to the way musicians play and singers sing, both in their tone and phrasing. That quality is as much evident in the un-relieved tragedy of the last act of *Otello* as it is in the comedy of *Falstaff*.

It has been reported that Levine knows more than seventy-five operas. Although he has not counted lately, he thinks that may be a low estimate. At any rate, in nine seasons at the Metropolitan, he has conducted an impressive total of thirty-one: 1970–71, *Tosca*; 1971–72, *Falstaff, Luisa Miller, Tosca*; 1972–73, *Otello, Rigoletto, Il Barbiere di Siviglia*; 1973–74, *Don Giovanni, Otello, Salome, Il Trovatore, I Vespri Siciliani*; 1974–75, *Falstaff, La Forza del Destino, La Traviata, I Vespri Siciliani, Wozzeck*; 1975–76, *Aida, Ariadne auf Naxos, La Bohème, Der Rosenkavalier*; 1976–77, *Andrea Chénier, La Bohème, La Forza del Destino, Il Trittico, Lohengrin, Lulu, Tosca, Il Trovatore;* 1977–78, *Cavalleria Rusticana, Pagliacci, Eugene Onegin, Pelléas et Mélisande, Otello, Rigoletto, Tannhäuser*; 1978–79, *Ariadne auf Naxos, The Bartered Bride, Don Carlo, Luisa Miller, Otello, Parsifal, Tannhäuser*.

Levine has conducted opera relatively little away from the Metropolitan. There were the San Francisco *Tosca* and *Simon Boccanegra*; *Aida* and *Il Barbiere di Siviglia* with the Welsh National Opera in 1970; and, from 1976 on, the Mozart operas at Salzburg—*La Clemenza di Tito* and *Die Zauberflöte*. He was forced by illness to cancel a *Rosenkavalier* scheduled in 1974 at Covent Garden. He has also done several operas in concert, notably *Les Troyens* at the Cincinnati May Festival and Ravinia and, some years ago in Cleveland, *Simon Boccanegra*. A major event in his career was a production of *Otello* in Hamburg in September of 1975, where he spent four weeks in rehearsal, three in performance. Peter Dannenberg reported on that production in the December issue that year of *Opera*:

> The new production of *Otello* (September 28) marked James Levine's debut as an opera conductor in Europe, and after the performance he received an ovation lasting over one-half hour. As a conductor his style is neither overtly personal nor instantly recognizable from small details. He does not put himself in the foreground; it is the work that counts. This *Otello* was tremendously dramatic, filled with an intensity which was felt even in the more intimate and lyrical moments in the score. Under Levine's direction, the strings breathed and spun their long drawn-out crescendos; both they and the wind groups took on an individual color. His cantabile was adept to the singers' voices without ever making musical concessions, and his ebullient temperament was never wasted on superficial or contrived effects. Nor did he once lose his feeling for the work as a whole, and one could give a hundred examples of this, from the dramatic struggle of the opening through to the calm, peaceful, almost resigned farewell of the dying *Otello*.

Nevertheless, Levine feels strongly that under the collaborative conditions he enjoys at the Metropolitan, his *Otello* performances there have been substantially better in every respect. Unquestionably they have also improved considerably from his first at the Metropolitan in December of 1972, when Harold C. Schonberg of the *New York Times* was less than completely enthusiastic:

> So the rotund Mr. Levine made his appearance and brought down his baton, and it was immediately apparent that we were going to be in for an exuberant evening. Exuberant it was, not always refined. Mr. Levine has strong ideas about the score, and he wanted to achieve its mixture of strength and brooding lyricism. . . . Often he sheerly overwhelmed

the singers by letting the brass dominate. It was good to hear the orchestra come to the fore, because too many conductors are content to
accompany rather than participate. . . . It was in the last act that Mr.
Levine settled down to his most impressive work. Having got the
fortissimos out of his system, he shaped the death scene with real
sensitivity, and the orchestra responded with some beautiful playing.

Levine's later productions of *Otello* in 1974 and 1978 were better
received, and when his recording of the opera was released in the fall of
1978, Peter G. Davis of the *Times* compared it in some detail to a
competitive issue conducted by Sir Georg Solti. His summary echoed
the general opinion of Levine's *Otello* in the preceeding spring and at
the beginning of the season:

> With all these pluses and minuses, it is really left to the conductors to
> capitalize on their respective casts' strong points and structure a cohesive
> entity. For this listener, Mr. Levine and the RCA recording in general
> get the nod—it has a greater measure of theatrical immediacy and the
> orchestra playing has more color, variety and sharply detailed profile
> than one hears on the London discs.

In his *High Fidelity* (February 1979) review David Hamilton was
more specific about Levine's handling of the orchestra in his recording
of *Otello*:

> I don't mean simply the matter of getting the notes (though that is
> certainly done to a fare-thee-well), but also such things as the way those
> syncopations "rub against" Levine's firm, forward-moving beat, as if
> they had a life of their own. They are always a palpable rhythmic event,
> no routine pattern. They sound fresh and significant in unexpected
> places, too: I don't recall ever before hearing them pulse so richly
> and vibrantly in the horns during the recapitulation of the vengeance
> duet, for example.
>   Making everything on the page sound is clearly one goal of
> Levine's conducting, and making it mean something is another; both are
> realized with remarkable consistency. I admire, too, the specificity of

orchestral color, the way timbres are more vividly and sharply realized than in most performances: the lustrous vibrato of the cellos at the start of the love duet, or the many varieties of string staccato, differentiating the percussive pounding of the storm (some of this played rather louder than Verdi's dynamic, I am afraid) from the seething rush in Otello's mind (after "Ora e per sempre addio").

Levine's only Mozart at the Metropolitan was *Don Giovanni,* with Sherrill Milnes in the title role, in the spring of 1974. This was originally planned as a new production to be conducted by Karl Böhm, but financial considerations dictated that the old Eugene Berman decor be refurbished instead. Deprived of a promised new production, Böhm withdrew, and Levine agreed to take over, providing he was given the same rehearsal time that would be scheduled for a new production. In his *New York Times* review, Harold Schonberg reported:

James Levine conducted his first "Don Giovanni" at the Metropolitan, and turned in an impressive piece of work. Rhythmically steady, beautifully coordinated, his work had cumulative impact. He led a sound, though not particularly revelatory performance of the Overture, but, as the opera proceeded, he loosened up. In the final scene he was absolutely brilliant. He fully achieved the strength and horror without forcing; here his conception was genuinely big, yet under total control.

Nevertheless, says Levine, "I feel that Mozart is the one standard operatic style that the Met does not do as well as other places," and outlines plans to inaugurate a complete overhaul of Mozart repertory with *Die Entführung aus dem Serail* in 1979–80: "Let me put it this way. The acoustics of this house are quite amazing. Especially considering it's a four-thousand-seat house. We've discovered that intimate dramatic things can be done here if they're thrust forward enough on the stage, and if they're acoustically backed up enough. The idea is to try to design some Mozart for this theater that would allow one to use great Mozart singers in these productions even if they happened at various times to be very good actors whose voices weren't the most gigantic. You get much better ensemble, you get much better detail if you don't have to use a huge performing force for Mozart. I think we now have in our quasi-*stagione* scheduling a much better way of putting together a Mozart ensemble and rehearsing it. There were, even in the previous so-called golden period of Met history, plenty of harrowing examples, such as Reiner and a lovely cast getting together to do *Don Giovanni* but one member not coming until the last two days before. We're out of that now. I think there is a chance to put some Mozart productions in the repertoire which would be at the same standard with the other things that we are doing."

Modern opera has always been a problem at the Metropolitan, more so possibly than in heavily subsidized European theaters. Yet, in the 1976–77 season both *Lulu* and *The Dialogues of the Carmelites* were superbly performed and box-office successes. *Lulu* had never been performed at the Met in the more than forty years since Berg's death. Likewise, after its premiere at the Met in 1959, *Wozzeck* had been revived only twice before Levine conducted it in the fall of 1974, when Schonberg reviewed it for the *Times*:

One significant difference, however, is the presence of James Levine as conductor. Several things have been working in his favor. The orchestra does not find Berg's writing as puzzling as it did the first time around. And musicians these days have been exposed to music of much greater novelty and technical demands than *Wozzeck*. Audiences, too, have been exposed to the new music. They no longer greet *Wozzeck* as though it was a two-headed monster. . . . Mr. Levine and the orchestra, far from fighting the score, handled it in an almost easy-going, post-Romantic manner. There was none of the hysteria, neuroticism and tightness that earlier performances of *Wozzeck* used to show. Mr. Levine approached the score as it should be approached—as a part of the mainstream of music. He conducted a kind of warm, colorful performance that put into highlight the Wagnerian influence that went into *Wozzeck*. As Mr. Levine went on through the evening, one did not think in terms of modern music. One thought only in terms of music.

Even more important to Levine, however, was to bring the Metropolitan up to date with *Lulu* in the spring of 1977. For this production, he worked with the musicologist George Perle, an expert on Berg, for advice on musical questions as well as staging. Perle was one of the few scholars ever to have studied Berg's materials for the unfinished third act of *Lulu* and was able to advise Levine and Dexter on the importance of the structural aspects of the opera as a whole in influencing the staging and music. It was not only possible to stage fragments of the originally published *Lulu* Suite as an abbreviated third act but also to design the entire production to fit into plans, now set for 1980–81, eventually to stage the full three-act version of the opera. In his *Newsweek* review of the 1977 *Lulu,* Hubert Saal wrote:

> The Met's orchestra, under James Levine, attacked the prodigious twelve-tone music as if the composer himself were in the audience. The marvelous score starts off with an enormous surge of energy and rarely flags thereafter. Concentrated, dense, hectic, descriptive, the music is deeply involved in the drama on the stage, and the wild trumpet and saxophone keenings are as expressive as the human voices.

However, several critics have noted that, despite Levine's extraordinary ability with such difficult twentieth-century scores, the young music director of America's leading opera company has yet to schedule a world premiere of a new opera, native or foreign.

Levine's first Wagner productions, *Lohengrin* and *Tannhäuser,* have been great successes, in considerable part thanks to his direction of the orchestra, as Andrew Porter noted in his *New Yorker* review of *Tannhäuser* in January 1978:

> All season, the Met orchestra has been playing supremely well, with uncommon richness and beauty of tone, and for Mr. Levine they gave their best. At Cincinnati two years ago, he showed himself to be a remarkably impressive conductor of *Tannhäuser,* and once again his combination of breadth and energy, of lyricism and grandeur proved irresistible. . . .
>
> Under his baton the music flowed, surged, sank, rose again naturally, convincingly, with unforced urgency. One small point: he must persuade

his trombones to play the big tune in the Overture more smoothly, to hold the notes for something like their full value.

After a visit to New York in the fall of 1977, Peter Heyworth wrote a general review of musical activity there for the *London Observer*, which included a report on the achievements of the new regime at the Metropolitan Opera:

In the past, the effect of the way in which New York finances its musical pleasures has been nowhere more evident than at the Metropolitan Opera. That is hardly surprising; opera is the most costly of all the arts and is accordingly more dependent on its sources of funds than any other. Under Rudolf Bing the Metropolitan set out to pander to the tastes of its subscribers, and an unparalleled procession of great singers paraded across its boards like models at a dress show, without much trace of any other artistic preoccupation. There was no musical director, no director of productions, only an assistant to an artistic director, who himself paradoxically remained anonymous. It was a case of *Bing über alles* and the results were usually deplorable, considering the stature of the artists involved.

In the last two or three years, the Metropolitan has, however, been undergoing a transformation that has attracted less attention than the reforms that Rolf Liebermann has brought about in Paris. But in some ways hardly less remarkable. The source of this renewal is James Levine, American-born and still only thirty-four, Levine made his debut at the Metropolitan in 1971 and was last year appointed its musical director, a post that had hitherto been non-existent, apart from Rafael Kubelik's brief tenure after Bing's retirement.

As an opera conductor, Levine is a natural. His approach is vigorous yet sensitive, dramatic yet direct. In the opening bars of *Pelléas and Mélisande* my ear was immediately seized by the warmth and responsiveness of an orchestra which I recall as distinctly mediocre in the Bing era. The chorus has also been transformed beyond recognition. But Levine is much more than a first-rate craftsman. His *Pelléas* was translucent in texture and supple in phrase, and if his grip of the work's architecture is not quite the equal of Boulez's, his articulation of detail and firm rhythms give the music a proper sense of backbone. His handling of a new production of *Rigoletto* was even more impressive, for here he matched fiery rhythms and a bold sense of line to fine-grain shadings of timbre and dynamics.

Not everything he does is on this level. His *Eugene Onegin,* for instance, suffered from oddly unconvincing tempi that robbed the score of its dramatic pace and unity. But Levine has brought the Met a new sense of musical discipline, so that, even when he himself is not in the pit, standards remain high. He has also successfully extended an unduly narrow repertoire. Last season, Berg's *Lulu* and Poulenc's *Carmelites* drew virtually sold-out houses, something of a triumph, considering the notorious tastes of the theatre's subscribers. . . . But as well as the superb register of singers the house still commands, there is now an entirely new sense of musical purpose.

Levine's current contract with the Metropolitan Opera, running until 1981 with an option for another five years, calls for him to be on hand from late August until May each season with time out for occasional guest appearances with such orchestras as the Boston Symphony, the New York Philharmonic, and the Philadelphia Orchestra. But he must be available the year round to the Metropolitan officials, who sometimes travel to Ravinia or Salzburg to confer with him in person when a long-distance call does not suffice.

James Levine was born June 23, 1943, in Cincinnati. Both of his parents had been involved in performance arts, his mother as a young actress in New York, where she had also studied at Martha Graham's school, and his father as a violinist and dance-band leader. After they met and married, his parents settled down in Cincinnati, where his father joined the family clothing business. Jimmy showed his talent early, beginning his piano lessons at the age of four, and shortly stopped stuttering. Although his parents did not push him, they gave him every encouragement, including arrangements for early release from school so that he could practice the piano more. When he was ten, he played Mendelssohn's Second Piano Concerto with the Cincinnati Symphony

Orchestra under Thor Johnson at a youth concert. He arranged that engagement with his teacher's help, without his parents' knowledge; the first they knew of it was when they overheard their son discussing over the phone whether he should be listed as James or Jimmy in the program.

Cincinnati was a good city for a musically oriented youngster to grow up in. It had a long tradition of musical activity, thanks to the many Germans who settled there before the Civil War. One of the first musicians' unions was organized there: Local no. 1 of the American Federation of Musicians. Cincinnati was one of three cities, along with New York and Chicago, where Theodore Thomas had his greatest impact in the decades after the Civil War: he visited there frequently with his own touring orchestra; founded its May Festival, which he conducted from 1873 until his death in 1905; and was for a short time director of a conservatory there. A later conservatory has long been one of the finest professional music schools in this country. The Cincinnati Symphony Orchestra and the summer opera, which used to perform at the zoo but now appears in the Music Hall, have long been mainstays of the city's cultural life, which has been strongly supported by private philanthropy. The Music Hall, built to accommodate the May Festival, is one of the most notable gems of American Victorian architecture to survive intact and well preserved.

When the May Festival celebrated its one-hundredth anniversary in 1973, its director, Robert Shaw, asked Levine, as an outstanding musician from Cincinnati, to participate by performing the Mahler Eighth Symphony. This he did with such great success that he was shortly invited to become director of the festival, a post he held from 1974 through 1978, when he reluctantly gave it up because of the pressure of his work at the Metropolitan and elsewhere. Levine was of course well aware of the unique tradition of the May Festival—a gathering together of a number of amateur choruses from all over Cincinnati for a little more than a week of performances of large-scale choral and operatic music. Levine gave his own first concert performances of *Lohengrin, Tannhäuser,* and *Parsifal* there, thus carrying on the tradition of Thomas, who crusaded on Wagner's behalf a century ago by bringing to

(243)

America major Wagnerian singers for memorable performances of this then new and controversial music.

By the time Levine was ten, his parents were deeply aware that they had a prodigy in the family and were concerned with his training. To celebrate his debut with the Cincinnati Symphony, they took him to New York during spring vacation for a visit that included performances at the Metropolitan Opera, a recital by Rudolf Serkin in Carnegie Hall, and several Broadway shows: "I heard *Così fan Tutte*, *Faust*, *La Bohème*, *Cavalleria* and *Pagliacci*, and a gala with scenes from *Don Carlo*, *Rigoletto*, and the second act of *La Traviata* with the same cast as the Toscanini recording. I had a wonderful time and a very interesting experience. Even though I had never been to New York, I felt somehow at home there, more so than I've ever felt anywhere else. It was sort of as though I had been there before."

The Levines also arranged an advisory audition for their son at the Juilliard School of Music, after which the dean, Mark Schubart, recommended against moving their son from Cincinnati at that time. The La Salle String Quartet, a group trained at Juilliard, was moving to Cincinnati as quartet-in-residence, and Schubart recommended that the youth's piano lessons be supplemented with training in chamber music and general musicianship with Walter Levin, its first violinist: "And when my parents called him, he said, 'The ten-year-old has not been born that I would teach." But my parents persuaded him to come over and have dinner at our house, after which he said yes. He was kind of intrigued, and we started then and there a relationship that still flourishes to this day. He really opened the doors to all of the cultural world to me, not only by the direct teaching of theory, harmony, score-reading, repertoire, stylistic issues but by simply referring to things that stimulated me to read and study when he was away on his tours. Even now we find when we meet a couple of times a year—I sometimes visit him in Switzerland in the summer; when I go to Cincinnati for the May Festival he is there; and he comes to New York once or twice a year—that we still confer about music and what was a teacher-student relationship has turned into something great."

Attending the Marlboro School of Music in the summer of 1956 provided a major turning point in Levine's youthful development as an artist. Then as now, Marlboro was built around the idea of chamber music, fervently pursued night and day by a mixture of very talented young musicians and a few very experienced older ones, many of them of Austro-German background. The school had been the creation of Adolf Busch and his son-in-law, Rudolf Serkin, who continues his unique leadership to this day. If chamber music became indispensable to young Levine at Marlboro, another experience had an equally important long-range impact on him: "The opera department at Marlboro was very small, just enough people to put on *Così fan Tutte* with one keyboard player in the pit to play the recitatives. The conductor Carl Bamberger had seen me hanging around the rehearsals and asked me if I wanted to conduct the chorus backstage and work on the production, which I agreed to do. After all, I'd been exposed to Cincinnati summer opera and had been studying a lot of music with Walter Levin that had nothing to do with the piano."

Although he was from then on committed to conducting as an objective, the following summer found him starting piano lessons with Rosina Lhevinne at Aspen. She wanted him to move to New York to study full time with her, but his parents thought it better for him to stay in Cincinnati and attend high school there. Consequently, he flew to New York every other weekend for his lessons with Madame Lhevinne and, of course, went every summer to Aspen to continue his studies there. Rosina Lhevinne was an extraordinary person and teacher; she was seventy-seven when Levine started studying with her. She had for years taught jointly with her husband, Josef, at the Juilliard Graduate School. After his death in 1944 she came into her own as one of the most renowned teachers of piano anywhere in the world. She was devoted to "Jeemey," the only pupil she accepted who was not aiming for a career as a solo pianist. Once he graduated from high school in Cincinnati, he enrolled for four years at Juilliard, majoring in conducting, but continuing his piano classes with Madame Lhevinne. At that time, only piano majors were eligible to compete in hotly contested auditions to select soloists for appearances with the Juilliard Orchestra, and Madame Lhevinne lobbied assiduously to get that rule changed so that Levine could compete. She never succeeded, and Levine had to content himself with playing second piano—often much better—for fellow students in the auditions.

Levine suspects that his relation with Rosina Lhevinne may have differed from that of students for whom the piano was their major concern. Sometimes she would exclaim, "It's such a pity that you're not going to spend all your time with the big solo repertoire because your hand is so perfect for it."

According to Levine, "She had a great respect for Walter Levin, and because of my relationship with Walter, my relationship to her developed a very unique bent. She thought his kind of thought, musically, represented a more comprehensive, more modern education than she had had. As a result, I think she was much more interested in musical discussion and two-way contact with me than she was with her students in general. For example, she never played in public in all the years I spent with her without closeting herself with me in a room and playing her piece for me and asking me to comment. I think she thought it was part of her own need for growth and for longevity to be in touch with some input from my generation, which was most fascinating and touching because it made our musical relationship much more stimulating than for a lot of her students."

At Juilliard, Levine was a conducting student in the class of Jean Morel, a Frenchman who also conducted from time to time at the Metropolitan and the New York City Opera. Although Morel was never a big-name conductor, he was a superb teacher. In over twenty years at Juilliard, he taught such important young conductors as Jorge Mester of the Louisville Orchestra; Leonard Slatkin of the St. Louis Symphony; John Nelson of the Indianapolis Symphony; Dennis Russell Davies, former conductor of the St. Paul Chamber Orchestra and now active in Germany; and James Conlon, who guest-conducts frequently and is on the staff of the Metropolitan. One great advantage that Morel's conducting class enjoyed was the chance to work regularly with the excellent instrumentalists in the Juilliard student orchestras. The conducting students were also encouraged to organize their own ensembles and orchestras and prepare them for performance in public concerts at the school. Levine was especially assiduous in employing his talent for organization and persuasion, and he produced a number of memorable performances during his four years at Juilliard. He also had the opportunity to study chamber music with the members of the Juilliard String Quartet and to play in ensembles with such talented fellow students as Itzhak Perlman and Pinchas Zukerman.

Nevertheless, Levine's central purpose at Juilliard was to learn conducting with Morel, to whom he still acknowledges a great debt. Morel, he recalls, had a rare technical ability. "He had," says Levine, "an extraordinary grasp of conducting technique and knew how to apply theory of conducting to practical situations." Despite some weakness in the classical German repertory, he had a thorough and enthusiastic knowledge of the French repertory from Berlioz to Debussy, Ravel, and French contemporaries. Levine found his grasp of *Carmen* and *Pelléas et Mélisande* quite extraordinary. Finally, the young student was captivated by the cultivated urbanity of the French conductor. While Morel was conducting French opera at the Met, Levine attended all of his rehearsals, which were followed by long discussions of the finer points of the music. They also attended many other performances at the old Thirty-ninth Street house and sat up most of the night with scores discussing the performances they had just heard.

Beginning in 1957, Levine spent nine summers at the Aspen School of Music, formally as Rosina Lhevinne's piano student but increasingly involved in a variety of chamber music and conducting activities. By his last summer there he was on the conducting staff. "My work at Aspen," says Levine, "in tandem with what I was doing with Walter in Cincinnati and with Rosina in New York, very largely shaped my *musical* personality. In those days, Aspen was something phenomenal. Aspen was something like a fantasy utopia. I owe a huge part of my musical makeup to what went on there, to what I experienced there. I started as a student when I was fourteen. I went nine consecutive summers. In the course of those nine summers, I began as a student and finished as a faculty member in opera and conducting and chamber music. In those days, there was a large faculty of performers who taught. There were very few people who performed and didn't teach, or taught and didn't perform. The music school was integrated into the town. We lived in the town, we ate in the town, our rehearsal and practice buildings were in the town. This was before they came up with a campus outside the town itself. In those days it was limited to three hundred students, which meant a little community in which there could be real interaction. When you are in your teens, your adolescence, this interaction that comes on every level is very significant for your growth. And there were a hell of a lot of musicians with whom my relationships started there, like Lynn Harrell, Adele Addison, the Juilliard Quartet, Bobby Mann, Rudi Firkusny, Jennie Tourel, Mack Harrell, Vronsky and Babin, Leonard Shure, Szymon Goldberg, not to mention a lot of orchestra first-chair players like Ray Still, Jimmy Chambers, Phil Farkas, Anshel Brusilow, Leonard Sharrow—fabulous musicians of various sorts—Darius Milhaud and Madeleine Milhaud, with whom I was in daily contact for all those years.

"I studied conducting and piano—piano with Rosina, of course, and conducting with Wolfgang Vacano, who taught for many years at Indiana University. He gave me my first opportunity actually to conduct opera performances because it was his theory that I was cut out for a certain involvement in opera and that if I was going to coach in the opera department, the last performance should be turned over to me, which he began doing in 1961, when I was eighteen. In Aspen there were seminars, there were master classes, there were rehearsals, there were concerts, there was this constant interaction. And Jennie, for example, I started working with because I played lessons for her. I played lessons for her students. And then I played in her master class. And then she began to call on me to prepare her own concerts for her a little bit, and then, years later when I was conducting, I invited her as soloist a couple of times with me and we did the Mahler *Wayfarer* songs and the Second Symphony, and then I played a recital with her in New York, which was actually the only time we ever appeared in recital together.

"There was a kind of indescribable community and the repertoire was fabulous because in order to get a really stimulating refueling kind of artistic experience, the repertoire tended to be minor works by major composers or major works by minor composers, rather than those same pieces that get overworked year after year in the winter season. You were lucky if you heard a Schubert Ninth Symphony or a Beethoven piano concerto when it came to standard repertoire. For the most part, those performances were very few and far in between. It was mostly chamber music. Many special concerts—concerts of all the Bartók quartets, concerts of Wolf lieder in the opera house, and an unforgettable evening when Mack Harrell and Leonard Shure performed *Winterreise*. Countless things like that."

At Aspen, Levine formed a close friendship with Lynn Harrell—son of the American baritone—who later became principal cellist of the Cleveland Orchestra when Levine was there as Szell's assistant. The two play sonata recitals whenever possible, and their association has given Harrell a strong notion of what he wants in collaborating with a pianist, as he told Henahan of the *Times* in 1977: "For me, a pianist must have his own strong musical ideas, and this is contrary to the way most accompanists are trained. The pianist who is subservient, who gives up his personality to the soloist, is all wrong. That's the way it used to be in the old days, but it doesn't work now. A pianist who plays *Winterreise* or *Die Schöne Müllerin* does as much as one who plays a solo in a Beethoven sonata recital—maybe more, because the accompanist also has to adjust to the singer."

After nine summers at Aspen, Levine spent much of the next four traveling in Europe, visiting with musicians and attending the major festivals. He still returns to Aspen to visit and occasionally teaches there briefly when he can find time in an increasingly crowded schedule.

During his fourth year at Juilliard, Levine participated in a Ford Foundation workshop for young conductors at the Peabody Conservatory of Music and Baltimore Symphony Orchestra. One of the instructors there was George Szell, who immediately asked Levine to audition for an assistantship with the Cleveland Orchestra that was then vacant.

As a result of a successful audition, in the fall of 1965 Levine joined the Cleveland Orchestra conducting staff, which included Robert Shaw, Louis Lane, and Michael Chary. He remained there until Szell's death in the summer of 1970. Despite differences of personality, Levine and Szell shared certain basic approaches to music: clarity of line and texture, and carefully controlled expression. Both were great admirers of Toscanini and his sense of fidelity to the composer. From the outset, Szell was extremely impressed both by Levine's natural talent and by a command of repertory that he had never encountered in such a young musician. Both were also pianists of solo caliber who were dedicated to conducting.

Assistantships under Szell were very active posts. Levine not only conducted the youth concerts that seem to be the obligatory lot of the assistant conductors but also had a few chances to conduct the orchestra in regular concerts. But most important was Szell's personal interest and the training he imparted. Simply to watch him at work was an educational experience for a young conductor, and Szell was always constantly available for discussion of music, pieces he was himself rehearsing or works outside his current programs that Levine was working on. On other occasions, Szell would drill Levine in passages of particular instrumental complexity. "Let's hear the oboe part," he would say, and Levine would sing a phrase. "Now let's hear the second clarinet," Szell would continue. A prodigy conductor himself, he had at twenty staggered Richard Strauss with his ability to play *Till Eulenspiegel* from memory at the piano, reproducing the sound of the ratchet by running his cufflinks over the keyboard. In Levine, he encountered a youth who had a similarly prodigious command of music.

Inevitably there were conflicts between two such strong artistic personalities, tensions in the conductor-assistant, teacher-student, or master-protégé relationship. Levine recalls conducting the final movement of the Beethoven Seventh Symphony at a youth concert in Severance Hall: Szell had dropped in to listen, standing at the back of the auditorium, and afterward tore into the young conductor for "mistreating" Beethoven with his Cleveland Orchestra. As Levine gained experience in

(250)

Cleveland and word of his ability began to spread, Szell received inquiries from colleagues about his assistant. On several occasions he recommended Levine very highly to Kurt Herbert Adler, director of the San Francisco Opera: "If you want a conductor who will know the score cold by memory before he comes and if you want somebody young and brilliant, take him." Then, at one point, Szell became angry with Levine and responded to Adler's next inquiry: "Yes, but his personality is very unreliable." Nevertheless, Szell took a warm personal interest in Levine, who recalls one evening at the conductor's home after a concert at which Peter Serkin had been soloist. Mrs. Szell retired early, leaving the three musicians talking and playing music. As Levine and young Serkin played four-hand piano music for Szell, he became so excited that he woke Mrs. Szell to come and hear their impromptu performance.

To Levine, Szell's relationship with the Cleveland Orchestra represented one of the last of what he viewed as the "Golden Age" of American symphony orchestras—a close and long-lasting affiliation of a great conductor with a great orchestra. Working with Szell in Cleveland, Levine learned how great orchestras operate on a day-to-day basis. Szell's encyclopedic mastery of the Austro-German classics was important to Levine after Morel's concentration on the French repertory. However, fantastic as Szell's grasp of various musical styles was, Levine found in the end that his own conception of working with an orchestra was quite different from Szell's. "I don't force, but I want big contrasts," he has said, "because I find that forcing an orchestra shuts it down. The sound shuts down and becomes crushed, dry, grainy, hard, not vocal, and that was one of my biggest objections to Szell's music-making—the lack of vocal legato, vocal line, breath. It was interesting because, of course, the man was phenomenally perceptive and illuminating about structure—classical structure particularly—and the chamber-style balances that he could get were fabulous, but I always wished for a greater line, greater vocality, greater breath, and greater physical sensuality, less abstraction."

Levine recalls encountering Szell immediately after he had been rehearsing with the Berlin Philharmonic at Salzburg. " 'Jimmy,' said Szell, 'You'll never be able to get that beautiful, big warm fiddle tone like that in Cleveland.' I bit my tongue. It was all I could do not to say, 'But, Uncle George, it's because whenever a violinist auditions with you who has that kind of sound, you reject him in favor of one who comes in with a little wiry sound, who has all the sixteenth notes in the right place.' Of course, I didn't say that, but it was interesting how he appreciated the Berlin Philharmonic sound and didn't realize that everything he did in Cleveland was counterproducing that sort of sound."

Like other assistants at the Cleveland Orchestra, Levine was approached to conduct semiprofessional orchestras in outlying communities. He declined these offers, but when Victor Babin of the Cleveland Institute of Music approached him with another proposal, both he and Szell agreed it was a remarkable opportunity. Babin, of course, knew Levine well from Aspen and engaged him to establish an orchestra program for the institute's students. This gave Levine an opportunity to explore repertory in actual performance as he could not have with the Cleveland Orchestra. It made it posssible for him to remain with Szell without feeling pressed to get out and find another orchestra of his own. With Aspen as a model, Levine had, by the time he left Cleveland in 1970, built this student orchestra at the institute to a level that he could conduct it in public performances of Mahler, Stravinsky, Ligeti, Berg, and Schoenberg. Colleagues from the Cleveland Orchestra, some of them on the institute faculty, worked as coaches and, when needed, as principals in this student orchestra. Some of its activity was sponsored jointly by Case-Western Reserve University. Levine also conducted a chamber orchestra and an opera theater—all outside his regular duties at the Cleveland Orchestra.

In the summer of 1967, his Cleveland colleague Robert Shaw was invited to organize a summer music institute at the University of Oakland in Meadowbrook, a suburb of Detroit. He asked Levine to join him and train a student orchestra there. Although Shaw remained only one year, Levine spent part of three summers at Meadowbrook, instructing in orchestra, chamber music, and opera. Both there and in Cleveland, he organized opera performances—some staged and some in concert form—using established professionals as well as students.

By the time he was twenty-six Levine had amassed an impressive variety of training and experience—study with Walter Levin in Cincinnati, piano with Rosina Lhevinne, conducting with Jean Morel, Marlboro and Aspen, Cleveland with Szell and the Cleveland Institute, Meadowbrook, and extensive travel in Europe. He had also established certain gods in his pantheon, musical figures of the past whom he literally worships to this day as having a seminal influence on his own music-making. They are Arturo Toscanini, Maria Callas, and Wieland Wagner.

Levine never heard Toscanini in person; the NBC Symphony had ceased before he was making his biweekly trips to New York. He therefore knows Toscanini only from records and tapes and from the reminiscences of such musicians as bassoonist Leonard Sharrow, cellist Frank Miller, and tenor Jan Peerce. To Levine, "Toscanini epitomizes what a conductor should be. A conductor's job is to put before the public as perceptive an account of the composer's intentions as possible, as vital an account, as true an account. Now, we can argue all the semantics of a statement like that, but Toscanini was faithful to that definition, to that concept. I would be the first to say he made mistakes; everybody does. I'd be the first to say, not all of it is that great; what is? But Toscanini, more consistently than anyone, laid the composer's work before the listener without filtering it through small-mindedness, pettiness, imperception, willful subjective superimposing. The thing that made him so controversial is that unfortunately people like to have things in generalities, which you can't have in art. Everything is specific, and they like to have things in pigeonholes and therefore they like to say, this conductor is subjective and that's Stokowski; that conductor is objective and faithful to the score and that's Toscanini. Fortunately Toscanini's personality was too volatile, too vital to be in any way academic. Why people should ever imagine someone performing something academically as being faithful to the score is the last thing in the world any composer ever wanted. Dry as dust is not why a person writes a piece.

"Basically it's a question of attitude. I admire Toscanini because he was the epitome of the right attitude. It's not a question of always making the right decision. God knows, there have been from Reiner and Szell and Monteux and Mitropoulos and Klemperer and Knappertsbusch and Furtwängler and Kleiber and Rodzinski wonderful performances, but Toscanini represented the apex, the top of what a conductor should be in my opinion."

Such is Levine's devotion to Toscanini that he regards the Bayreuth recording of *Tannhäuser* conducted by Karl Elmendorff as a quasi-Toscanini recording, because it was of a production that Toscanini had prepared and conducted but could not record. "The playing is so fabulous," Levine declares. "That orchestra really sounds like an orchestra that had rehearsed and performed that piece with Toscanini, and there are some stunning things in that performance."

Levine also finds of interest "pirate" tapes of Toscanini's rehearsals: "I find they give you almost the same stimulus you get from discussing knotty musical problems with a colleague. You come in contact with that person's grappling with those very same problems. What happens is that you may discover certain places where you agree and certain places where you don't agree. You go back to the score, and you look again. You hear something you are toying with as a possibility, but it doesn't work. Or you hear something you toy with as a possibility and it does work. And there is a certain stimulus from it.

"But I think people have a whole misconception about what we do when we listen to rehearsals and performances, something about mimicking or copying. You can't mimic or copy. It's just nonsense. You're dealing with your own pulse and your own ear and a completely different set of musicians and a completely different set of singers, and the only sense in which one copies or mimics is that you hear something with which you absolutely agree, you go in that direction."

Knowing as he does from secondhand but authentic accounts of

Toscanini's autocratic control of an orchestra—of his rages and personal abuse of players—Levine still feels that it is not necessary to instill fear into an orchestra in order to obtain good performance: "One can get as good results based on mutual respect, empathy, rapport, communication. Frankly, for me it would have to be that way because the other way I can't function. I am totally shut down in a hostile atmosphere. If the air is crackling with hatred, I can't work. Therefore I think it wrong to equate a lack of fear with a lack of discipline. But I do see a basic problem here. Go back to the era when there was a lot of fear. There have been great results from some of the great disciplinarians, but I don't believe for a minute that if Toscanini or Reiner appeared at this moment, they would get any less good results than they got before, but they would in certain respects have to use other means. The trouble with that era was that a lot of small, petty, sadistic conductors, who didn't have the greatness of that handful, terrorized people way out of proportion to their value.

"I have found in the moments in which I have done gratifying music-making that when I felt I got close to the composer's wishes in any way, I didn't find a fear response would have improved it."

Levine declares with enthusiasm, "Callas was sort of the singing counterpart to what I said of Toscanini. I'm a singer freak. I love the human voice; I love singers. I think there have been an enormous number of great singers. I could make a very long list. But in our time, Callas had a level of expression, a level of communication of the composer's essential point. In other words, if you read what composers write on the subject of what was important to them in performances of their works, it always is, in various words, fidelity to the point—not fidelity to the letter but only fidelity to the letter when it is in fact fidelity to the point. Now this is a very complicated area because there are certain things in which fidelity to the letter is an absolute must, but other times when that falls short of the ultimate perception. Callas had a way of harnessing her personality, her skills, her technique, her extraordinarily colorful instrument to perform something that was like the ultimate of what the composer imagined, wanted. It functions for me as a kind of model of what the expressive substance—the character of expression—as a kind of model of what the expressive substance of music is really all about.

"Now, once again, you can break that apart too. She didn't have a beautiful voice? To me, it was a very beautiful voice—it was a human voice, it was a voice of incredible expressive power, which is what beauty is all about to me. There are singers who can make abstracted sounds that some people say are beautiful, but to me they sound like interplanetary space communication. I can't feel the emotion behind them; therefore, its beauty is limited for me. I could name a lot of singers who may have made objectively more beautiful sounds, but if you listen to Callas sing *Lucia* on the 'pirate' recording with Karajan from Berlin, if you listen to her sing *Butterfly* on her early recording with Karajan, if you listen to her sing *Forza del Destino* on her recording with Serafin, or *Vespri* on the 'pirate' recording with Kleiber in the Maggio Musicale, you hear that she *is* these people. And I don't mean that in some kind of mystical bullshit baloney sense. If you hold the score in front of you, she was faithful to the musical values, she was faithful to the rhythmic values. She had the ultimate perception of the verbal values."

Wieland Wagner's productions at Bayreuth made a very great impression on Levine: "He opened to me what a theatrical experience could be. For many years, a conflict had arisen in me between the opera I saw in my head and the opera I saw when I walked into a theater. In my head I could see the incredible drama of human conflicts, human passions, and human problems—psychological layers and visceral layers. But when I walked into a theater, I saw wigs and fake beards and fake sword fights. Blue back-cloths hang across the back of the stage, and somebody says, 'That's a blue sky.' But to me, it looks like a blue back-cloth. People were trying to sort of imitate cinematic art on the stage. But from the first thing I ever saw of Wieland's, I realized that he was turning on the theater in your imagination, was giving you those cues, those stimuli that would interact with the music the way the music, after all, goes directly into your bloodstream, like alcohol. If somebody speaks in words, there is a moment when it filters through your brain in order for you to understand what the words mean. You cannot just interpret the words as sound. When people play music, it goes directly to your nervous system without being filtered through the question of what does the music mean.

"Wieland understood that effect, that the stage should function on a different level. I have seen only occasionally—from a John Dexter, from a Franco Zeffirelli, from a Jean-Pierre Ponnelle, from a Giorgio Strehler—productions that were in their way on that level. Now those men are all different, and I don't think Wieland would have been wonderful staging a Rossini comedy or Mozart operas. I don't think anyone can touch John Dexter's staging of *Lulu,* of *Dialogues of the Carmelites,* of *Vespri,* the kind of thing which is in his kind of vision. Strehler has done things—like his *Marriage of Figaro* or his *Abduction* in Salzburg—that were just incredible. Ponnelle's *Clemenza di Tito* in Salzburg.

"But for the most part, operatic stage direction immediately prior to Wieland aimed at a certain imitation of movie reality, which was mostly canvas and spirit gum and fake. Wieland showed that you could put a drama on the stage that fired the imagination, that drew you in, that magnetized you, that made you more perceptive dramatically— at one with the composer's vision musically, psychologically. I guess the other thing that attracts me to him is that he represents the kind of career that is undeniably historically important and, therefore, extremely controversial. Almost nothing which moves this art form ahead can exist without that kind of controversy."

By 1970, Levine's long contact with Wilford was beginning to produce engagements that he was happy to accept because, even before Szell's death, he was finally prepared to leave Cleveland. He was now ready to explore the American orchestral world before settling down in the kind of close affiliation that he always considered ideal. In June of 1970 he appeared with the Philadelphia Orchestra in Robin Hood Dell in the first of many appearances with that orchestra. Later that summer, he traveled to Cardiff to conduct the Welsh National Opera in productions of *Aida* and *Il Barbiere di Siviglia,* his first appearances with a fully professional opera company. In the early fall, his freedom from commitments in Cleveland finally made a San Francisco appearance possible, conducting the *Tosca* that Robert Herman of the Metropolitan heard. During this time he began appearances with orchestras all over the United States that eventually took him to Atlanta, St. Louis, Pittsburgh, Los Angeles, San Francisco, Boston, New York, Denver, Oakland, and Washington, D.C.

However, it was in the summer of 1971 that his career took a great leap with engagements that were to have long-range consequences for him. In June, he conducted *Tosca* at the Metropolitan Opera. Later that month, he made his first appearance at the Ravinia Festival. In July, he conducted another *Tosca,* this time in the Greek Theater of Griffith Park in Los Angeles; this was a production featuring Dorothy Kirsten.

"After the performance," Levine recalls, "a man came backstage and introduced himself with a very British accent. It was Ernest Fleischmann. He said, 'I am executive director of the Los Angeles Philharmonic, and I want to tell you to your face that I haven't seen conducting like that in many a year. You must come and work with the Los Angeles Philharmonic. Have lunch with me tomorrow.' So I did, and he called Ronald right there and booked me with the Philharmonic for the next summer, which was the first available opening. A month after we'd met, while I was on vacation in Michigan, Ernest called me. 'I have a problem. Zubin has hurt his back and cannot conduct his five Bowl concerts. Would you be willing to do them? All of them, or any of them?' Although it was my vacation, I couldn't resist such a show of faith. He'd just seen me conduct one Greek Theater *Tosca,* and here he was holding a *Traviata* for me with Sills, Domingo, and Milnes; and he had a Wagner concert with Ingrid Bjoner and Jess Thomas all set up for *Ring* excerpts. So I said, 'I'd like to do those opera concerts but, for the sake of balance, one symphonic concert too. Why don't I do three concerts, and somebody else the other two?' Ernest is a great colleague and a great friend. Of all the orchestras with whom I have a guest-conducting relationship, outside perhaps of Philadelphia, I have conducted the Los Angeles Philharmonic more often—nearly every year. I did many of my first performances there and have a wonderful rapport with the orchestra, which I love. Ernest created an atmosphere there for me where I could really work fully. The woman I live with, Sue Thomson, who plays the oboe, was out there on one occasion, on which she said, 'You rehearse this orchestra as if it was your own! It is so effortless.' "

Like the Metropolitan *Tosca* in early June of 1971, his debut at the Ravinia Festival later that month had very important consequences. Following Seiji Ozawa's departure as principal conductor in 1969, the post was taken by a fine Hungarian conductor, the late István Kertész, who failed, however, to bring the electric excitement that Ozawa had generated. Moreover, he had an exceptionally active career in Europe. Eugene Ormandy had been scheduled to open the 1970 Ravinia season with the Mahler Second Symphony but canceled, promising to return in 1971. That year he again canceled; he was having serious trouble with his hip, for which he subsequently had replacement surgery. However, the Ravinia manager Edward Gordon felt it imperative to give his patrons a Mahler Second on the opening night in 1971 with Kertész. When he fell ill in Europe and was forbidden by his doctors to fly to the United States, word reached Gordon about a week before the season was to open. "It was very short notice," Levine recalls, "and he rooted around trying to find another conductor associated with Mahler. Wilford told him, 'You know, I have a young conductor who did the piece with his student orchestra at Meadowbrook. He knows it by memory. He could do it.' Only as a last resort, Ed took me, and I remember him calling me up to verify that I had really done the piece and really did know it, because of course he was risking his neck with the Chicago Symphony Orchestra."

The first rehearsal for the Mahler Second was on Levine's twenty-eighth birthday. So impressed was Gordon by its beginning that he spent the intermission phoning Wilford: "Now that's the man I would like to have for a music director here." Bernard Jacobson reported the success of this debut in the *Chicago Daily News*:

This gifted twenty-eight-year-old musician earned every last resounding cheer. He had taken the concert over at a week's notice from István Kertész (who was himself a replacement for the originally scheduled Eugene Ormandy), and everything he did was proof of thorough preparation, fine artistic judgment and the ability to communicate ideas to the orchestra and, through it, to the audience. There were a number of unusual touches in the interpretation, but almost all of them proceeded from the conductor's exceptional clear-sightedness in his study of the score. A good instance was the end of the first movement, where those fateful descending triplets were for once performed at the main tempo of the movement, in exact accordance with Mahler's instructions, and not at the much faster speed we commonly hear. What does matter is the depth and vividness of his knowledge, and his capacity to convey it to his listeners. In these respects, Levine is already a master, and if he can escape the damaging effects of early celebrity that have corrupted more than one promising talent, he will someday be a great one.

As Gordon's call to Wilford prophesied, Levine was indeed engaged as music director of Ravinia after a second series of concerts in 1972. His engagement, announced in October 1972 to take effect the following summer, resulted as much from the imaginative ideas he put forth for Ravinia's future as from the excitement generated by his conducting.

Under Levine's direction, and fully supported by the managerial expertise of Gordon, Ravinia has developed into the kind of diversified music activity that its sponsors had talked about for years but never achieved. The Chicago Symphony remains the centerpiece of the festival, but its concerts are surrounded by a variety of chamber music and solo recitals—some involving the orchestra players themselves, others offering visiting soloists and ensembles. Levine himself plays the piano frequently in chamber music or as collaborator in recitals. The twelve-week season also offers a number of "popular" attractions and performances of modern dance and ballet. Levine's special contribution has been the variety and vitality of his music programming. In 1978, he and the orchestra presented with soloists and chorus a complete performance of *Les Troyens,* in two evenings, as well as Bach's *St. Matthew Passion.* That being a Schubert year, the composer's music was featured in the orchestral programs, chamber concerts, and song recitals. Some of the evening concerts are preceded by one-hour "Previews," in which music related to the program is played by some of the soloists and members of the orchestra; Levine plans the Previews and appears in some of them.

Levine's basic responsibility is conducting the Chicago Symphony Orchestra, which plays three concerts a week—usually on four rehearsals—for the first eight weeks of the festival season. Levine generally conducts the first four of the weeks before leaving for Europe to conduct Mozart operas in Salzburg and to make recordings in London. His program has frequently been very imaginative, as when, on one night in 1972, he prefaced a concert version of the first act of *Die Walküre* with a performance of the Bach D-minor Clavier Concerto conducted from the piano. Given the limited rehearsal time, he must rely on repertory that the orchestra already knows, but he manages each season to program music new to the players: Berlioz's *Les Troyens,* Schoenberg's *Gurrelieder,* and all of the orchestral songs of Berg, for instance. However, novelty alone is by no means Levine's only forte at Ravinia. In 1972, he conducted a performance of the Schubert Ninth Symphony of which Jacobson commented:

[Levine] had an opportunity to show his mettle in the sort of music by which a performer's full range and depth may be fairly judged. He responded with one of the most profound and comprehensive realizations of a large-scale classical symphony in several years of Chicago concert life. Like other conductors who have become disenchanted with the mythical "objectivity" of the Toscanini school, Levine is not afraid to bend a tempo when it suits his expressive purpose. He did this several times, very gently, in a generally mobile reading of the slow movement, evoking the sense of so many corners around which the listener might peer to see what new beauties were in prospect. He did it again, more dangerously but I think with success, at the stark denouement of the finale, where the pounding repeated unisons seemed intent on arresting the headlong course of the music.

But these touches and others like them had to be apprehended in the context of Levine's conception as a whole. Thus, though the lilt of the Scherzo—given, for once, with all its repeats intact—sounded more lilting than ever, yet the threatening overtones in the development section emerged from the dance with complete inevitability. This was the conducting of a master. Levine's previous exploits here, impressive as they were, involved works that can be brought off by sheer craftsmanship. But Schubert's Ninth yields its secrets only to an artist.

On another occasion, in 1975, Levine programmed the Mahler Third Symphony at Ravinia in order to record it for RCA. Although the record producer scheduled six three-hour sessions for this work, Levine thought it could be completed in five and asked that the orchestra material for the Brahms First, also in the Ravinia repertory that summer, be on hand for the recording session. Despite the doubts of everyone else, a fine record of the Mahler was taped in five sessions, and the sixth was used for the Brahms symphony, recorded in virtually one basic take for each movement with a few inserts by way of correction. The record was so successful that it became the first of a complete series of Brahms symphonies. In addition to Mahler and Brahms symphonies, RCA has also recorded some of the chamber music that Levine has made such an important part of the Ravinia Festival.

A measure of Levine's growth at Ravinia was taken by Thomas Willis in the *Chicago Tribune* when the Mahler Second Symphony was repeated in 1977:

It was conductor Levine's evening, nevertheless, and nothing should be allowed to obscure the fact. This was the work with which he opened the 1971 season, pinch-hitting at the last moment while he was still based in Cleveland. For a conductor still in his twenties, the fact that he could bring this gigantic, challenging score to a successful performance under Ravinia's current rehearsal conditions was in itself amazing. Amazing is one thing, superbly paced and moving to the point of tears is another. In the intervening years, Levine has matured in giant steps until today he is one of the three or four major interpreters of his generation. There was a time when this undeniable facility and earlier developing talent seemed to have limits. A major career could be predicted without risk, but no more. One felt the presence of a confident but static personality, who would be satisfied with an encyclopedic knowledge of the repertory and an inflexible standard of excellence.

Saturday he proved, as he has on two or three previous occasions in the last year or so, that he is a dynamic performer who is maturing as he grows. This was a performance of spaciousness, risk-taking, spiritual depth, and an expansive understanding of the score's deepest layers of musical meaning.

Despite the opportunity to work with the Chicago Symphony Orchestra and to make recordings with it, Ravinia is a still far from ideal setting for this young conductor to establish a symphonic affiliation comparable to his relation to the Metropolitan Opera. Levine must, therefore, do much of his purely orchestral conducting as a guest. In addition to his engagements with the Los Angeles Philharmonic, he now appears regularly with the New York Philharmonic, the Boston Symphony, and the Philadelphia Orchestra. Under his RCA contract, Levine records with both the Philadelphia Orchestra and the Chicago Symphony. His time abroad is very limited and he currently conducts only the Berlin Philharmonic, Vienna Philharmonic, and the London Symphony; the latter is another orchestra with which he records. The Boston Symphony has regularly engaged Levine as guest conductor since 1972. When it visited Chicago on tour in 1975, it played a benefit concert to raise funds for Ravinia in which a former music director of the festival, Seiji Ozawa, and the current one were featured, Levine playing a Mozart piano concerto. Later that year, Levine conducted the Boston Symphony at Symphony Hall in a performance of Debussy's *Images* that especially impressed Richard Dyer of the *Boston Globe*:

> What Levine did show was why he has a reputation as a complete, natural musician. One has heard more nuance in other performances of *Images*—but not all those nuances sounded natural; one has hardly heard more buoyancy, more sheer fluency. Levine clearly loves not only to mould the sounds of music but also to listen to them as well. He seemed well-pleased to be playing a great instrument like the BSO.

When Levine conducted the Mozart C-minor Mass with the Boston Symphony in the spring of 1978, Dyer ranked it "with the best Mozart performances I have heard in Symphony Hall":

> In nearly all the music I have heard him conduct or play, James Levine has either set or at least matched the present international standard of performance, because in him the musical impulse is so strong and so natural. After a Levine performance one hardly ever thinks of his interpretation; instead one thinks about the music and of how fresh it has been made to sound. Even the occasional defects and lapses in the performance are usually only exaggerations, generated by the excitement, of what is a right thing to do. And his positive qualities are such remarkable ones—a wide knowledge, love of all kinds and styles of music, a technique that enables his work to move in a clear, strong line, from intention to effect, an especially wonderful way of working with singers, is something that is at once reassuring and challenging.

Aside from tending to his artistic growth, Levine has a clear idea of what he wants to work toward in the next decade or so: "By the time I'm fifty, I want an approximately eight-month-a-year working period, with a guaranteed four months that I can deal with without advance planning, which means time to rest, time to travel, time to read, time to think, time to practice the piano consistently again, time to accept a project on the spur of the moment that's irresistible. In the other eight months, what I would want primarily to do is work with one opera company and one orchestra, and do all my media work, any television, records, etc., with those two organizations. It seems to me that the only way to do that is to build toward it. I don't expect it to appear full-blown."

Toward this end, Levine already organizes his life very thoroughly, with minimum distraction from music. He recalls from his childhood how he resented having to interrupt piano practice or study of scores to join the family at dinner, where he had to engage in small talk while his mind wanted to concentrate on more important matters. One afternoon, when his mother called for him at school, she noted that he was carrying a score of *Don Giovanni*. When she expressed concern about how he could get any work done at school that way, he replied, "Oh, mother. I got so much done on the second act just today." Summers at Marlboro and Aspen and the biweekly trips to New York gave him a welcome sense of independence early in his teens. Rather than providing a chance to dawdle or become diverted, such freedom was cherished as an opportunity to organize his time in the most productive way. Nowadays, with two major posts involving artistic administration, he needs good staff support in addition to that provided by the Metropolitan Opera and the Ravinia Festival. His younger brother, Tom, who studied accounting and business administration but has turned to painting, assists him a great deal in his rather diversified professional affairs.

Nevertheless, for all the pressures on him and demands for his time and attention, Levine is an extremely happy and gregarious person while he is making or administering music. Paradoxically, though he often seems to be spinning in orbit, there is nothing hectic or tense about him. Amidst a casting crisis at the Metropolitan, he can leave one meeting for another on a totally unrelated matter and relax completely, leaning back in his swivel chair, nibbling on a sandwich, and sipping a diet drink, seemingly without a care in the world while he concentrates on the immediate business before him.

Given such extraordinary talent and the rapid rise in his career since 1971, it is surprising that there have been as few mistakes on his part, so little unfortunate consequence of inevitable hubris. Although a London reporter visiting New York in 1974 was amazed to find no one with a bad word for Levine in New York, that is no longer the case. Some observers at and around the Met complain that he is undertaking too much, spreading himself too thin. Others have observed that although he can be very tough-minded about music, his very gregarious good-natured fondness for people makes it difficult at times for him to say no. He shares what seems to be an occupational desire of most conductors—to be liked—and this could undermine the kind of toughness that administering a vast and complex lyric theater requires. Nevertheless, Levine is learning to be tough, and there are unquestionably many more instances of his upholding the artistic standards of the Metropolitan Opera than the widely publicized complaints of Lucine Amara, Joan

Sutherland and her husband, and James McCracken indicate. (In each instance, it must be noted, the Metropolitan's position was officially put forth by Bliss, but there can be no question that all such artistic problems are decided with Levine's full participation.)

Early in his tenure as music director, Levine publicly set forth certain goals and a rough timetable for achieving them. Many outside the Met agree that he is, if anything, well ahead of schedule in establishing a higher general standard of performance in that theater. Moreover, his personal achievement as conductor in such productions as *Otello, Lulu, Tannhäuser,* and *Don Carlo* places him in the forefront of operatic conductors today. Given the way in which his artistic direction of the house is intertwined with his conducting there, it might be difficult to say whether he could have achieved his artistic successes without also having the administrative authority he wields. There is no question, however, that the Metropolitan Opera has benefited greatly from having as its music director a conductor so talented as Levine is. Nevertheless, much as he has contributed to the Metropolitan's well-nigh miraculous recovery, it is unfair and unrealistic to expect him to be a miracle-worker always, either as administrator or as conductor.

Toward his goal of eight months in opera and with orchestra and four for vacation and last-minute opportunities, Levine has yet to settle into an orchestral situation. Exciting as Ravinia is—for Levine and for those he serves—it is not the kind of affiliation that Levine talks about when he hankers for the Golden Age of Koussevitzky, Stokowski, and Stock. Although his name has come up on the short list for every important orchestral vacancy in the United States in recent years, he has not yet felt ready to take on that task. Although this unquestionably must be the next major step in his career, it may be difficult to coordinate it with his commitment—contractually, artistically, and personally—to the Metropolitan Opera. Moreover, as a young man who has come very far very fast, his artistic ambition may outrun the maturity needed to cope with the progress of his career once the honeymoon he has been enjoying at the Metropolitan is over. Thanks to extraordinary talent and training, plus shrewd management of his career so far, he is now at the top of a very slippery pole.

RECORDINGS

THE following lists include all performances conducted on records by the eight conductors in this book. They are based on a thorough review of the *Schwann Catalog* and *Artist Issue* and the composer and artist sections of the *Gramophone Classical Catalogue* from 1962 (the year of the Tartini concertos conducted by Abbado) to the end of June 1979. The German, French, and Italian counterparts of these catalogs have also been consulted in some instances. In an effort to present a complete listing, records no longer available are included, but within parentheses ( ) ; if a recording has never been issued in the United States or United Kingdom, the indication is "(No U.S.)" or "(No U.K.)," as the case may be.

If only one catalog number is given, it refers to American availability unless otherwise stated. Where two numbers appear, the first applies to the United States, the second to the United Kingdom; "id." signifies release in both countries under the same catalog number. Where a performance has been issued under different numbers, the latest and most likely to be encountered separately is given; if a performance is available only in a set, the number is preceded by "in."

As a guide to the *approximate* age of recordings, dates in parentheses indicate the month of review in *Gramophone* magazine, where such information is available. A few records issued after June 1979 are included, as are some recordings known to have been made but not released. This information should not be taken as complete or even accurate.

DANIEL BARENBOIM

BARENBOIM's recordings of the Beethoven piano sonatas are indispensable to any appreciation of the extraordinarily rich musicianship he had developed by his mid-twenties. Since the few excerpts from the complete series offered in the United States are not an adequate sampling, one must turn to English releases of the sonatas singly or to the complete set.

Equally important are the Mozart concertos with Barenboim as soloist and conductor. Although the full series, on single records or in a boxed set, is available only in England, the American release of the last eight concertos is an excellent example of Barenboim's work. Recorded somewhat later are the violin concertos with Pinchas Zukerman and the *Sinfonia Concertante,* in which Isaac Stern joins his young Israeli friends; here Barenboim's Mozart is firmer rhythmically, possibly responding to Zukerman's more aggressive style.

In fact, some of Barenboim's most interesting conducting has been in collaboration with Zukerman and Itzhak Perlman in well-integrated Bach concerto performances. And, of course, the Haydn, Boccherini, Elgar, and Dvořák concertos with Du Pré are unique treasures. The Elgar, being from a concert performance in Philadelphia, shows the individuality of the two musicians and the almost improvisatory spontaneity of their reaction to one another.

These concerto records have their counterpart in the ensemble records that Barenboim has made—the Brahms sonatas with Du Pré, Zukerman, and de Peyer; the Beethoven sonatas and trios with Du Pré and Zukerman. No overview of Barenboim as a musician can ignore these collaborations— uneven at times but frequently exciting.

Barenboim's exploration of Mozart and Haydn symphonies has been reasonably thorough. A comprehensive representation of Mozart is offered in Britain, but American listeners must be content with rather unconvincing readings of the G-minor and *Jupiter.* Likewise, Haydn is better represented in the U.K., although the two U.S. Haydn symphony releases are excellent.

With the Chicago Symphony, Barenboim's Schumann has been more successful than his Bruckner. The latter, of course, is beautifully projected by the Chicago orchestra, but Barenboim fails to maintain a consistent sense of the music's line. His Schumann is highly personal, but the young conductor's interpretive originality has convincing logic.

BACH: Concertos for Violin in A-minor, S. 1041, for Violin in D-minor, S. 1052, and for Violin and Oboe, S. 1060.* English CO (Perlman, *Black). Ang 37076; EMI ASD 3076 (6/75).

BACH: Concertos for Violin in E, S. 1042,* for Two Violins in D-minor, S. 1043, and for Violin in G-minor, S. 1056.** English CO (*Perlman, **Zukerman). Ang 36841; EMI ASD 2783 (12/72).

BACH: *Magnificat,* S. 243; BRUCKNER: *Te Deum.* New Philharmonia O (Popp, Baker, Tear, Hemsley; Pashley, Finnala, Tear, Garrard; New PO Cho). Ang 36615; EMI ASD 2533 (2/70).

BARTÓK: *Music for Strings, Percussion and Celesta* and *Divertimento.* English CO. Ang 36760; (EMI ASD 2670) (2/72).

BEETHOVEN: Piano Concerto in D-major, Op. 61*a.* English CO (Barenboim). DG 2530 457 id. (10/74).

BEETHOVEN: Piano Concertos nos. 1–5. London PO (Rubinstein). RCA CRL-5-1415 id. (5/76).

BEETHOVEN: Violin Concerto in D-major, Op. 61. New York PO (Stern). Col M-33587; 76477 (3/76).

BEETHOVEN: Violin Concerto in D-major, Op. 61. Chicago SO (Zukerman). DG 2530 903 id. (11/77).

BERLIOZ: *La Damnation de Faust,* Op. 24. O de Paris (Mathis, Domingo, Fischer-Dieskau, Bastin, O de Paris Cho). 2 DG 2709 087 id. (7/79).

BERLIOZ: *Harold in Italy,* Op. 16. O de Paris (Zukerman). Col M-34541; 76593 (6/77).

BERLIOZ: Excerpts from *Roméo et Juliette* and from *Les Troyens.* O de Paris. Col M-35112.

BERLIOZ: *Symphonie Fantastique,* Op. 14. O de Paris. DG 2531 092 id. (5/79).

BERLIOZ: *Te Deum.* O de Paris (Dupouy, Choruses). Col M-34536; 76578 (8/77).

BIZET: *Carmen* Suite, *L'Arlésienne* Suite, and *Jeux d'Enfants.* O de Paris. (Ang 36955) (EMI ASD 2915) (1/74).

BIZET: Symphony in C-major, *Patrie* Overture, and *Jolie Fille de Perth* Suite. O de Paris. (No U.S.) EMI ASD 3277 (10/76).

BOCCHERINI (arr. Grutzmacher): Cello Concerto in B-flat major; HAYDN: Cello Concerto in C-major. English CO (Du Pré). Ang 36439; EMI ASD 2331 (10/67).

BORODIN: Dances from *Prince Igor*; Mussorgsky: *A Night on Bald Mountain*; RIMSKY-KORSAKOFF: *Russian Easter* Overture and *Festival Overture.* Chicago SO. DG 2530 657 id.

BRAHMS: *Ein Deutsches Requiem,* Op. 45. London PO (Mathis, Fischer-Dieskau, Edinburgh Festival Cho). 2 DG 2707 066 id. (1/73).

BRAHMS: *Hungarian Dances*; DVOŘÁK: *Slavonic Dances*; LISZT: *Les Préludes*; SMETANA: *The Moldau.* Chicago SO. DG 2531 054 id.

BRUCKNER: Mass no. 2 in E-minor. English CO (Aldis Cho). Ang 37112; (EMI ASD 3079) (10/75).

BRUCKNER: Mass no. 3 in F-minor. New Philharmonia O (Harper, Reynolds, Tear, Rintzler, New Philharmonia O Cho). Ang 36921; (EMI ASD 2836) (12/72).

BRUCKNER: Symphony no. 4 in E-flat major, *Romantic*. Chicago SO. DG 2530 336 id. (8/73).

BRUCKNER: Symphony no. 5 in B-flat major. Chicago SO. (DG to be released.)

BRUCKNER: Symphony no. 6 in A-major. Chicago SO. DG 2531 043 id. (11/78).

BRUCKNER: Symphony no. 9 in D-minor. Chicago SO. DG 2530 639 id. (4/76).

CHAUSSON: *Poème*; FAURÉ: *Berceuse*; SAINT-SAËNS: Violin Concerto no. 3 in B-minor, Op. 61. O de Paris (Stern). Col M-34550; 76530 (4/77).

CIMAROSA: *Il Matrimonio Segreto*. English CO (Ayger, Varady, Hamari, Davies, Fischer-Dieskau). 3 DG 2709 069 id. (9/77).

DEBUSSY: Excerpts from *Le Martyre de Saint Sébastien* and *Printemps*. O de Paris. DG 2530 879 id. (10/77).

DEBUSSY: *La Mer* and *Nocturnes*.* O de Paris (*O de Paris Cho). DG 2531 056 id. (3/79).

DEBUSSY: *Prélude à l'Après-Midi d'un Faune;* CHABRIER: *España;* IBERT: *Escales;* RAVEL: *Daphnis et Chloé* Suite no. 2. O de Paris. Col M-34500.

DELIUS: *On Hearing the First Cuckoo in Spring, Summer Night on the River*, excerpts from *Fennimore and Gerda, Two Aquarelles*; WALTON: Excerpts from *Henry V*; VAUGHAN WILLIAMS: *Greensleeves* and *The Lark Ascending*.* English CO (*Zukerman). DG 2530 505 id. (4/75).

DVOŘÁK: Cello Concerto in B-minor, Op. 104, and *Silent Woods,* Op. 68. Chicago SO (Du Pré). Ang 36046; EMI ASD 2751 (1/72).

DVOŘÁK: Serenade in E-major, Op. 22; TCHAIKOVSKY: Serenade in C-major, Op. 48. English CO. Ang 37045; (EMI ASD 3036) (11/74).

DVOŘÁK: Violin Concerto in A-minor, Op. 53; Romances, Op. 11. London PO (Perlman). Ang 37069; EMI ASD 3120 (10/75).

ELGAR: Cello Concerto, Op. 85,* and *Enigma* Variations, Op. 36.**
*Philadelphia O (Du Pré) ; **London PO. Col M-34530; 76529
(11/76).

ELGAR: *Chanson de Nuit, Chanson de Matin, Elegy, Serenade, Salut
d'Amour, Romance, Rosemary, Carissima,* and *Sospiri.* English CO. Col
M-33584; 76423 (11/75).

ELGAR: *Falstaff,* Op. 68, and *Cockaigne* Overture. London PO. Col
M-32599; 76284 (9/74).

ELGAR: *Pomp and Circumstance* Marches 1–5, *Crown of India* Suite, and
Imperial March. London PO. Col M-32936; 76248 (9/74).

ELGAR: *In the South* and *Sea Pictures.** London PO (*Minton). U.K.
Col 76579 (8/77).

ELGAR: Symphony no. 1 in A-flat major, Op. 55. London PO. Col
M-32807;.76247 (9/74).

ELGAR: Symphony no. 2 in E-flat major, Op. 63. London PO. Col
M-31997 (73094) (3/73).

ELGAR: Violin Concerto, Op. 61. London PO (Zukerman). Col M-34517;
76528 (11/76).

FAURÉ: Requiem and *Pavane.* O de Paris (Armstrong, Fischer-Dieskau,
Edinburgh Festival Cho). Ang 37077; EMI ASD 3069 (6/75).

FRANCK: *Le Chasseur Maudit,* excerpts from *Psyché,* and *Nocturne.** O de
Paris (*Ludwig). DG 2530 771 id. (12/76).

FRANCK: Symphony in D-minor and *Rédemption.* O de Paris. DG 2530
707 id. (10/76).

HAYDN: Sinfonia Concertante in B-flat, Op. 84; MOZART: Sinfonia Concertante in E-flat, K. 297a. English CO. Ang 36582; (EMI ASD
2462) (5/69).

HAYDN: Symphonies no. 44 in E-minor, *Trauersymphonie,* and no. 49 in
F-minor, *La Passione.* English CO. DG 2530 708 id. (2/77).

HAYDN: Symphonies no. 45 in F-sharp minor, *Farewell,* and no. 48 in
C-major, *Maria Theresia.* English CO. DG 2531 091 id. (7/79).

HAYDN: *Paris* Symphonies, nos. 82–87. English CO. (No U.S.) (EMI
SLS 5065) (10/76).

HINDEMITH: *Trauermusik*;* SCHOENBERG: *Verklärte Nacht*; WAG-
NER: *Siegfried Idyll.* English CO (*Aronowitz). Ang 36484; (EMI
ASD 2346) (2/68).

MOZART: Concertone in C-major, K. 190; PLEYEL: Sinfonia Concertante in B-flat major, Op. 29. English CO (Stern, Zukerman). Col M-32937 (73310) (12/74).

MOZART: Concerto for Three Pianos in F-major, K. 242,* and Concerto for Two Pianos in E-flat major, K. 365. English CO (Ashkenazy, Barenboim, and *Fou T'Song). Lon 6937; Dec SXL 6716 (8/68).

MOZART: *Don Giovanni,* K. 527. English CO (Sgourda, Harper, Donath, Soyer, Evans, Alva, Scottish Op Cho). (Ang SDL 3811; EMI SLS 978) (4/75).

MOZART: Flute Concerto in D-major, K. 313,* and Oboe Concerto in C-major, K. 314.** O de Paris (*Debost, **Bourgue). Ang 37269; EMI ASD 3320 (3/77).

MOZART: *Le Nozze di Figaro,* K. 492. English CO (Berganza, Blegen, Harper, Evans, Fischer-Dieskau). (No U.S.) EMI SLS 995 (7/77).

MOZART: Piano Concertos nos. 1–6, 8, 9, 11–27, and Rondo in D-major, K. 382. English CO (Barenboim). (No U.S.) EMI SLS 5031.

Note: The following Mozart piano concertos by Barenboim are available on EMI as follows: 1, 2, 3, 4 (ASD 3218) ; 6, 26 (ASD 3032) ; 8, 25 (ASD 3033) ; 11, 16 (ASD 2999) ; 12, 19 (ASD 2956) ; 13, 17 (ASD 2357) ; 14, 15 (ASD 2434) ; 18, 24 (ASD 2887) ; 20, 23 (ASD 2318) ; 21, 27 (ASD 2465).

MOZART: Piano Concerto no. 20 in D-minor, K. 466, and Piano Sonata no. 17 in D-major, K. 576. English CO (Barenboim). Ang 36430.

MOZART: Piano Concerto no. 21 in C-major, K. 467,* and Symphony no. 40 in G-minor, K. 550. English CO (*Barenboim). Ang 36814.

MOZART: Piano Concertos nos. 21–27, and Rondo in D-major, K. 382. English CO (Barenboim). 4 Ang 3830.

MOZART: Requiem, K. 626. English CO (Armstrong, Baker, Gedda, Fischer-Dieskau). Ang 36842; EMI ASD 2788 (7/72).

MOZART: Serenade no. 10 for Thirteen Wind Instruments in B-flat major, K. 361. English CO. (No U.S.) EMI ASD 3426 (1/78).

MOZART: Serenade no. 13 in G-major, *Eine Kleine Nachtmusik,* K. 525, Divertimento no. 7 in D-major, K. 205, and Marches nos. 9 and 10 in D-major. English CO. (No U.S.) EMI ASD 2610 (11/70).

MOZART: Sinfonia Concertante in E-flat, K. 364; STAMITZ: Sinfonia Concertante in D-major. English CO (Stern, Zukerman). Col M-31369; 73030 (10/72).

MOZART: Symphonies no. 29 in A-major, K. 201, no. 30 in D-major, K. 202, and no. 34 in C-major, K. 334. English CO. (No U.S.) (EMI ASD 2806) (7/72).

MOZART: Symphonies no. 31 in D-major, *Paris,* K. 297, and no. 41 in C-major, *Jupiter,* K. 551. English CO. (No U.S.) EMI ASD 2379 (9/69).

MOZART: Symphonies no. 32 in G-major, K. 318, no. 35 in D-major, *Haffner,* K. 385, and no. 38 in D-major, *Prague,* K. 504. English CO. Ang 36512; EMI ASD 2327 (9/67).

MOZART: Symphonies no. 33 in B-flat, K. 319, and no. 36 in C-major, *Linz,* K. 425. English CO. (EMI ASD 2583) (9/70).

MOZART: Symphonies no. 39 in E-flat major, K. 543, and no. 40 in G-minor, K. 550. English CO. (No U.S.) EMI ASD 2424 (8/68).

MOZART: Symphony no. 41 in C-major, *Jupiter,* K. 551, and Serenade no. 13 in G-major, *Eine Kleine Nachtmusik,* K. 525. English CO. Ang 36761.

MOZART: Violin Concertos nos. 1–5, and Adagio in E, Rondo in C, and Rondo Concertante. English CO (Zukerman). U.K. 3 Col 77381.

MOZART:Violin Concertos no. 1 in B-flat major, K. 207, and no. 3 in G-major, K. 216. English CO (Zukerman). Col M-32301.

MOZART: Violin Concerto no. 2 in D-major, K. 211, Rondo in C-major, K. 373, Rondo Concertante, K. 261*a,* and Adagio in E-major, K. 261. English CO (Zukerman). Col M-33206.

MOZART: Violin Concertos no. 4 in D-major, K. 218, and no. 5 in A-major, K. 219. English CO (Zukerman). Col M-30055.

RODRIGO: *Concerto de Aranjuez;* VILLA-LOBOS: *Concerto for Guitar.* English CO (Williams). Col M-33208; 76369 (1/75).

SAINT-SAËNS: Cello Concerto no. 1 in A-minor, Op. 33; SCHUMANN: Cello Concerto in A-minor, Op. 129. English CO (Du Pré). Ang 36642; EMI ASD 2498 (11/69).

SAINT-SAËNS: Symphony no. 3 in C-minor, Op. 78. Chicago SO (Litaize). DG 2530 619 id. (4/76).

SCHUMANN: Symphonies nos. 1–4, *Manfred* Overture, and *Konzertstück for Four Horns.* Chicago SO. (U.S. only) 3 DG 2709 075 (also separately no. 1 and no. 4 on 2530 660 id., no. 2 and *Konzertstück* on 2530 939 id., and no. 3 and *Manfred* Overture on 2530 940 id.) (3/78, 4/78).

SIBELIUS: Violin Concerto in D-minor, Op. 47; BEETHOVEN: Two Romances. London PO (Zukerman). DG 2530 552 id. (10/75).

TCHAIKOVSKY: Symphony no. 4 in F-minor, Op. 36. New York PO. Col M-30752; (72926) (6/71).

VAUGHAN WILLIAMS: Oboe Concerto (Black), *The Lark Ascending* (Zukerman), and Tuba Concerto (Jacobs).* English CO, *Chicago SO. DG 2530 906 id. (2/78).

VIEUXTEMPS: Violin Concertos no. 4 in D-minor, Op. 31, and no. 5 in A-minor, Op. 37. O de Paris (Perlman). Ang 37484; EMI ASD 3555 (11/78).

ANDREW DAVIS

IN his still limited representation on recordings, Andrew Davis has produced a superlative reading of Shostakovich's Tenth Symphony, a major master-piece of our time. He captures the brooding tragedy and nobility of this music possibly better than any other conductor on recordings. The London Philharmonic plays superbly for him. On a budget label, this is a rare bargain.

Davis's Franck and Borodin are straightforward performances, sensitive to the respective styles and idioms, expressive but neither subjective nor idiosyncratic in interpretation. Although he is an enthusiastic Elgarian, his record of *Falstaff* and the *Enigma* Variations is a disappointment. He does not quite convey the necessary Edwardian plush with his rather literal approach. Moreover, the reproduction of the orchestral sound is constricted, probably in the effort to squeeze two long works onto one disc.

BORODIN: Symphonies nos. 1–3 and excerpts from *Prince Igor*. Toronto SO (Mendelssohn Choir). 2 Col M2-34587; 79214 (11/77).

BRITTEN: *Young Person's Guide to the Orchestra*; PROKOFIEV: Excerpts from *Cinderella*. London SO. Col M-33891; 76453 (12/75).

DURUFLÉ: Requiem and *Danse lente*. New Philharmonia O (Te Kanawa, Nimsgren, NP Cho). Col M-34547; 76633 (10/77).

ELGAR: *Enigma* Variations, Op. 36, and *Falstaff*, Op. 68. New Philharmonia O. HNH 4049; Lyr SRCS 77 (9/75).

FAURÉ: Requiem and *Pavane*. Philharmonia O (Popp, Nimsgren, Ambrosian Singers). Col M-35153; 76754 (12/78).

FRANCK: Symphony in D-minor; FAURÉ: Excerpts from *Pelléas et Mélisande*. New Philharmonia O. Col M-34506; 76526 (10/76).

God Save the Queen; HANDEL: *Zadok the Priest*; ELGAR: *Pomp and Circumstance* March no. 1; ARNE: *Rule, Britannia*; WALTON: *Crown Imperial*; PARRY: *Jerusalem*. London PO. (No. U.S.) EMI CFP 198 (5/72).

GRIEG: Excerpts from *Peer Gynt*. New Philharmonia O (Söderström). Col M-34531; 76527 (2/77).

HODDINOTT: Symphony no. 5, Piano Concerto no. 2 (Jones), and Horn Concerto (Tuckwell). Royal PO. U.K. Dec SXL 6606 (3/74).

JANÁČEK: *Taras Bulba* Suite and *Cunning Little Vixen* Suite. Toronto SO. Col M-35117 (No U.K.).

RACHMANINOFF: Piano Concerto no. 2 in C-minor, Op. 18. New Philharmonia O (Vered). Lon 21099; Dec PFS 4327 (3/75).

SHOSTAKOVICH: Symphony no. 10 in E-minor, Op. 93. London PO. Sera 60255; EMI CFP 40216 (5/75).

CLAUDIO ABBADO

UNQUESTIONABLY, Claudio Abbado's most important recordings are two Verdi operas, two Mahler symphonies, and *Carmen*. High as the standard of his earlier work has been, these five releases, all dating from the past few years, mark a substantial advance in his work.

Both *Macbeth* and *Simon Boccanegra* have strong fiber without being heavy, expression without sentimentality, and a supple singing line free of prima donna (or primo tenore) indulgence. In both instances, his casts are first-rate, and because he insists on preceding recording with plenty of actual performance, the ensemble is excellent and the atmosphere vividly theatrical. The La Scala orchestra and chorus perform beautifully, a tribute to Abbado's work as principal conductor and artistic director. The single record of Verdi choruses is a thrilling sampler of grand opera at La Scala.

Although the Rossini operas may be a trifle bland, the new recording of *Carmen* must rank among Abbado's top achievements on records. It has fine style, and again because it was preceded by well-prepared production, the overall ensemble is a delight.

Abbado's Mahler is singularly free of hysteria. Phrasing is expressive, rhythm exciting, and the conductor and recording engineers vividly project Mahler's orchestral palette. The Second and Fourth begin a Mahler series that will feature both the London and Chicago orchestras: a Sixth was taped in Chicago during March 1979.

Although Abbado has expressed dissatisfaction with his Brahms symphonies, the Second is worth seeking out, both for its sweeping interpretation and for the plangency of the Berlin Philharmonic under his direction. All four of his Tchaikovsky symphonies are good, but the Fourth is outstanding, regarded by many as the best current version.

To two earlier London Symphony recordings of Stravinsky, Abbado has added *Pulcinella*; he now plans a comprehensive recorded survey of this composer's orchestral music. His *Le Sacre du Printemps* is one of the best performed and reproduced on records, somewhat richer in texture and color than the composer preferred, but completely honest and free of interpretive self-indulgence.

Abbado's concerto recordings—especially those involving Martha Argerich in Ravel, Prokofiev, Chopin, and Liszt and Maurizio Pollini in Brahms—are notable both for superb pianism and Abbado's alert collaboration.

Finally, Abbado's record of Nono's *"Como una ola de fuerza y luz"* is a brilliant and authoritative documentation of important contemporary music.

BACH: *Brandenburg* Concertos nos. 1–6. La Scala O. (No U.S.) Col 79215 (8/78).

BARTÓK: Piano Concertos nos. 2 and 3. Chicago SO (Pollini). (DG to be released.)

BEETHOVEN: Symphony no. 7 in A-major, Op. 92, and Overture to *Die Geschöpfe des Prometheus*, Vienna PO. (Lon 6510); Dec SXL 6270 (11/67).

BEETHOVEN: Symphony no. 8 in F-major, Op. 93. Vienna PO. (No U.S.) Dec SXL 6549 (1/73).

BERG: *Lulu* Suite,* *Three Pieces for Orchestra*, and *Five Orchestral Songs*.* London SO (*M. Price). (U.S.) DG 2530 146 (4/72).

BIZET: *Carmen*. London SO (Berganza, Cotrubas, Domingo, Milnes). DG 2709 083 id. (11/78).

BRAHMS: Piano Concerto no. 2 in B-flat major, Op. 83. Vienna PO (Pollini). DG 2530 790 id. (8/77).

BRAHMS: *Rinaldo*,* Op. 50, and *Schicksalslied*, Op. 54. New Philharmonia

O (*King, Ambrosian Singers). Lon 26106; Dec SXL 6386 (1/70).

BRAHMS: Serenade no. 2 in A-major, Op. 16, and *Academic Festival* Overture. Berlin PO. (DG 139 371 id.) (10/68).

BRAHMS: Symphony no. 1 in C-minor, Op. 68. Vienna PO. (No U.S.) DG 2530 424 (6/73).

BRAHMS: Symphony no. 2 in D-major, Op. 73. Berlin PO. (U.S.) DG 2530 125 (10/71).

BRAHMS: Symphony no. 3 in F-major, Op. 90, and *Variations on a Theme of Haydn,* Op. 56a. Dresden Staatskapelle. DG 2535 293; 2530 452 (8/74).

BRAHMS: Symphony no. 4 in E-minor, Op. 98. London SO. (*Note*: Although this has not been issued separately in the U.S., Germany, or the U.K., it is included in a set of all four Brahms symphonies issued by the International Preview Society of Great Neck, New York.)

BRUCKNER: Symphony no. 1 in C-minor. Vienna PO. Lon 6706; Dec SXL 6494 (1/71).

CHOPIN: Piano Concerto no. 1 in E-minor, Op. 11; LISZT: Piano Concerto no. 1 in E-flat major. London SO (Argerich). DG 139 383 id. (1/69).

DEBUSSY: *Nocturnes**; RAVEL: *Daphnis et Chloé* Suite no. 2* and *Pavane.* Boston SO (*New England Conservatory Cho). DG 2530 038 id. (12/70).

HINDEMITH: *Symphonic Metamorphoses on Themes of Carl Maria von Weber*; JANÁČEK: *Sinfonietta.* London SO. Lon 6620; Dec SXL 6398 (5/69).

MAHLER: Symphony no. 2 in C-minor, *Resurrection.* Chicago SO (Neblett, Horne, CSO Cho). 2 DG 2707 094 id. (6/77).

MAHLER: Symphony no. 4 in G-major. Vienna PO (Von Stade). DG 2530 966 id. (6/78).

MENDELSSOHN: Symphonies no. 3 in A-minor, *Scotch,* Op. 56, and no. 4 in A-major, *Italian,* Op. 90. London SO. Lon 6587; Dec SXL 6363 (9/68).

MENDELSSOHN: Violin Concerto in E-minor, Op. 64; TCHAIKOVSKY: Violin Concerto in D-major, Op. 35. Vienna PO (Milstein). DG 2530 359 id. (12/73).

MOZART: Mass no. 4 in C-minor, *Waisenhaus,* K. 114a(139). Vienna PO (Janowitz, Von Stade, Ochmann, Moll, St Op Cho). DG 2530 777 id. (3/77).

MOZART: Piano Concertos no. 20 in D-minor, K. 466, and no. 21 in C-major, K. 467. Vienna PO (Gulda). DG 2530 548 id. (11/75).

MOZART: Piano Concertos no. 25 in C-major, K. 503, and no. 27 in B-flat major, K. 595. Vienna PO (Gulda). DG 2530 642 id. (7/76).

NONO: *"Como una ola de fuerza y luz."* Bavarian Radio O (Taskowa, Pollini). DG 2530 436 id. (7/74).

PROKOFIEV: *Buffoon,* Suite no. 1, Op. 21, and excerpts from *Romeo and Juliet,* Op. 64. London SO. Lon STS-15477; Dec JB 56 (5/67).

PROKOFIEV: Piano Concerto no. 3 in C-major, Op. 26; RAVEL: Piano Concerto in G-major. Berlin PO (Argerich). DG 139 349 id. (2/68).

PROKOFIEV: *Scythian* Suite and *Lieutenant Kije* Suite. Chicago SO. DG 2536 967 id. (11/78).

PROKOFIEV: Symphonies no. 1 in D-major, *Classical,* Op. 25, and no. 3 in C-major, Op. 44. London SO. Lon 6679; Dec SXL 6469 (10/70).

RACHMANINOFF: Piano Concerto no. 3 in D-minor, Op. 30. London SO (Berman). Col M-34540; 76597 (6/77).

ROSSINI: *Il Barbiere di Siviglia* (ed. Zedda). London SO (Berganza, Alva, Prey, Montarsolo). 3 DG 2709 041 id. (10/72).

ROSSINI: *La Cenerentola* (ed. Zedda). London SO (Berganza, Capecchi, Alva, Trama). 3 DG 2709 039 id. (6/72).

ROSSINI: Overtures to *Il Barbiere di Siviglia, La Gazza Ladra, L'Italiana in Algeri, Il Signor Bruschino, La Cenerentola,* and *L'Assedio di Corinto.* London SO. DG 2530 559 id. (1/76).

SCRIABIN: Symphony no. 4, *Poème de l'Extase,* Op. 54; TCHAIKOVSKY: *Romeo and Juliet.* Boston SO. DG 2530 137 id. (4/72).

STRAVINSKY: *Jeu de Cartes* and *L'Oiseau de Feu* Suite (1919). London SO. DG 2530 537 id. (8/75).

STRAVINSKY: *Pulcinella.* London SO (Berganza, Davies, Shirley-Quirk). DG 2531 087 id. (4/79).

STRAVINSKY: *Le Sacre du Printemps.* London SO. DG 2530 635 id. (5/76).

TARTINI: Violin Concertos in D-major and F-major. Milan Angelicum O (Gulli). MHS 3223; Italy: Ars Nova UST 6118.

TCHAIKOVSKY: Symphony no. 2 in C-minor, Op. 17, *Little Russian.* New Philharmonia O. (U.S.) DG 139 381 (2/70).

TCHAIKOVSKY: Symphony no. 4 in F-minor, Op. 36. Vienna PO. DG 2530 651 id. (11/76).

TCHAIKOVSKY: Symphony no. 5 in E-minor, Op. 64. London SO. DG 2530 198 id. (4/72).

TCHAIKOVSKY: Symphony no. 6 in B-minor, Op. 74, *Pathétique*. Vienna PO. DG 2530 350 id. (7/74).

VERDI: Arias from *Nabucco, Macbeth, I Vespri Siciliani,* and *Simon Boccanegra.* London SO (Ghiaurov). Lon 26146; Dec SXL 6443 (9/70).

VERDI: Choruses from *Nabucco, Il Trovatore, Otello, Ernani, Aida, Macbeth, I Lombardi,* and *Don Carlo.* La Scala. DG 2530 549 id. (11/75).

VERDI: *Macbeth.* La Scala (Verrett, Domingo, Cappuccilli, Ghiaurov). 3 DG 2709 062 id. (10/76).

VERDI: Overtures to *Aida, Nabucco, La Forza del Destino, Aroldo, Luisa Miller,* and *I Vespri Siciliani.* London SO. RCA ARL1-3345; 31378 (2/79).

VERDI: *Simon Boccanegra.* La Scala (Freni, Carreras, Cappuccilli, Ghiaurov, Van Dam, Foiani). 3 DG 2709 071 id. (11/77).

RICCARDO MUTI

RICCARDO MUTI himself regards Verdi's *Macbeth* and the Mendelssohn *Scotch* Symphony as the best recorded representation of his work. In *Macbeth,* Muti produces a cohesive, well-balanced sound and has full control of the total ensemble. This performance carries greater theatrical impact than, for instance, *Aida* or *Nabucco,* the first and last of his four Verdi recordings.

Symphonically, Muti is systematically building a diversified repertory. If his Mendelssohn *Scotch* stands out, it does not outstrip his fine *Italian* and Schumann Fourth by far. He has made an impressive beginning on a complete Tchaikovsky symphony cycle.

In Philadelphia, he has recorded two Beethoven symphonies, the Seventh and Sixth, again probably part of another series. He is also exploiting the extraordinary orchestral virtuosity of the Philadelphia Orchestra in some colorful Russian music: a coupling of the Mussorgsky-Ravel *Pictures* and the 1919 *Oiseau de Feu* may herald still another planned series. The first of these Philadelphia records, the Beethoven Seventh and the Russian works, were well received in both the United States and England when they were released early in 1979, shortly before Muti's Philadelphia appointment was announced.

CONDUCTORS

Although the *Ivan the Terrible* cantata may not be Prokofiev at his best, Muti's performance is extremely effective. Nor should two records of Italian choral music be ignored: both the Cherubini Requiem and the Vivaldi *Gloria* and *Magnificat* are fine examples of Muti's work.

American listeners should be warned that Angel processing of Muti's orchestral recordings, with the Philharmonia at least, frequently gives a wrong impression of his command of texture. The murky acoustic that is apparently caused by Angel's processing of the original EMI tapes is not heard on the British counterparts of these recordings, which frequently do better justice to the lighter and more transparent sound that Muti elicits from the Philharmonia Orchestra.

BEETHOVEN: Piano Concerto no. 3 in C-minor, Op. 37. Philharmonia O (Richter). Ang 37512; HMV ASD 3543 (12/78).

BEETHOVEN: Symphony no. 7 in A-major, Op. 92. Philadelphia O. Ang 37538; EMI ASD 3646 (4/79).

CHERUBINI: Requiem. New Philharmonia O (Ambrosian Singers). Ang 37096; EMI ASD 3073 (5/75).

DVOŘÁK: Symphony no. 9 in E-minor, *From the New World,* Op. 95. New Philharmonia O. Ang 37230; EMI ASD 3285 (1/77).

MENDELSSOHN: Symphony no. 3 in A-minor, *Scotch,* Op. 56, and *Meeresstille* Overture. New Philharmonia O. Ang 37168; EMI ASD 3184 (6/76).

MENDELSSOHN: Symphony no. 4 in A-major, *Italian,* Op. 90; SCHUMANN: Symphony no. 4 in D-minor, Op. 120. New Philharmonia O. Ang 37412; EMI ASD 3365 (7/77).

MOZART: Symphonies no. 25 in G-minor, K. 183, and no. 29 in A-major, K. 201. New Philharmonia O. Ang 37257; EMI ASD 3326 (5/77).

MUSSORGSKY-RAVEL: *Pictures at an Exhibition;* STRAVINSKY: *L'Oiseau de Feu* (1919 Suite). Philadelphia O. Ang 37539; EMI ASD 3645 (4/79).

SCHUMANN: Symphony no. 2 in C-major, Op. 61, and *Hermann und Dorothea* Overture. Philharmonia O. Ang 37602; EMI ASD 3648 (2/79).

SCHUMANN: Symphony no. 3 in E-flat major, *Rhenish,* and overture to *The Bride of Messina.* Philharmonia O. (Ang to be released.) EMI ASD 3696 (6/79).

TCHAIKOVSKY: Symphony no. 1 in G-minor, *Winter Dreams,* Op. 13.

New Philharmonia O. Ang 37114; EMI ASD 3213 (7/76).

TCHAIKOVSKY: Symphony no. 2 in C-minor, *Little Russian,* Op. 17, and *Romeo and Juliet.* New Philharmonia O. Ang 37472; EMI ASD 3488 (6/78).

TCHAIKOVSKY: Symphony no. 3 in D-major, *Polish,* Op. 29. Philharmonia O. Ang 37496; EMI ASD 3449 (3/79).

TCHAIKOVSKY: Symphony no. 5 in E-minor, Op. 64. Philharmonia O. (Ang to be released.) EMI ASD 3717 (6/79).

VERDI: *Aida.* New Philharmonia O (Caballé, Cossotto, Domingo, Cappuccilli, Ghiaurov). 3 Ang 3715; EMI SLS 977 (2/75).

VERDI: *Un Ballo in Maschera.* New Philharmonia O (Arroyo, Cossotto, Domingo, Cappuccilli, Royal Op Cho). 3 Ang 3762; EMI SLS 984 (12/75).

VERDI: *Macbeth.* New Philharmonia O (Cossotto, Milnes, Carreras, Raimondi, Ambrosian Cho). 3 Ang 3833; EMI SLS 992 (12/76).

VERDI: *Nabucco.* New Philharmonia O (Scotto, Obraztsova, Maniguerra, Ghiaurov). 3 Ang 3850; EMI SLS 5132 (10/78).

VERDI: Overtures to *Nabucco,· Giovanna d'Arco, La Bataglia di Legnano, Luisa Miller, I Vespri Siciliani,* and *La Forza del Destino.* New Philharmonia O. Ang 37407; EMI ASD 3366 (10/77).

VIVALDI: *Gloria* and *Magnificat.* New Philharmonia O (Terrani, Berganza, NPO Cho). Ang 37415; EMI ASD 3418 (12/77).

ZUBIN MEHTA

THE music of Richard Strauss, Mahler, Bruckner, and Schoenberg shows Mehta at his best on records. The coupling of the Schoenberg *Kammersymphonie,* Opus 9, and the *Variations,* Opus 31, is one of the best recordings of this composer's orchestral music. Some of Mehta's Strauss is exceptionally good, especially the *Alpensymphonie,* a seldom-heard work. His early Bruckner Ninth from Vienna is marginally more supple in phrasing than the Eighth from Los Angeles. In Mahler, Mehta avoids subjective excess, but some may find him somewhat too matter-of-fact. His Vienna Second is very good, and the Fifth from Los Angeles is a fine example of the Philharmonic's overall quality.

In *Il Trovatore,* Mehta has produced one of the best Verdi opera performances on records. He masterfully brings out the best—individually and in ensemble—of a fine cast in an opera in which fine singing is indispensable.

Stravinsky is a composer whose music Mehta has always played well, except for his second version of *Le Sacre du Printemps,* his first venture before the microphones with the New York Philharmonic, undertaken before he had actually taken over as music director. Unlike an earlier Los Angeles performance, this one shows Mehta at his flamboyant worst.

BARTÓK: *Concerto for Orchestra* and *Hungarian Sketches.* Los Angeles PO. Lon 6949; Dec SXL 6730 (12/76).

BEETHOVEN: Excerpts from *Die Geschöpfe des Prometheus,* Op. 43. Israel PO. Lon 6660; Dec SXL 6438 (7/70).

BEETHOVEN: Piano Concerto no. 4 in G-major, Op. 58. Israel PO (Lupu). Lon 7108; Dec SXL 6886 (9/78).

BEETHOVEN: Piano Concerto no. 5 in E-flat major, *Emperor,* Op. 73. Vienna Pro Musica (Brendel). Turnabout 34402; TV 34209 (4/68).

BEETHOVEN: Piano Concerto no. 5 in E-flat major, *Emperor,* Op. 73. Los Angeles PO (De Larrocha). Lon 7121; Dec SXL 6899 (4/79).

BEETHOVEN: Symphony no. 7 in A-major, Op. 92, and *Egmont* Overture. Los Angeles PO. Lon 6870; Dec SXL 6673 (10/74).

BERLIOZ: *Harold in Italy.* Israel PO (Benyamini). Lon 6951; Dec SXL 6732 (8/75).

BERNSTEIN: *Candide* Overture; COPLAND: *Appalachian Spring* Suite; GERSHWIN: *An American in Paris.* Los Angeles PO. Lon 7031; Dec SXL 6811 (9/76).

BLOCH: *Schelomo* and *A Voice in the Wilderness.* Israel PO (Starker). Lon 6661; Dec SXL 6440 (7/70).

BRAHMS: Piano Concerto no. 1 in D-minor, Op. 15. Israel PO (Rubinstein). Lon 7018; Dec SXL 6797 (10/76).

BRAHMS: Piano Concerto no. 2 in B-flat major, Op. 83. London SO (Ashkenazy). Lon 6539; Dec SXL 6309 (9/67).

BRAHMS: Symphony no. 1 in C-minor, Op. 68. Vienna PO. Lon 7017; Dec SXL 6796 (3/79).

BRAHMS: Symphony no. 2 in D-major, Op. 73. New York PO. Col M-35158 (5/79).

BRAHMS: Violin Concerto in D-major, Op. 77. New York PO (Stern). Col M-35146 (5/79).

BRUCH: Violin Concerto no. 1 in G-minor, Op. 26; LALO: *Symphonie Espagnole,* Op. 21. Los Angeles PO (Zukerman). Col M-35132 (5/ 79).

BRUCKNER: Mass no. 2 in E-minor and *Te Deum.* Vienna PO (Blegen, Lilona, Ahnsjö, Meier, Vienna St Op Cho). Lon 26506; Dec SXL 6837 (12/77).

BRUCKNER: Symphony no. 4 in E-flat, *Romantic.* Los Angeles PO. Lon 6695; Dec SXL 6489 (4/71).

BRUCKNER: Symphony no. 8 in C-minor. Los Angeles PO. 2 Lon 2237; Dec SXL 6671/2 (9/74).

BRUCKNER: Symphony no. 9 in D-minor. Vienna PO. Lon 6462; Dec SXL 6202 (1/65).

"Canadian Music"—MOTTON: *Mouvement Symphonique* no. 2; MER-CURE: *Lignes et Points.* Montreal SO. (VICS 1040 id.).

COPLAND: *A Lincoln Portrait* (Peck) ; KRAFT: Concerto for Four Percussion and *Contextures.* Los Angeles PO. Lon 6613; Dec SXL 6388 (9/69).

DVOŘÁK: Symphony no. 7 in D-minor, Op. 70. Israel PO. Lon 6607; Dec SXL 6381 (4/69).

DVOŘÁK: Symphony no. 8 in G-major, Op. 88, and *The Wood Dove,* Op. 110. Los Angeles PO. Lon 6979; Dec SXL 6750 (2/77).

DVOŘÁK: Symphony no. 9 in E-minor, *From the New World,* Op. 95, and *Carnival* Overture. Los Angeles PO. Lon 6980; Dec SXL 6751 (11/ 76).

EINEM: *Philadelphia Symphony*; SCHUBERT: Symphony no. 8 in B-minor, *Unfinished.* Vienna PO. (No U.S.) (Dec SXL 6418) (1/70).

ELGAR: *Enigma* Variations, Op. 36; IVES: Symphony no. 1. Los Angeles PO. Lon 6816; Dec SXL 6592 (9/73).

"The Fourth of July"—IVES: Symphony no. 2, "Decoration Day," and Variations on "America"; COPLAND: *Appalachian Spring*; BERN-STEIN: Overture to *Candide*; GERSHWIN: *An American in Paris.* Los Angeles PO. 2 Lon 2246; Dec SXL 6753 (7/76).

"Greatest Hits"—RAVEL: *Boléro*; TCHAIKOVSKY: *Marche Slave*; BIZET: *Carmen* Preludes; VERDI: *La Forza del Destino* Overture; SUPPÉ: *Poet and Peasant* Overture. Los Angeles PO. Lon 6823; Dec SXL 6568 (2/73).

"Hits at the Bowl." Los Angeles PO. Lon XPS-613.

HOLST: *The Planets,* Op. 22. Los Angeles PO. Lon 6734; Dec SXL 6529 (11/71).

LISZT: *Hunnenschlacht, Mazeppa,* and *Orpheus.* Los Angeles PO. Lon 6738; Dec SXL 6535 (4/72).

LISZT: *Les Préludes;* WAGNER: Excerpts from *Lohengrin, Parsifal* Prelude, and *Meistersinger* Prelude. Vienna PO. Lon 6529; Dec SXL 6298 (4/68).

MAHLER: Symphony no. 1 in D-major. Israel PO. Lon 7004; Dec SXL 6779 (9/76).

MAHLER: Symphony no. 2 in C-minor, *Resurrection.* Vienna PO (Cotrubas, Ludwig, St Op Cho). 2 Lon 2242; Dec SXL 6744/5 (12/75).

MAHLER: Symphony no. 4 in G-major. Israel PO (Hendricks). Lon LDR 10004 (U.S. release 6/79).

MAHLER: Symphony no. 5 in C-sharp minor and Symphony no. 10: Adagio. Los Angeles PO. 2 Lon 2248; Dec SXL 6806 (11/77).

MOZART: Symphony no. 34 in C-major, K. 338, and Symphony no. 39 in E-flat major, K. 543. Israel PO. Lon 7055; Dec SXL 6833 (3/77).

MOZART: Symphony no. 40 in G-minor, K. 550, and Serenade no. 13 in G-major, *Eine Kleine Nachtmusik.* Israel PO. Lon 7066; Dec SXL 6844 (5/78).

MUSSORGSKY-RAVEL: *Pictures at an Exhibition.* Los Angeles PO. Lon 6559; Dec SXL 6328 (12/67).

NIELSEN: Symphony no. 4, *The Inextinguishable,* Op. 29. Los Angeles PO. Lon 6848; Dec SXL 6633 (12/74).

PAGANINI: Violin Concerto no. 1 in D-major. Israel PO (Belkin). Lon 7019; Dec SXL 6798 (2/76).

"Philharmonic Solo"—HAYDN: Trumpet Concerto in E-flat major (Stevens) ; VIVALDI: Piccolo Concerto (Zentner) ; WEBER: Clarinet Concerto, Op. 73 (Zukovsky) ; H. WIENIAWSKI: *Polonaise de Concert* and *Scherzo-Tarantelle* (Dichterow). Los Angeles PO. Lon 6967; Dec SXL 6737.

"Pops Concert"—MENDELSSOHN: Excerpts from *A Midsummer Night's Dream;* ROSSINI: *La Scala di Seta* Overture; VERDI: *La Traviata* Preludes and *I Vespri Siciliani* Overture; WEBER: *Oberon* Overture. Los Angeles PO. Lon 7065; Dec SXL 6843.

PUCCINI: *La Fanciulla del West.* Royal Opera (Neblett, Domingo, Milnes). 3 DG 2709 078 id. (9/78).

PUCCINI: *Tosca.* New Philharmonia O (Price, Domingo, Milnes, Aldis Cho). 2 RCA ARL2-0105 id. (3/74).

PUCCINI: *Turandot.* London PO (Sutherland, Caballé, Pavarotti, Ghiaurov, Aldis Cho). 3 Lon 13108; Dec SET 561-3 (9/73).

RAVEL: *Boléro,* etc. Los Angeles PO. Lon 7132; Dec KSXC 6568.

RAVEL: *Daphnis et Chloé* Suite no. 2, *Ma Mère l'Oye* Suite, and *La Valse.* Los Angeles PO. Lon 6698; Dec SXL 6488 (3/71).

RESPIGHI: *Feste Romane*; R. STRAUSS: *Don Juan.* Los Angeles PO. RCA AGL1-1276; LSB 4109 (1/66).

RIMSKY-KORSAKOFF: *Scheherazade.* Los Angeles PO. Lon 6950; Dec SXL 6731 (11/75).

SAINT-SAËNS: Symphony no. 3 in C-minor. Los Angeles PO (Priest). Lon 6680; Dec SXL 6482 (1/71).

SCHMIDT: Symphony no. 4 in C-major. Vienna PO. (Lon 6747); Dec SXL 6544 (2/73).

SCHOENBERG: *Kammersymphonie,* Op. 9, and *Variations for Orchestra,* Op. 31. Los Angeles PO. Lon 6612; Dec SXL 6390 (8/69).

SCHOENBERG: *Verklärte Nacht*; SCRIABIN: Symphony no. 4, *Poème de l'Extase.* Los Angeles PO. Lon 6552; Dec SXL 6325 (1/68).

SCHUBERT: Symphonies no. 1 in D-major and no. 2 in B-flat major. Israel PO. Lon 7114.

SCHUBERT: Symphonies no. 3 in D-major and no. 5 in B-flat major. Israel PO. Lon 7020; Dec SXL 6799 (3/78).

SCHUBERT: Symphonies no. 4 in C-minor, *Tragic,* and no. 8 in B-minor, *Unfinished.* Israel PO. Lon 7067; Dec SXL 6845 (4/79).

SCHUBERT: Symphony no. 6 in C-major and incidental music from *Rosamunde.* Israel PO. Lon 7115.

SCHUBERT: Symphony no. 9 in C-major. Israel PO. Lon 6948; Dec SXL 6729 (7/77).

SCHUMANN: Symphonies no. 1 in B-flat major, *Spring,* Op. 38, and no. 4 in D-minor, Op. 120. Vienna PO. Lon 7039; Dec SXL 6819 (6/77).

R. STRAUSS: *Eine Alpensinfonie,* Op. 64. Los Angeles PO. Lon 6981; Dec SXL 6752 (4/76).

R. STRAUSS: *Also Sprach Zarathustra,* Op. 30. Los Angeles PO. Lon 6609; Dec SXL 6379 (3/69).

R. STRAUSS: *Don Quixote,* Op. 35. Los Angeles PO (Reher). Lon 6849; Dec SXL 6634 (4/74).

R. STRAUSS: *Ein Heldenleben,* Op. 40. Los Angeles PO. Lon 6608; Dec SXL 6382 (5/69).

R. STRAUSS: *Symphonia Domestica,* Op. 53. Los Angeles PO. Lon 6663; Dec SXL 6442 (9/70).

STRAVINSKY: *Petrouchka* (1947 vers.) and *Circus Polka.* Los Angeles PO. Lon 6554; Dec SXL 6324 (1/68).

STRAVINSKY: *Le Sacre du Printemps* and *Instrumental miniatures.* Los Angeles PO. Lon 6664; Dec SXL 6444 (3/70).

STRAVINSKY: *Le Sacre du Printemps.* New York PO. Col XM-34557; 76676 (7/78).

TCHAIKOVSKY: *1812* Overture, Op. 49, and *Romeo and Juliet.* Los Angeles PO. Lon 6670; Dec SXL 6448 (5/70).

TCHAIKOVSKY: Symphonies nos. 1–6. Los Angeles PO. 5 Lon CSP-10; 5 Dec D9506 (2/79).

TCHAIKOVSKY: Symphony no. 4 in F-minor, Op. 36. Los Angeles PO. Lon 6553; Dec SXL 6323 (1/68).

TCHAIKOVSKY: Symphony no. 5 in E-minor, Op. 64. Israel PO. Lon 6606; Dec SXL 6380 (4/69).

VARÈSE: *Arcana, Ionization,* and *Intégrales.* Los Angeles PO. Lon 6752; Dec SXL 6550 (9/72).

VERDI: *Aida.* Rome Opera (Nilsson, Bumbry, Corelli). 3 Ang 3716; (EMI SAN 189–91) (11/67).

VERDI: *Quatro Pezzi Sacri.* Los Angeles PO (Master Cho, Minton). Lon 26176; Dec SET 464 (11/70).

VERDI: *Il Trovatore.* New Philharmonia O (Price, Cossotto, Domingo, Milnes, Giaiotti). 3 RCA LSC 6194; SER 5586 (7/70).

"Virtuoso Overtures"—J. STRAUSS, Jr.: *Die Fledermaus;* MOZART: *Le Nozze di Figaro;* ROSSINI: *La Gazza Ladra;* WEBER: *Der Freischütz;* WAGNER: *Rienzi.* Los Angeles PO. Lon 6858; Dec SXL 6643.

WILLIAMS: *Star Wars* Suite and *Close Encounters* Suite. Los Angeles PO. Lon 1001; Dec SXL 6885 (3/78).

SEIJI OZAWA

IN many respects, Ozawa's most interesting recordings were done early in his career—the Messiaen *Turangalîla* from Toronto; and, from Chicago, the

Janáček-Lutoslawski coupling and the Bartók and Schoenberg concertos with Peter Serkin. These convey a freshness and youthful excitement of discovery that make these performances highly enjoyable.

In Boston, conditions have been far more favorable to recording than in San Francisco or in ad hoc sessions with orchestras in London and Paris. Among Ozawa's best recent work with the Boston Symphony are his Berlioz performances, especially the *Roméo et Juliette* and *La Damnation de Faust*. There and in the Brahms First Symphony one can hear vivid documentation of the superb condition that the Boston Symphony has attained under Ozawa.

BARTÓK: *Concerto for Orchestra*; KODÁLY: *Dances from Galánta*. Chicago SO. Ang 36035.

BARTÓK: *Music for Strings, Percussion and Celesta* and *The Miraculous Mandarin* Suite. Boston SO. DG 2430 887 id. (12/77).

BARTÓK: Piano Concertos no. 1 and no. 3. Chicago SO (P. Serkin). RCA LSC-2929.

BEETHOVEN: Piano Concerto in D-major, Op. 61*a*. New Philharmonia O (P. Serkin). RCA LSC-3152.

BEETHOVEN: Piano Concerto no. 5 in E-flat major, *Emperor,* Op. 73. Boston SO (Eschenbach). DG 2530 438; 2535 276 (8/74).

BEETHOVEN: Symphony no. 3 in E-flat major, *Eroica,* Op. 55. San Francisco SO. (Phi 9500 002). U.S. only cassette 7750095.

BEETHOVEN: Symphony no. 5 in C-minor, Op. 67; SCHUBERT: Symphony no. 8 in B-minor, *Unfinished.* Chicago SO. RCA LSC-3132; GL 25002 (10/76).

BEETHOVEN: Symphony no. 9 in D-minor, Op. 125. New Philharmonia O (Napier, Reynolds, Brilioth, Ridderbusch, Ambrosian Singers). (2 Phi 6747 119).

BERLIOZ: *La Damnation de Faust,* Op. 24. Boston SO (Mathis, Burrows, McIntyre, Paul, Tanglewood Cho). (U.S.) 3 DG 2709 048 (12/74).

BERLIOZ: *Roméo et Juliette,* Op. 17. Boston SO (Hamari, Dupouy, Van Dam, New England Conservatory Cho). 2 DG 2707 089 id. (11/76).

BERLIOZ: Excerpts from *Roméo et Juliette,* Op. 17; PROKOFIEV: Excerpts from *Romeo and Juliet*; TCHAIKOVSKY: *Romeo and Juliet.* San Francisco SO. DG 2530 308 id. (5/73).

BERLIOZ: *Symphonie Fantastique,* Op. 14. Boston SO. DG 2530 358 id. (12/73).

(287)

BERLIOZ: *Symphonie Fantastique,* Op. 14. Toronto SO. Odys Y-31923 (U.K. Col 61659).

BERNSTEIN: Ballet Music, *West Side Story*; RUSSO: *Three Pieces for Blues Band and Orchestra.* San Francisco SO. DG 2530 309; on 2530 210 (U.K.) (4/75).

BRAHMS: Symphony no. 1 in C-minor, Op. 68. Boston SO. DG 2530 889 id. (8/78).

BRITTEN: *Young Person's Guide to the Orchestra*; MUSSORGSKY-RAVEL: *Pictures at an Exhibition.* Chicago SO. RCA LSC-2977.

BRUCH: Violin Concerto no. 1 in G-minor, Op. 26; SIBELIUS: Violin Concerto in D-minor, Op. 47. Japan PO (Ushioda). (No U.S.) (EMI SXLP 30137) (4/72).

DVOŘÁK: Symphony no. 9 in E-minor, *From the New World,* Op. 95, and *Carnival* Overture. San Francisco SO. Phi 9500 001.

FALLA: *El Sombrero de Tres Picos.* Boston SO (Berganza). DG 2530 823 id. (6/77).

FREEDMAN: *Images*; MACMILLAN: *Two Sketches*; MERCURE: *Triptych*; MOREL: *L'Etoile Noire.* Toronto SO. (CBS 3211 0038).

GERSHWIN: *An American in Paris*; RUSSO: *Street Music.* San Francisco SO. DG 2530 788 id. (12/77).

GRIFFES: *The Pleasure Dome of Kubla Khan* and *Three Poems of Fiona MacLeod.** Boston SO (*Bryn-Julson). New World 273.

HONEGGER: *Jeanne d'Arc au Bûcher.* London SO (Harper, Watts, Aneer, Young, Robinson, LSO Cho). (No U.S.) (Col 77216 U.K.) (12/76).

ICHIYANAGI: *Life Music*; LIGETI: *Atmosphères*; TAKEMITSU: *Arc*; XENAKIS: *Strategie.* Yomiuri Nippon SO. Var/Sara 81060.

IVES: Symphony no. 4 and *Central Park in the Dark.* Boston SO. DG 2350 787 id. (2/77).

JANÁČEK: *Sinfonietta*; LUTOSLAWSKI: *Concerto for Orchestra.* Chicago SO. Ang 36045.

KHATCHATURIAN: Piano Concerto; LISZT: *Hungarian Fantasy.* New Philharmonia O (Entremont). Col M-31075.

MAHLER: Symphony no. 1 in D-major. Boston SO. DG 2530 993 id. (5/78).

MENDELSSOHN: Violin Concerto in E-minor, Op. 64; TCHAIKOVSKY: Violin Concerto in D-major, Op. 35. London SO (Friedman). (RCA LSC-2865); SB 6666 (6/66).

MESSAIEN: *Turangalîla* (Y. and J. Loriod); TAKEMITSU: *November Steps.* Toronto SO. RCA LSC-7051; (SB-6761/2) (9/68).

MOZART: Symphonies no. 28 in C-major, K. 200, and no. 35 in D-major, *Haffner,* K. 385. New Philharmonia O. (RCA VICS-1630 id.) (3/72).

ORFF: *Carmina Burana.* Boston SO (Mandac, Kolk, Milnes, New England Conservatory Cho). RCA LSC-3161; LSB 4006 (11/70).

PROKOFIEV: Piano Concerto no. 3 in C-major, Op. 26; RAVEL: Piano Concerto in G-major. O de Paris (Weissenberg). Ang 36785; [EMI ASD-2701] (9/71).

RACHMANINOFF: Piano Concerto no. 3 in D-minor, Op. 30. New York PO (Watts). Col M-30059; (72857) (1/71).

RAVEL: *Boléro, Rhapsodie Espagnole,* and *La Valse.* Boston SO. DB 2530 475 id. (4/75).

RAVEL: *Daphnis et Chloé.* Boston SO. DG 2530 563 id. (11/75).

RESPIGHI: Ancient Airs and Dances, Suites 1–3. Boston SO. DG 2530 891 id. (6/79).

RESPIGHI: *Roman Festivals, The Pines of Rome,* and *The Fountains of Rome.* DG 2530 890 (6/79).

RIMSKY-KORSAKOFF: *Scheherazade.* Boston SO. DG 2530 972 id. (11/78).

RIMSKY-KORSAKOFF: *Scheherazade;* BORODIN: Dances from *Prince Igor.* Chicago SO. Ang 36034; (EMI ASD 2756) (11/71).

SCHOENBERG: *Piano Concerto.* Chicago SO (P. Serkin). (RCA LSC-3050; SB-6816) (3/70).

SCHUMANN: Piano Concerto in A-minor, Op. 54; R. STRAUSS: *Burleske.* London SO (Pennario). (RCA LSC-2875; SB 6675) (10/66).

SESSIONS: *When Lilacs Last in the Dooryard Bloom'd.* Boston SO (Hinds, Quivar, Cossa, Tanglewood Festival Cho). New World 296.

SHOSTAKOVICH: Cello Concerto no. 2; GLAZOUNOV: *Chant du Ménestrel,* Op. 71. Boston SO (Rostropovich). DG 2530 653 id. (11/76).

STRAVINSKY: *Capriccio, Concerto for Piano and Winds,* and *Movements for Piano and Orchestra.* O de Paris (Beroff). (Ang 36875; EMI ASD 2770) (6/72).

STRAVINSKY: *L'Oiseau de Feu.* O de Paris. Ang 36910; (EMI ASD 2845) (6/73).

STRAVINSKY: *L'Oiseau de Feu* Suite (1919 vers.) and *Petrouchka* (1947 vers.). Boston SO. RCA LSC-3167; in DPMK 1027 (LSB 4009) (12/70).

STRAVINSKY: *Le Sacre du Printemps* and *Fireworks,* Op. 4. Chicago SO. RCA LSC-3026; (SB-6791), *Sacre* only in DPMK 1027 (3/69).

TAKEMITSU: *Requiem, Green for Orchestra, The Dorian Horizon,* and *Asterism.* Toronto SO. (RCA LSC-3099); SB 6814 (2/70).

TCHAIKOVSKY: *Nutcracker* Suite, Op. 71a, and Excerpts from *The Sleeping Beauty.* O de Paris. Phi 6500 851; 7300 340 (cassette only).

TCHAIKOVSKY: Piano Concerto no. 1 in B-flat minor, Op. 23. London SO (Browning). (RCA LSC-3069).

TCHAIKOVSKY: Piano Concerto no. 1 in B-flat minor, Op. 23 (Browning), and Violin Concerto in D-major, Op. 35 (Friedman). London SO. (U.K. RCA LSB 4016). (4/71, 6/66).

TCHAIKOVSKY: Symphony no. 5 in E-minor, Op. 64; MUSSORGSKY: *A Night on Bald Mountain.* Chicago SO. RCA LSC-3071; (SB 6802) (9/69).

TCHAIKOVSKY: Symphony no. 5 in E-minor, Op. 64. Boston SO. DG 2530 888 id. (1/78).

TCHAIKOVSKY: Symphony no. 6 in B-minor, *Pathétique,* Op. 74. O de Paris. Phi 6500 850 id. (4/75).

TELEMANN: Oboe Concerto in D-minor; VIVALDI: Oboe Concerto, P. 306. Columbia CO (H. Gomberg). Col MS-6832.

H. WIENIAWSKI: Violin Concertos no. 1 in F-sharp minor, Op. 14, and no. 2 in D-minor, Op. 22. London PO (Perlman). Ang 36903; EMI ASD 2870 (5/73).

EDO DE WAART

CONDUCTING the Netherlands Wind Ensemble and the Dresden State Orchestra, Edo de Waart has produced some exceptionally fine performances of "lesser" Mozart works, although that term hardly applies to the great wind Serenades in B-flat (K. 361), C-minor (K. 388), and E-flat major (K. 375). Similarly, the "orchestral" serenades recorded in Dresden—and, unfortunately, mostly no longer available—are delightful in their own right while demonstrating the young Dutch conductor's remarkable grasp of the Mozartean idiom.

De Waart's range of repertory is evidenced by a series of Rachmaninoff performances with the Rotterdam Philharmonic that are beautifully played but possibly somewhat restrained in expression. The same may be said of his only opera recording, *Der Rosenkavalier,* a work that shows great potential only partly fulfilled.

However, in the more contemporary idiom of Stravinsky and Kurt Weill, de Waart is completely at home.

BACH: Concerto for Two Violins in D-minor, S. 1043 (Grumiaux and Toyoda), and Concerto for Oboe and Violin in C-minor, S. 1060 (Grumiaux and Holliger) ; VIVALDI: Concerto for Violin, P. 1. New Philharmonia O. Phi 6500 119 id. (9/71).

BACH: Violin Concertos in A-minor and E-major and Concerto for Two Violins in D-minor.* New Philharmonia O (Grumiaux, *Toyoda). Phi 7300 304 id. (cassette only).

BEETHOVEN: Marches, German Dances, etc.; MOZART: Dances, Marches, Minuets. Rotterdam PO. Phi 9500 080 (id.) (1/77).

BEETHOVEN: *Romances* nos. 1 and 2; BERLIOZ: *Rêverie et Caprice;* SVENDSEN: *Romance;* TCHAIKOVSKY: *Sérénade Mélancholique;* H. WIENIAWSKI: *Légende* and *Romance* from Violin Concerto no. 2 in D-minor, Op. 22. New Philharmonia O (Grumiaux). (U.S.) Phi 6500 047 (1/72).

BRAHMS: Piano Concerto no. 1 in D-minor, Op. 15. London PO (Lupu). Lon 6947; Dec SXL 6728 (11/75).

BRUCH: Violin Concerto no. 1 in G-minor, Op. 26; TCHAIKOVSKY: Violin Concerto in D-major, Op. 35. Rotterdam PO (Fujikawa). (U.S.) Phi 6500 708 (1/75).

DVOŘÁK Serenade in D-minor, Op. 44; GOUNOD: *Petite Symphonie;* SCHUBERT: *Octet.* Netherlands Wind Ens. (No U.S.) Phi 6500 163 (5/71).

GERSHWIN: *An American in Paris, Cuban Overture,* and *Porgy and Bess* Symphonic Picture. Monte Carlo Op O. (Phi 6500 290 id.) (2/73).

GERSHWIN: Piano Concerto in F, *Rhapsody in Blue,* and "I Got Rhythm" Variations. Monte Carlo Op O (Haas). Phi 6500 118.

GERSHWIN (arr. Bennett): *Porgy and Bess* Symphonic Picture. Monte Carlo Op O. (No U.S.) Phi 7300 189 (cassette).

HAYDN: Cello Concertos in C-major and D-major. English CO (Walewska). Phi 6500 381.

HAYDN: Piano Concerto in D-major, Op. 21; MOZART: Piano Concerto no. 8 in C-major, K. 246. Rotterdam PO (Vera). Phi 6833 199.

M. HAYDN: Violin Concerto in A-major; VIOTTI: Violin Concerto no. 22 in A-minor. Concertgebouw O (Grumiaux). Phi 839 757; (SAL 3804) (12/70).

MOZART: Adagio in B-flat major, K. 410, and Divertimentos in E-flat major, K.Anh. 226, in B-flat major, K.Anh. 227, and no. 14 in B-flat major, K. 270. Netherlands Wind Ens. Phi 6500 004 (id.) (7/70).

MOZART: Adagio in F-major, K. 411, and Divertimentos no. 4 in B-flat major, K. 186, no. 13 in F-major, K. 253, and no. 16 in E-flat major, K. 289. Netherlands Wind Ens. Phi 6500 003 (id.) (7/70).

MOZART: Arias. English CO (Ameling). Phi 6500 544 (id.) (10/74).

MOZART: Arias; ROSSINI: Arias. Rotterdam PO (Von Stade). Phi 9500 098 id. (2/77).

MOZART: Divertimentos for Winds no. 3 in E-flat major, K. 166, no. 8 in F-major, K. 213, no. 9 in B-flat major, K. 240, and no. 12 in E-flat major, K. 252. Netherlands Wind Ens. Phi 6500 002.

MOZART: Masonic Music. New Philharmonia O (Hollweg, Partridge, Dean). Phi 6570 063 (6500 020) (2/71).

MOZART: Oboe Concerto in C-major, K. 314; R. STRAUSS: Oboe Concerto. New Philharmonia O (Holliger). Phi 6500 174 id. (1/72).

MOZART: Serenade no. 4 in D-major, K. 203, and March in D-major. Dresden St O. (Phi 6500 965); in cassette 7699 049 (3/76).

MOZART: Serenade no. 5 in D-major, K. 205, and March, K. 215. Dresden St O. (Phi 6500 967); in cassette 7699 049 (3/76).

MOZART: Serenade no. 7 in D-major, Haffner, K. 250, and March in D-major. Dresden St O. Phi 6500 966; in cassette 7699 049.

MOZART: Serenade no. 9 in D-major, Posthorn, K. 320, and March in D-major. Netherlands Wind Ens. (U.S.) Phi 6500 627 (4/75).

MOZART: Serenade no. 10 for Thirteen Wind Instruments in B-flat major, K. 361. Netherlands Wind Ens. Phi 839 734 id. (10/71).

MOZART: Serenades no. 11 in E-flat, K. 375, and no. 12 in C-minor, K. 388. Netherlands Wind Ens. Phi 802 907 id. (5/72).

MUSSORGSKY-RAVEL: Pictures at an Exhibition; RAVEL: Boléro. Rotterdam PO. Phi 6500 882 (id.) (11/75).

PROKOFIEV: Excerpts from Romeo and Juliet. Rotterdam PO. Phi 6500 640; in cassette 7300 305 (3/74).

RACHMANINOFF: Piano Concertos nos. 1–4 and *Rhapsody on a Theme of Paganini,* Op. 43. Rotterdam PO (Orozco). (No U.S.) 3 Phi 6747 397.

RACHMANINOFF: Piano Concerto no. 2 in C-minor, Op. 18, and *Rhapsody on a Theme of Paganini,* Op. 43. Rotterdam PO (Orozco). Phi 6570 046 id. (12/77, 10/78).

RACHMANINOFF: Piano Concerto no. 3 in D-minor, Op. 30. Rotterdam PO (Orozco). (U.S.) Phi 6500 540 (7/74).

RACHMANINOFF: *Symphonic Dances,* Op. 45, and *Caprice Bohémien,* Op. 12. London PO. Phi 6500 362; in cassette 7300 292.

RACHMANINOFF: *Symphony* no. 2 in E-minor, Op. 27. Rotterdam PO. Phi 9500 309 id. (12/78).

RACHMANINOFF: Symphony no. 3 in A-minor, Op. 44, and *The Rock,* Op. 7. Rotterdam PO. Phi 9500 302 id. (5/78).

SAINT-SAËNS: Symphony no. 3 in C-minor, Op. 44, and *Wedding Cake,* Op. 76. Rotterdam PO (Chorzempa). Phi 9500 306 id. (5/78).

SCHUBERT: Operatic Excerpts from *Die Freunde von Salamanka, Claudine von Villa Bella, Die Bürgschaft, Alfonso und Estrella, Die Verschworenen, Die Zwillingsbrüder,* and *Der Vierjährige Posten.* English CO (Ameling, Ahnsjö). Phi 9500 170 id. (2/77).

R. STRAUSS: *Der Rosenkavalier.* Rotterdam PO (Lear, Welting, Von Stade, Bastin). 4 Phi 6707 030 id. (8/77).

R. STRAUSS: Serenade for Thirteen Winds in E-flat and Sonatina no. 2 for Sixteen Winds in E-flat. Netherlands Wind Ens. (Phi 6500 097 id.).

R. STRAUSS: Sonatina no. 1 for Sixteen Winds in F-major and Suite for Thirteen Winds in B-flat major. Netherlands Wind Ens. (Phi 6500 297 id.).

STRAVINSKY: Concerto for Piano and Winds (Bruins), *Ebony Concerto, Octet,* and *Symphonies of Wind Instruments.* Netherlands Wind Ens. Phi 6500 841 (id.) (3/76).

TCHAIKOVSKY: Piano Concerto no. 1 in B-flat minor, Op. 23 (Orozco), and Violin Concerto in D-major, Op. 35 (Fujokawa). Rotterdam PO. (No U.S.) Phi 6570 028 (10/78, 1/75).

WEILL: Symphonies no. 1 and no. 2. Leipzig Gewandhaus O. Phi 6500 642 id. (7/75).

JAMES LEVINE

LEVINE'S *Otello,* well cast and vividly recorded, may well be one of the best all around opera recordings of recent years. It climaxes a series of Verdi operas that began with a somewhat overexuberant and noisy *Giovanna d'Arco* and proceeded through an excellent uncut (except for the ballet music) *Vespri* and a beautifully controlled *Forza.* Levine's two other complete operas are less impressive: he tends to take the bombast and tawdriness of *Andrea Chénier* too seriously and, in the *Barbiere di Siviglia,* with Sills in less than optimum voice, Levine passes up wit in favor of more obvious belly laughs.

Symphonically, Levine has seldom made a weak recording. His four Brahms symphonies with the Chicago are all very good in the conductor's straightforward but fluent manner. His Mahler symphonies are first-rate—lyrical, beautifully colored, and exceptionally sympathetic to Mahler's visionary expression and characteristic structure. All are fine performances, but the Third is extraordinary in every respect—especially for the balance between the moment-to-moment beauties of this sprawling score and the structural unity of Mahler's conception.

The Ravinia Festival Ensemble consists of players from the Chicago Symphony; its Bach record features Kathleen Battle in a beautifully sung *Wedding* Cantata, stunning solo playing by principals from the orchestra, notably Adolph Herseth in the Second *Brandenburg* Concerto, and Levine's performance at the harpsichord in the Fifth.

Levine's fondness for collaborative music-making is also evident in the Dvořák Cello Concerto that he made with Lynn Harrell, a lively but controlled reading. Harrell has also been Levine's partner in sonatas by Beethoven, Schubert, Debussy, Prokofiev, and Mendelssohn.

BACH: Cantata no. 202, *Weichet Nur,** and *Brandenburg* Concertos no. 2 in F-major and no. 5 in D-major.** Ravinia Festival Ens (*Battle, **Levine). RCA ARL1-2788.

BRAHMS: Symphony no. 1 in C-minor, Op. 68. Chicago SO. RCA ARL1-1326 id. (6/76).

BRAHMS: Symphony no. 2 in D-major, Op. 73. Chicago SO. RCA ARL1-2864.

BRAHMS: Symphony no. 3 in F-major, Op. 90. Chicago SO. RCA ARL1-2097 id. (2/78).

BRAHMS: Symphony no. 4 in E-minor, Op. 98. Chicago SO. RCA ARL1-2624 id. (4/79).

CILÈA: *Adriana Lecouvreur*. Philharmonia O (Scotto, Obraztsova, Domingo, Milnes). Col M3-34588; 79310 (6/78).

DVOŘÁK: Cello Concerto in B-minor, Op. 104. London SO (Harrell). RCA ARL1-1155 id. (2/76).

GIORDANO: *Andrea Chénier*. National PO (Scotto, Domingo, Milnes, Aldis Cho). 3 RCA ARL3-2046; RLO2046 (8/77).

MAHLER: Symphony no. 1 in D-major. London SO. RCA ARL1-0894 id. (5/75).

MAHLER: Symphony no. 3 in D-major. Chicago SO (Horne, CSO Cho, Glen Ellyn Children's Cho). 2 RCA ARL2-1757; RKO 1757 (3/77).

MAHLER: Symphony no. 4 in G-major. Chicago SO (Blegen). RCA ARL1-0895 id. (10/75).

MAHLER: Symphony no. 5 in C-sharp minor and Symphony no. 10: Adagio. Philadelphia O. 2 RCA ARL2-2905.

MAHLER: Symphony no. 6 in A-minor. London SO. RCA ARL2-3213.

ROSSINI: *Il Barbiere di Siviglia*. London SO (Sills, Barbieri, Gedda, Milnes, Capecchi, Raimondi. 3 Ang SX3761; EMI SLS 985 (11/75).

STRAVINSKY: *Petrouchka* (1947 vers.) Chicago SO. RCA ARL1-2615 id. (5/78).

VERDI: *La Forza del Destino*. London SO (Price, Cossotto, Domingo, Milnes, Giaiotti, Bacquier, Aldis Cho). 4 RCA ARL4-1864; RLO 1864 (8/77).

VERDI: *Giovanna d'Arco*. London SO (Caballé, Domingo, Milnes). 3 Ang S 3791; EMI SCS 967 (5/73).

VERDI: *Otello*. National PO (Scotto, Domingo, Milnes). 3 RCA CRL3-2951 id. (10/78).

VERDI: *I Vespri Siciliani*. New Philharmonia O (Arroyo, Domingo, Milnes, Raimondi). 4 RCA ARL4-0370 id. (9/74).

INDEX

As in the Recordings section, throughout the index "SO" is used for "Symphony Orchestra," "PO" for "Philharmonic Orchestra," and "CO" for "Chamber Orchestra"; "O" is used for "Orchestra" and "Orchestre," "Op" and "St Op" for "Opera" and "State Opera," and "Ens" for "Ensemble."

Abbado, Claudio: at Accademia Chigiana with Barenboim and Mehta, 73; authentic editions, 82–83; authentic texts, 88–91; at Berkshire Music Center, 75, 130; Berlin debut with RIAS, 77; on Cantelli, 86; Chicago SO, 79; conducting style, 86–88; on conductors, 47, 85–86; Edinburgh Festival, 83; European Community Youth O, 83–85; on Furtwängler, 85; hears Furtwängler, 72; B. Jacobson on, 79; Kennedy Center, 80; La Scala artistic director, 94–100, 101, 112; London SO, 80–83; Mahler Symphony no. 4, xvii, 85, 86–87; Mehta invitation to Montreal and Los Angeles, 76; Metropolitan Op, 79–80; Milan debut, 75; Mitropoulos Competition, 76; on music, 102–3; on New York City, 78–79; New York Philharmonic assistant conductor, 76; Parma Conservatory, 75; political views, 71, 101–2; A. Porter on, 86–87, 90; recordings, 79, 82, 93–94; rehearsal, 87–88; repertory, 91–93; Salzburg Festival debut, 77; Salzburg study, 73; Second Viennese School, 91; study, early, 71–72; on Toscanini, 85; hears Toscanini, 72; Trieste debuts, 75; L. Tuck on, 89–90; in United States, 78–80; at Verdi Conservatory, 72; Verdi *Don Carlo*, 89–91; at Vienna Academy, 73–75; Vienna PO principal conductor, 77–78; on Bruno Walter, 85–86; T. Willis on, 79; youth and family in Milan, 71
Abbado family, 70–72, 101

Accademia Chigiana (Siena), 8, 73
Adler, Kurt Herbert, 251
Alioti, Joseph L., 177
Allen, Woody, *Manhattan,* 128
America Israel Cultural Foundation, 8
Ančerl, Karel, 57–58
Arons, Max, 158
Ashkenazy, Vladimir, 14, 24
Aspen School of Music, 245, 247–49
Babin, Victor, 252
Bamberger, Carl, 245
Barbirolli, Sir John, 54
Barenboim, Daniel, xvi; Accademia Chigiana, 8; appearance, 4; Australia, 10, 24; Austro-German tradition, 14; Beethoven concerto recordings, 23; on Beethoven *Eroica,* 22; Beethoven *Hammerklavier* Sonata, 9–10; Beethoven piano sonatas, 10, 11; Beethoven trios, 23–24; Bruckner Symphony no. 5, xvii; Buenos Aires, debut in, 6; Buenos Aires, music in, 6; on career, 44; as celebrity, 3; Chicago SO, 27–28; childhood, 5–7; conducting technique, 29–31; P. G. Davis on, 37; Jacqueline du Pré, marries, 18; Edinburgh Festival, 36; English CO, 11–12, 52; friends, circle of, 14–16; on Furtwängler, 33–35; Furtwängler, influence of, 16; Furtwängler, meets, 7; E. Greenfield on, 11; Haifa, conducting in, 24; D. Henahan on, 35–36; A. Hughes on, 13; S. Hurok, 9; on interpretation, 33; Israel, move to, 6; as Israeli, 16; B. Jacobson on, 27–28; and Klemperer, 23; London residence, 14; managements, popularity with, 28; on Mehta, 8–9; memory, 4, 9, 32; Mozart *Don Giovanni,* 36–37; Mozart piano concertos, 13; on music, 4; New Philharmonia O, 24; New York conducting debut, 24–25; New York Philharmonic, 27; O de Paris, 38–43; Paris debut, 9; pianist and conductor, 12, 43; popularity with orchestra players, 28–30; recordings,

CONDUCTORS